Secondary School Examinations

Secondary School Examinations
International Perspectives on Policies and Practice

Max A. Eckstein and Harold J. Noah

Yale University Press   New Haven and London

Published with assistance from the Louis Stern Memorial
Fund.

The authors acknowledge permission to use material from
work previously published by: The University of Chicago
Press, Pergamon Press, Routledge, and the State University
of New York Press.

Designed by Sonia L. Scanlon.
Set in Times Roman type by Maple-Vail, Binghamton,
New York.
Printed in the United States of America by Edwards Brothers,
Ann Arbor, Michigan.

Library of Congress Cataloging-in-Publication Data

Eckstein, Max A.
    Secondary school examinations : international
perspectives on policies and practice / Max A.
Eckstein and Harold J. Noah.
        p.   cm.
    Includes bibliographical references and index.
    ISBN 0-300-05393-2
    1. High schools—Examinations.   2. General
Certificate of Secondary Education.   3. Educational
tests and measurements.   4. Education and state.
5. Comparative education.   I. Noah, Harold J.
II. Title.
LB3060.28.E25   1993
373.12′64—dc20   92-38889

A catalogue record for this book is available from the British
Library.

The paper in this book meets the guidelines for permanence
and durability of the Committee on Production Guidelines for
Book Longevity of the Council on Library Resources.

10 9 8 7 6 5 4 3 2 1

Contents

Preface

When we began thinking about a study of examinations, we considered the scarcity of international comparative work on examinations to be somewhat curious. In the words of one of our favorite authors, we thought, "Here is a paradox we should not pass without inquiry."[1] But after four years of study, we now understand why there has been relatively little published work along these lines. The subject is not at all simple, if only because examinations are so embedded in their national educational and social contexts. In addition, the comparative data are often ambiguous: in some countries examination systems are extremely durable and resistant to change; in others they are undergoing substantial, even rapid, restructuring. Moreover, the direction of change often differs from country to country.

Our work on this project began in 1988, just at the time when political upheavals in the Soviet Union and in Eastern Europe began occurring more rapidly and to a greater extent than anyone could ever have expected. We selected eight countries for study, and in four of the eight the political and social contexts of examination systems altered dramatically during the last stages of our work. When we began, we did not anticipate the unification of the two Germanys, the disintegration of the Soviet Union, the abrupt turn away after the student demonstrations in Tiananmen Square from what had seemed to be liberalization policies in China, and the growing public dissatisfaction in Sweden with the policies of the Social Democrats, leading to their replacement in power by a right-wing coalition. Each of these political upheavals has had profound implications for change in educational policy. Some of these implications have already begun to show themselves: China has modified its heavily merit-based policy of university admissions; the Swedish National Board of Education (the central ministry), which ruled for decades over the nation's educational policies and programs, has been abolished, decentralization of administration and finance of the schools from Stockholm to the municipalities has been accelerated, and the option to take aptitude tests for university admission has been extended to secondary school graduates.

The Soviet Union formally came to an end at the close of 1991, dis-

1. William S. Gilbert, from *Princess Ida,* act 3. We introduce each of our chapters with citations from the works of Gilbert and Arthur Sullivan.

solving into its constituent republics. The standard practices in education
and examinations developed during seventy years of Soviet rule will surely
disappear, completely in some jurisdictions but less so in others. The former German Democratic Republic (GDR) *Länder* are taking giant steps toward
integration with the school policies of the western Länder. Since 1945, the
two Germanys had gone distinctly different ways in their educational systems, not least in their arrangements for secondary education. In the western part of the country, the pre–World War II tripartite structure of *Gymnasium, Realschule,* and *Hauptschule* was largely restored, whereas East
Germany followed the Soviet model of a common (comprehensive) secondary school until age sixteen. Students then transferred to the senior
secondary school, which prepared them for the leaving examinations at the
end of twelfth grade, compared with the West, where the *Abitur* examinations are usually taken after thirteen years of schooling. Although educational arrangements in the five new Länder will no doubt not become
mere carbon copies of arrangements in any of the original eleven Länder,
it is already clear that most of the former GDR content, practices, and structures eventually will give way to those of the West.

We have taken note of these and similar developments and report the
most recent data and structures. But since the political changes are so recent and their effects, if any, upon the examination systems have not yet
been clearly demonstrated, the information we present on examinations
describes the scene to about the end of 1990. Thus, our presentation ap-
plies to the former Soviet Union and not to the emergent Commonwealth
of Independent States, and to the former Federal Republic and not to the
current unified Germany.

This study is *not* about testing and *not* about evaluating school programs. It is also *not* about techniques of test construction or other psychometric features. It is, rather, centered on external examinations at the end
of secondary school and what they stand for in eight major countries. It is
a study of alternative examination policies and practices and their implications. It is, above all, a study of how examination systems control and
are controlled, of the different ways they fulfill often similar functions,
and of how these differences are related to major aspects of education and
society.

There are still those who believe that "they" have nothing to teach
"us," a belief held either out of conviction of the superiority of "our"
practices or from stubborn belief in the uniqueness of "our" condition.
This work is based on the contrary position: that there is much to be learned
about the dynamics of education in society through comparative study, not

least that we can understand our own problems better with the help of such knowledge.

The book is the culmination of a four-year project in the course of which we held work conferences in Malaga, Frankfurt, and Paris; arranged an international symposium in Montreal; and organized a series of working papers and articles. Chapters 1, 7, and 8 contain parts of previously published work.[2]

Very little could have been accomplished without the contributions of many individuals, none of whom, we hasten to add, bears any responsibility for the deficiences in our work, particularly for our errors of omission and commission. These are entirely our own. We acknowledge first those who were our consultants and who provided information and insight on examination systems in the eight countries, responded to questions, and commented on our findings. These colleagues, some of whom worked with us at meetings in Europe, included Oskar Anweiler, Emeritus, Ruhr-Universität Bochum; Katsuhiro Arai, National Institute for Educational Research, Tokyo; W. D. Halls, formerly of University of Oxford Department of Education; Dennis Kallen, University of Paris VIII, Vincennes; Edmund J. King, Emeritus, King's College, University of London; Friedrich Kuebart, Ruhr-Universität Bochum; Mikhail Levitskii, State Pedagogical Institute, Moscow; Lu Zhen, National Education Examinations Authority, China International Examinations Coordination Bureau, Beijing; Thierry Malan, Ministère de l'Education Nationale, Paris; Sixten Marklund, Institutionen för internationell pedagogik, University of Stockholm; Wolfgang Mitter, Deutsches Institut für Internationale Pädagogische Forschung, Frankfurt; Leonid Novikov, Deutsches Institut für Internationale Pädagogische Forschung, Frankfurt; David Phillips, University of Oxford Department of Education; Dieter Schultz, Ruhr-Universität Bochum.

We thank also the following, especially for their contributions to the 1989 Montreal symposium, the papers from which were recently published:[3] Patricia Broadfoot, University of Bristol; Ingemar Fägerlind, Institutionen för internationell pedagogik, University of Stockholm; Philip J. Foster, State University of New York, Albany; Peter Frost, Williams Col-

2. Max A. Eckstein and Harold J. Noah, "Forms and Functions of Secondary-School-Leaving Examinations," *Comparative Education Review* 33, no. 3 (1989), pp. 295–316; Harold J. Noah and Max A. Eckstein, "Tradeoffs in Examination Policies: An International Comparative Perspective," *Oxford Review of Education* 15, no. 1 (1989), pp. 17–27; also Patricia Broadfoot et al., eds., *Changing Educational Assessment: International Perspectives and Trends* (London: Routledge, 1990), pp. 84–97.

3. Max A. Eckstein and Harold J. Noah, eds., *Examinations: Comparative and International Studies* (Oxford: Pergamon Press, 1992).

lege, Massachusetts; Stephen P. Heyneman, the World Bank, Washington, D.C.; Huang Shiqi, State Education Commission, Beijing; Thomas Kellaghan, St. Patrick's College, Dublin; Joan Knapp, Educational Testing Service, Princeton, New Jersey; Angela Little, Institute of Education, University of London; Angela W. Ransom, the World Bank, Washington, D.C.

In addition, we express our appreciation to Jacques Hallak, Director of the International Institute for Educational Planning (IIEP), Paris, who was our gracious host and active participant in a seminar reviewing a major portion of the book in draft, together with Gabrielle Göttelman-Duret, IIEP; John Nisbet, King's College, Aberdeen; Desmond Nuttall, University of London Institute of Education; John Smythe, United Nations Educational, Scientific, and Cultural Organization; and Alan Wagner, Organization for Economic Cooperation and Development.

Throughout the four years of this project, we have received assistance of outstanding value from Juan Manuel Moreno, the Universidad Nacional de Educacion a Distancia, Madrid. His close association with the project began with his work comparing examinations in the "Mediterranean-Latin" and "Anglo-Saxon" countries, a study that became a prize-winning doctoral dissertation. Our first work conference in Malaga would not have been possible without his initiative, and we acknowledge with thanks his contribution at other meetings. Most important, acting as a persistent yet ever-gracious critic in a series of extended and detailed reviewing sessions, he gave us valuable comments as our manuscript evolved.

We also had assistance throughout the project from Jeanne Weiler, and at various times from Mark A. Ashwill and Lalita Ramdas, all at the time doctoral students at the University at Buffalo, State University of New York. At various times, too, graduate students, including Ya Ling Li, Sofia Nayer, and Zemin Zhang, translated and interpreted foreign documents for us. As we prepared our final manuscript, Mary Metcalf supplied needed editorial help, as did Gladys Topkis of Yale University Press. We thank them all.

Over the long period devoted to this study, we enjoyed periods of stimulating and productive work in various locations with colleagues abroad and in the United States. Hidden behind the words of this text are pleasant memories of working together in Gascony, France, first at "Sonnard," Castera-Verduzan, where we were hosted by Michelle and Marcel Guiraud, and then in the tranquil surroundings of the Domaine de Bentenac, Simorre; in Malaga and Almunecar, Spain; in Frankfurt, Paris, and Montreal; in Amenia, New York, and in Colrain, Massachusetts, and, most particularly, halfway between Amenia and Colrain on the spacious stoop of the Red Lion Inn in Stockbridge, Massachusetts. Our appreciation is also due to Teachers College, Columbia University, and to the Comparative Education Center at the University at Buffalo, State University of New York for the facilities they provided us separately and jointly in the course of the work. Both institutions are distinguished in their contributions to comparative and international education. The first has a rich and lengthy history in this field; the second, though a relative newcomer, has already achieved an outstanding record of teaching and research in comparative education.

In particular, we thank colleagues at both institutions for their support and encouragement: Philip G. Altbach, the late Gail P. Kelly, Hugh Petrie, and Lois Weis, all at the University of Buffalo; Lambros Comitas and other members of the Department of Philosophy and the Social Sciences at Teachers College, and especially Dianne Sadnytzsky, Administrative Assistant to the department; and Ellen Condliffe Lagemann, Director of the Institute of Philosophy and Politics of Education at Teachers College.

We acknowledge with gratitude the generous support of the Spencer Foundation and the cooperation and forbearance of its officers, especially Marion M. Faldet, Vice-President, and Linda M. Schumacher, Treasurer, in all matters concerning the administration of the grant of funds for this project.

Finally, we wish to record our profound personal, intellectual, and professional indebtedness to the late Professor and President of Teachers College, Columbia University, and President of the Spencer Foundation, Lawrence A. Cremin, to whom we dedicate this book.

Max A. Eckstein
Harold J. Noah

Chapter 1

Introduction: The Comparative Study of Examinations

If you wish in the world to advance,
Your merits you're bound to enhance.
  You must stir it and stump it,
    And blow your own trumpet,
Or, trust me, you haven't a chance!
—Robin, *Ruddigore,* act I

This book is a study of external end-of-secondary-school examination systems in eight countries: England/Wales, France, the Federal Republic of Germany, Japan, the People's Republic of China, the (former) Soviet Union, Sweden, and the United States. Its focus is on the implications of examination systems for schooling in these countries. The central themes are those of examinations as instruments and as targets of control: their relation to curriculum, to student learning and teacher activities, and to individual life chances. In the course of the chapters that follow, we draw attention to the contextual changes that influence examination policy: increasing participation in upper secondary schooling, the growing "publicness" of examinations, and how efforts to achieve reforms in society and education affect attitudes and practice in respect to examinations.

The structure, content, and effects of examinations are currently matters of much concern in the United States. In particular, the potential use of examinations to improve educational performance is being widely discussed and acted upon. But interest in the role of examinations is not limited to the United States. It extends to other nations as different from one another as England/Wales, France, Japan, and China. Nor is such intense interest a new phenomenon. In past decades, Sweden and the Federal Republic of Germany had serious concerns about their examination systems, and during the years leading up to its dissolution the Soviet Union was engaged in vigorous debates about new directions for education.

Examinations are important, pervasive, and persistent. Educators are inclined to think that they provide a measure of student learning of content and skills. This is both true and obvious, and as a result, much of the study of and debate over examinations focus on the kinds of content and skills to be assessed. Debates tend to center on distinctions between common, basic learning on the one hand and specialized learning on the other, between "useful" and "academic" knowledge. At least as common is the work of psychometricians on the technical topics of norms, reliability, validity, and comparability of results and the debate over the effects of various examination formats on teaching and learning. But students, their parents, school administrators, and large sectors of the public are well aware that content and form are not all that matter in examinations. These examinations are also about student selection, educational change, legitimation of knowledge, and above all, as we shall see, about control in education.

The Origins of External Examinations

How old are examinations? If we define them as noncompetitive tests of knowledge or skill set, administered, and graded by adults who know the candidates, we cannot give even an approximate date, for they probably existed at least as far back as the early hunters who tested their children's skills in the chase or who used such tests as a part of the rite of passage to maturity. But if we rephrase the question to ask: "How old are *written, public, competitive* examination *systems?*" we can be reasonably precise: the Han emperors of China (206 B.C. to A.D. 220) established the first centrally organized system having all of these characteristics.[1]

Designed to select candidates for government service, the Chinese system lasted for two thousand years. Given this extraordinary longevity, we might expect that many nations would have learned sooner rather than later from the Chinese, copying their invention while making suitable adaptations to local conditions. Surprisingly, this did not happen. Only in the eighth century A.D., after almost a millennium, did the Japanese adopt a version of the Chinese system, but the innovation was short-lived. Examinations did not appear again in Japan until modern times.[2]

In the late sixteenth century, the Chinese system may have had some influence on education in European countries through the reports of Matteo Ricci, a Jesuit traveler to China. He witnessed the metropolitan examinations held in Peking in 1604, and his descriptions of the Chinese examinations may have supported the Jesuits' practice of using individual com-

1. Wolfgang Franke, "The Reform and Abolition of the Traditional Chinese Examination System." East Asian Research Center, Harvard University (dist. Cambridge: Harvard University Press, 1968).

2. Ikuo Amano, *Education and Examination in Modern Japan* (Tokyo: University of Tokyo Press, 1990), p. 43.

petition to stimulate pupils' efforts.[3] Three centuries later, toward the end of the nineteenth century, European writers on examinations (Max Weber most prominently) referred to the way China selected its mandarin class.[4] But other than these scattered and tardy instances, there is little evidence of Chinese influence on examinations, in striking contrast to the alacrity and thoroughness with which such other Chinese inventions as gunpowder, pottery, and papermaking were taken up in the West.

Modern examination systems were substantially reinvented between the second half of the eighteenth and the middle of the nineteenth centuries in Western Europe, initially in Prussia, then in France and England. Frederick the Great was the first European ruler to use competitive examinations to select government officials, and examinations had an important role in Napoleon's reconstruction of the French government. As modern states industrialized, improved communications, and evolved their large bureaucracies, the practice of selection by written, public examinations, previously confined to China, became increasingly common.[5]

There were substantial differences, however, between the classical Chinese and the reinvented European systems. In China, examinations were used narrowly, to select government bureaucrats. In Europe and Japan, while at first selection for public service was also the most important function, examinations were quickly extended to the selection of personnel for private employment and to the awarding of professional licenses. In China the competitive principle was the defining characteristic of the examination system, whereas in the European and American models examinations were sometimes competitive, but as often qualifying.

The institutional context of competitive examinations in China also differed from that in Europe and Japan, where examinations were tied to specific courses of study. Examination candidacy was restricted to those who had completed the appropriate course. Thus, there arose in Europe and Japan mutually sustaining relations between schools and universities on the one side and examinations on the other: the restrictions placed on access to examinations increased the demand for admission to particular types of schools, and the subsequent growth in the numbers of schools and universities, pupils and students, in turn favored the growth of examinations. Indeed, without the device of examinations there would not have been the spectacular expansion of schooling of the past century and a half.

3. Jonathan D. Spence, *The Memory Palace of Matteo Ricci* (New York: Penguin Books, 1985) provides excerpts from Ricci's reports on the examinations in China.

4. Max Weber, *The Religion of China* (Glencoe, Ill.: Free Press, 1968).

5. Ibid.

In Europe and Japan, establishment of an ordered set of elementary, secondary, and higher-education institutions required some mechanism for allocating scarce places at each successive level. Examination results provided a defensible way of doing this, reducing though not eliminating accusations of nepotism, bribery, and preferential treatment for the children of the wealthy. Wherever the number of candidates greatly exceeded the number of places, difficult competitive examinations could convince most aspirants and their families that failure to secure a particular study place or job was due more to their objectively measured level of achievement than to some nefarious system that gave other candidates unfair access. "Fair" examinations increasingly took the form of public sessions in which anonymous candidates faced the same questions or exercises, providing responses that were evaluated according to the same externally determined criteria.

Such examinations were also favored as a means of "quality control" of school graduates. To pass the examination, candidates had to have studied a stated syllabus. Employers, university admissions officers, administrators of the educational system, taxpayers, parents, politicians—all felt more comfortable when they knew that the credential awarded at the end of secondary school was based on the results of a public examination of performance on that syllabus.

Furthermore, examination systems were valued (at least in England and the United States) because candidates' marks could be regarded as an index of teachers' effectiveness. Examination results could be used to guide the allocation of public funds among schools or school districts or to inform parents of the scholastic quality of one school compared with another. More to the point, promotion and pay increments for teachers could be tied to the examination results for the school or even to each teacher's students.

Examination systems were particularly useful in countries where schools and universities exercised considerable autonomy in defining their curricula. In such circumstances, a private examination system could find favor with government as a way to restrain curricular experimentation and differentiation. The national character of examinations and their associated credentials was equally valued in countries with central control of school curricula. They played an important role in the consolidation of the nation-state, helping to transcend regional and religious divisions by attaching a nationally recognized imprimatur to those who had passed.

As we shall see, different combinations of these motives were present in the eight countries of our study when they introduced their examination systems and as those systems became established.

Replacing Monopolies of Birth and Wealth. Government authorities in imperial China, Prussia, France, and Japan introduced examinations primarily to break the monopoly over government jobs enjoyed by an aristocratic or feudal class. The emperor Kao-tsu was the first ruler to use examinations to select candidates for positions in government service. In 196 B.C. he issued an edict requesting local dignitaries to nominate men "of proven virtue" to come to the capital as aspirants for official positions. A half-century or so later, study of the Confucian classics was required, and candidates were awarded positions in the imperial service according to their examination success.[6] The result was a bureaucracy, the mandarinate, which owed its allegiance to the emperors, thereby curtailing the aristocracy's influence on government. Testimony to the success of this device is its longevity: the final administration of the imperial examinations took place only in 1904, two thousand years after their beginning.

The early style of Chinese examination set during the Han dynasty required candidates to discuss practical problems of statecraft:

> Now all within the four seas are unified and public opinion is alike in all the localities. The whole realm follows the right way more than ever before. But in the North are uncontrolled warriors and in the West are peoples of vulgar practices. Because of the threats, it is impossible to sleep in peace. What measures should be used to put an end to these dangers and clear up trouble in the remote areas?[7]

Later examinations introduced by the Sui emperors (A.D. 581–618) turned away from such practical questions to more abstract and literary assignments. Candidates were required to complete three exercises: an oral exam, the sentence test (*T'ieh*), and an exercise in the form of a project (*T'se*). The T'ieh presented incomplete lines from a Confucian classic, the blanks to be filled in with the correct words. The T'se required lengthy written answers.

Although changes in the system with respect to content and regulations occurred over its long history, three distinguishing marks of the imperial Chinese examinations remained constant: the burden of study imposed on candidates was heavy and prolonged; the examinations were highly competitive; and they were designed to select for government service. Successful candidates advanced through a system of local and provincial exami-

---

6. Francke, "Reform and Abolition of the Traditional Chinese Examination System," p. 2.

7. J. Lloyd Brereton, *Exams! Where Next?* (Victoria, British Columbia: Pacific Northwest Humanist Publications, 1964), p. 43.

nations to the imperial examinations held at the capital. Although many entered, few succeeded at each stage. Those who were successful in the imperial examinations were appointed to powerful, lucrative, and prestigious positions in government. The emperors transformed a system of inherited appointment based on aristocratic birth into one that made appointment a prize to be won in a meritocratic competition of academic skills.[8]

More than a thousand years later, in 1748, Frederick the Great, also concerned to reduce the power of the landed aristocracy and to centralize power in his own person, instituted selection of all government officials in Prussia by two-stage examination. The first stage (the *Abitur*) qualified candidates for entry into the university training programs in law and public administration, and the second, a strictly competitive examination, selected them for appointment. By 1812, under Napoleonic influence, the Abitur in Prussia had assumed its basic form, and in 1834 admission to the universities and the learned professions was made conditional on passing it.[9] Other German states followed the Prussian example and developed similar systems, as did Sweden.[10]

From its inception, the Abitur was partly written and partly oral. Candidates who performed outstandingly well in the written portions could be excused from the oral examination. Although the candidates' teachers graded the examinations, their marks were subject to change by the inspector of schools. The regulations governing the conduct of the oral examinations were detailed and carefully set out to minimize favoritism. "Successful candidates receive a diploma (*Reifezeugnis*) signed by the provincial inspector of schools and other members of the examining committee. This diploma certifies to the character, conduct, attention and industry of the holder; to his standing in each subject of the examination, and to the quality of his work in the *Oberprima* [final year of the *Gymnasium*]."[11] Few held the Reifezeugnis,[12] and they enjoyed important privileges: the right to

8. For further details, see C. T. Hu, "The Historical Background: Examinations and Control in Pre-modern China." *Comparative Education* 20, no. 1 (1984): 7–26.

9. James E. Russell, *German Higher Schools: The History, Organization and Methods of Secondary Education in Germany* (New York: Longmans, 1907), p. 179.

10. The *studentexamen,* Sweden's equivalent of the Abitur, was originally taken at the university (that is, it functioned as a qualifying entrance examination). In 1862 the examination began to be taken at school. Leon Boucher, *Tradition and Change in Swedish Education* (Oxford: Pergamon, 1982), p. 10.

11. Russell, *German Higher Schools*, p. 185.

12. Fritz Ringer points out that in 1885 in Prussia only 30 pupils in 10,000 attended the Gymnasium, and only about 5 percent of these eventually obtained the Abitur. Fritz Ringer, *The Decline of the German Mandarins* (Cambridge: Harvard University Press, 1979), p. 39.

study at a university and the right to apply for admission to all posts in the state service.

In France the Revolution of 1789 destroyed the privileged access to positions in the royal government that the aristocracy had enjoyed. The principle of *égalité* implied that all *citoyens* of the new France were now free to compete on an equal basis for qualifications, positions, and wealth. Availability of schooling was to become liberal and free. Although the revolutionary government did not last long enough to bring these ideals to fruition, Napoleon, like Frederick the Great, was determined to build a modern unitary state, staffed on the basis of talent. The accident of birth was no longer to be the major determinant of occupation or position in society.

An important instrument of this great social and administrative change was the *baccalauréat* qualification, reestablished and reformulated by Napoleon in 1808. In the Middle Ages *bacheliers* were young clerics admitted as probationers to ecclesiastical establishments. In the sixteenth century the title was reserved for junior scholars (*maîtres ès arts*), who had already studied logic for two years and were now studying for a further two years to receive their *licence*. Napoleon revived the maîtres ès arts qualification, renamed it the baccalauréat, attached to it a process of formal examination, and assigned to it the status of a university degree. Indeed, during most of the nineteenth century the major function of universities in France was to administer the baccalauréat degree for pupils completing their secondary education.

Initially there were five types of baccalauréat—in letters, science, medicine, law, and theology—but substantial changes were made to the subjects, content, and format of the degree throughout the nineteenth and twentieth centuries. Until 1821 the examination was purely oral in format and literary in content. Candidates were required to answer questions on the life and works of Latin or Greek authors. In 1821 the scope of the examination was widened, adding oral examinations in mathematics and physics. Written examinations were introduced in 1830 in the form of compositions and translations to and from the classical languages, as well as an obligatory oral examination on Aristotelian syllogisms. In 1840 the Latin translation examination was used as an elimination device, and an oral examination in French authors was introduced. The written subjects in 1852 were Latin translation and French or Latin composition, and the oral subjects were logic, history-geography, arithmetic, geometry, and elementary physics. In 1857 Latin composition was changed from an optional to a compulsory subject, and in 1864 the *décret Duruy* established one of the most characteristic and long-lasting features of the baccalauréat (surviving to this day)—the compulsory philosophy essay.

A reform in 1874 set up two distinct tracks, or *séries,* of the examination: (1) Latin translation or composition and (2) philosophy and modern foreign language translation. Other previously required subjects remained common to the two séries, which were renamed in 1880. They were now called "rhetoric" (requiring Latin translation *and* composition and a theme in a modern foreign language) and "philosophy" (composition papers in science and philosophy), respectively. In 1896 the "classical" and the "modern" baccalauréats were created. The *baccalauréat modern* permitted the substitution of two modern languages in place of Latin. The contemporary practice of identifying each série by a letter of the alphabet was introduced in 1902.[13]

Throughout all the changes, preparation for the baccalauréat has continued to represent a nationally recognized rite of passage for an ever-growing number of young men and women in France and in its overseas territories and possessions.[14] From its inception, the baccalauréat carried with it not only the right to be admitted to study at a university at public expense, but also a certain civil status. It was in effect a certificate of academic and civic maturity, available to anyone who could pass the examinations.

Napoleon also encouraged the development of the *grandes écoles* to provide a cadre of knowledgeable and skilled officials for service to the state. The ancien régime had already established a number of grandes écoles, for example, Ecole des ponts et chaussées (1747), Ecoles des mines de Paris (1783), and Ecole d'arts et métiers (1780), to provide more practical

13. At that time they were called *sections:* A—(Latin, Greek); B—(Latin, languages); C—(Latin and science); D—(science and modern languages). In 1925 a section A' permitted Latin without Greek, and section B was reformulated as French, plus two modern languages. One should emphasize that other common subjects (mathematics, philosophy, history-geography, and science) were also required in all sections.

Other postwar changes have been the establishment (1945), then the abolition (1965) of a first-stage selection examination (*examen probatoire*) within the baccalauréat framework; the introduction (1969) of a paper in French language to be taken in the year before the main examination (*épreuve de francais anticipée*); and in 1983 the abolition of grades, but 1984 their reintroduction. Most important, the first *baccalauréats* for *techniciens* (in industrial studies, social and medical sciences, music, dance, secretarial work and accountancy, and computer science) were established in 1968. Guy Neave, "France," in Burton R. Clark, ed., *The School and the University: An International Perspective* (Berkeley: University of California Press, 1985).

14. When the *baccalauréat* was first administered in 1809, there were 32 successful candidates. In 1850, already 4,147; in 1900, 15,352; in 1939, 47,081; in 1950, 72,695; in 1985, 172,919; and in 1991, 571,428 sat for the baccalauréat. *Le Monde de l'Education,* supp. (February 1992): 72.

study of engineering, mining, and bridge-building than was available in the universities. Napoleon emasculated the universities, reducing them to weak *facultés,* and in their place he promoted the establishment of additional grandes écoles, establishing the Ecole normale supérieure in 1794 and the Ecole polytechnique in 1795. Entry was on a strictly competitive basis. The curricula were closely tied to the specific administrative, military, and engineering needs of government. Upon graduation, students were assigned to positions in order of academic merit. The social standing of the family counted for little; advancement was based on demonstrated achievement during the course work and in the final examinations.

This meritocratic spirit survived Napoleon's regime. Even though the monarchy was restored, the governmental institutions and practices of post-Napoleonic France could never simply revert to those of royal France before the Revolution. Nineteenth-century France under, successively, the restored Bourbon monarchy, the Second Empire, and the Third Republic was ready to accept examination success as a legitimate road to preferment and social status, an acceptance that continues today.

When Japan embarked on its process of modernization after 1868, the German model of examinations (together with borrowings from the French and English systems) helped shape the general direction and details of Japanese education.[15] Before the Meiji restoration, educational opportunities in Japan reflected the feudal arrangements of society, with strong elements of caste organization. Children were expected to follow the occupations of their fathers. The former warrior class, the samurai, monopolized both the highest educational opportunities and positions in government service. Within three years of the Meiji restoration the government swept away this restrictive system. Samurai could now enter any occupation; in turn, their privileged access to learning was abolished in favor of opening educational opportunities to any Japanese male willing and able to make the necessary substantial investment of time and effort. Within twenty-five years Japan had developed a thoroughgoing competitive examination system to select individuals for appointment to government positions.

Although an important motive of this reform had been to remove the samurai class from its dominant position in government, the result of the educational reforms and the introduction of competitive examinations was not quite so radical. Samurai families, though now deprived of their privileged access to positions of authority and high income, were nevertheless

15. See Amano, *Education and Examination in Modern Japan,* pp. 19, 56, 59, 124–126.

able to conserve much of their former advantage by encouraging their sons to achieve success in the new system.

> Which class or social group made the best use of the examination system? Various materials show that the former samurai class—that is, the former ruling class—was the first to take advantage of this system. The Japanese population structure in the early Meiji era consisted of 6 percent samurai. . . . But the majority of those studying at the various schools were from the samurai class . . . 84 percent of those admitted to the Law School of the Ministry of Justice in 1880 . . . 72 percent of the students of the Engineering College in 1885 . . . the pattern was the same at Tokyo University. . . . Even in 1900 . . . the number of students from the samurai class was still remarkably high [due to] the strength of their desire to rise socially: the drive to succeed in life enabled the children of the former samurai class to make the necessary effort.[16]

Checking Patronage and Corruption. Well into the nineteenth century, positions in British government service, both civil and military, and in the East India Company were bought and sold. Patronage was common practice, and the open buying and selling of government jobs (the term used was *jobbery*) was the excuse for corruption in the execution of official business, since those who had paid hard cash for their positions felt justified in seeking an appropriate return on their investment.

After 1849 passing an examination became a standard requirement before one could purchase a military commission, and in 1853 examinations for entry into the Indian administration were approved by Parliament. This was followed in 1858 by the introduction of examinations to control entry into Sandhurst and Woolwich (respectively, the army and navy officer-training schools).[17] Finally, the practice of buying positions in the Indian administration, the army, and navy was abolished in 1871. From then on, examinations were progressively introduced for entry into the home civil service.[18] These governmentally organized examinations were effective in checking nepotism and open corruption, though they could not eliminate

16. Ibid., pp. 192–93.

17. Jo Mortimore et al., *Secondary School Examinations: The Helpful Servants, Not the Dominating Master* (London: Institute of Education, University of London, 1986), pp. 11–12.

18. Rupert Wilkinson, *Gentlemanly Power: British Leadership and the Public School Tradition: A Comparative Study in the Making of Rulers* (London: Oxford University Press, 1964), pp. 89–90.

the advantages that derived from social status and wealth. For example, the well-connected young Winston Churchill experienced some difficulty entering Sandhurst in the 1890s. Family position and resources enabled him to make no fewer than three attempts, while enrolling in intensive cramming establishments, before he passed with sufficiently high marks to gain a place.[19] Nor was his experience rare. The sons of the British upper classes patronized the crammers to "get up" their mathematics and foreign languages in the months before the civil and military service examinations, much as today Japanese young people attend *juku* and *yobiko* (private, after school institutions providing extra training for university entrance examinations).

Similar motives were present in the United States. At every level of government, examinations were instituted in the hope that this would check the pervasive practice of politicians favoring their supporters with jobs. The federal government introduced examinations in the early 1870s for appointments to the Patent Office, the Census Bureau, and the Indian Office.[20] The Pendleton Act of 1883 extended examinations as minimum conditions of entry into the U.S. Civil Service for all candidates except those at the highest levels. Today, work in the postal, sanitation, police, and fire services, as well as in innumerable other types of employment offered by government authorities, is open only to those who have first passed written, competitive examinations.

Raising Levels of Knowledge and Skills. Although we have associated a major motive for the introduction of examination systems with particular countries, nowhere was just one motive at work. For example, although the elimination of patronage and corruption was the primary goal in the introduction of civil and military service examinations in Britain, other goals were present, particularly the encouragement of higher levels of competence and knowledge. However, in Britain this enjoyed nowhere near the attention it received in France and Germany, where improvement of the level of skill and knowledge of those appointed to government service was the major objective.

Although the courses of study in the grandes écoles were closely tied to the needs of the major specialized branches of government administration,

19. Robert J. Montgomery, *Examinations: An Account of Their Evolution as Administrative Devices in England* (London: Longmans, Green, 1965), p. 30.

20. Samuel Kavruck, "Thirty-three Years of Test Research: A Short History of Test Development in the U.S. Civil Service Commission," *American Psychologist* 2 (July 1956): 329–333. Cited in David A. Goslin, *The Search for Ability: Standardized Testing in Social Perspective* (New York: Russell Sage Foundation, 1963), p. 34.

finance, civil engineering, education, and so forth, the entrance examinations were strictly academic, though not exclusively focused on the traditional classical curriculum. "Higher scientific education had developed within the lycées to prepare boys for the entrance examinations to the government's *grandes écoles.*"[21] One result has been close correspondence between the content of the entrance examinations and the actual work of government administrators. In Germany the examinations given at the universities were (and still are) considered less important than the *Staatsexamen*, the licensing examinations given by the government authorities. These examinations cover material relevant to the future work of civil servants or members of the professions. In contrast to France and Germany, for decades the British government examinations for civil service entry focused exclusively on the humanities, especially on classical language and literature. The natural sciences, law, economics, and even applied mathematics were generally slighted. Indeed, some observers have criticized this bias toward literary skills and knowledge as an unfortunate, if unconscious, repetition of the emphasis on the Chinese classics in the examinations for appointment in the imperial government, even using the term *mandarinate* to describe the upper reaches of the British civil service.[22]

Allocating Scarce Places in Higher Education. Rapid increases in the number of students completing secondary education and wishing to continue into higher education promoted the use of end-of-secondary-school examinations as selection devices. This function of examinations was exceptionally important in Japan and Russia (and subsequently the Soviet Union).

The development of Japanese education was dominated by preparation to take competitive entrance examinations for admission to secondary schools and to higher education. Initially, too, admission to lower secondary schools was subject to successful performance in an entrance examination. Currently, the critical examinations come at the point of transfer from junior to senior secondary school and from senior secondary school to college or university. The focus on entrance examinations originated in the early years of modern Japanese education, when demand for places in schools far ex-

21. R. D. Anderson, *Education in France, 1848–1870* (Oxford: Clarendon Press, 1975), pp. 58, 66–72.

22. "Until World War I, most high achievers in Britain's higher civil service had studied classics, and once again, having come from professional or aristocratic backgrounds, they were characterized as mandarins." Carolyn Webber, "The Mandarin Mentality: Civil Service and University Admissions Testing in Europe and Asia," in Bernard R. Gifford, ed., *Test Policy and the Politics of Opportunity Allocation: The Workplace and the Law* (Boston: Kluwer Academic Publishers, 1989), pp. 47–48.

ceeded supply. Even though the absolute shortage of places has largely disappeared, competitive entrance examinations continue to characterize the Japanese system. Japanese parents are acutely conscious of the prestige and job value of their children's attending the "right" schools and higher education institutions, and they know that admission depends on good performance on the entrance examination.

In nineteenth-century Russia, the examination for the secondary-school-completion credential (the *attestat zrelosti,* or maturity certificate) was structured along the lines of the German Abitur.[23] Examinations were both written and oral. Because opportunities for higher education expanded more slowly than the number of secondary school graduates, places were rationed. Although provincial administrators occasionally enjoyed some discretion and could exercise a certain degree of autonomy, throughout the century the Imperial Ministry of Public Instruction followed a policy of increasing control over the content and regulation of the maturity examinations, especially under the formidable centralizing administration of Count Dmitry Tolstoy.[24] The purpose of this control was both to hold in check often rebellious students and alienated faculty and to reduce the pressure of admissions on the universities. The authorities were somewhat more successful in achieving the second goal than the first![25]

Immediately following the Revolution of 1917, the Bolshevik government abolished examinations at the end of secondary school and for university entrance. The 1920s were a period of active educational experimentation, much of it influenced by the progressive educational thought of Europe and America. The reformers, led by Lenin's wife, Krupskaia, directed their efforts at replacing what they regarded as an overacademicized, harmfully competitive curriculum with one that encouraged pupils to work cooperatively on socially useful projects. Teachers were to abandon their roles as didactic instructors, instead becoming facilitators, their authority subordinated to that of the pupil council, or *soviet.* Grades for schoolwork were abolished as oppressive; admission to the universities and higher technical institutes depended on social class origin and demon-

23. For the development of the Russian school system under the czars, see Nicholas A. Hans, *The Russian Tradition in Education* (London: Routledge and Kegan Paul, 1963).

24. Allen Sinel, *The Classroom and the Chancellery: State Educational Reform in Russia under Count Dmitry Tolstoi* (Cambridge: Harvard University Press, 1973), esp. chaps. 5 and 6.

25. For analysis of educational goals, programs, and policies in late nineteenth- and early twentieth-century Russia, see Patrick L. Alston, *Education and the State in Tsarist Russia* (Stanford: Stanford University Press, 1969). Also, Paul Monroe, *A Cyclopedia of Education* (New York: Macmillan, 1911), has a detailed article on Russia.

strated enthusiasm for the new political order, rather than on examination results.

By the end of the 1920s, Stalin's rise to power had put an end to this program. Soviet policy (summed up in the slogan "build Socialism in one country") now sacrificed idealism to the goal of rapid construction of an industrialized economy. This, it was announced, required a disciplined work force with technical competence. The progressivists in education were dismissed from their posts (or worse), and by 1933 the school and university systems had settled into a structure that, while it differed in many important ways from the czarist pattern, nevertheless had reinstated essential features of the czarist examination system for certifying satisfactory completion of secondary school and for university entrance.

Measuring and Improving the Effectiveness of Teachers and Schools. Following its introduction of examinations for positions in the civil service and armed forces, the British government imposed a system of examinations on state-subsidized elementary schools as part of the notorious Revised Code of 1862. Elementary schools served the children of the poor, while the middle and upper classes educated their children at home or in private schools. Throughout the 1840s and 1850s, the government had been providing increasing grants-in-aid to the elementary schools, despite the reluctance in mid-nineteenth-century England to provide taxpayer support for the poor.

There was much concern about the quality of education in the elementary schools, and particularly about the quality of the teaching. Most schools were small, church-run establishments, staffed by teachers who were undertrained or in too many schools even untrained. The Revised Code was intended to respond to these concerns: if the government was to provide money, it should know what results were being achieved. The code called for each school to be visited by a government inspector who would test the pupils in reading, writing, and arithmetic, and then report his findings. The code went further and provided a cash incentive to teachers to improve their own and their pupils' performance. The size of the government's subsidy to each elementary school was tied to the number of pupils who passed the inspector's tests, and teachers' salaries in turn were tied to the size of the subsidy. This was the much maligned system of "payment by results," which despite all criticism lasted until 1897.

Secondary education also changed during the Victorian era, expanding greatly under the auspices of a host of church-related, charitable, and private organizations. The "public" (that is, independent) schools grew in number and size as the middle and upper classes enrolled their sons either as day pupils or, increasingly, as boarders.

Because it was not providing financial support, the government did not intrude into the operation of the secondary schools as it did in elementary education. Instead, it took the view that it was up to the parents to ensure that they were getting value for their money and that their children were getting a satisfactory education. As in other spheres of English life, the principle of caveat emptor applied.

Parents, teachers in the private schools, and the schools' governing bodies were, like the government, ready to accept examination results as valid indicators of school quality and teachers' effectiveness. Their needs were served by nongovernment bodies. The College of Preceptors began to provide examinations for pupils in 1854. But these examinations were designed for presecondary (private) education, and the more influential secondary schools needed some other authority to establish the quality of their education. At first they found this in the original mode of Local Examinations, in which a school's governing body would pay for an Oxford or Cambridge college fellow to carry out an on-site inspection of the school premises, facilities, teacher qualifications, and level of the students' knowledge. "Locals" of this kind were hardly a *system* of examination, and in 1857 Exeter University collaborated in the so-called Exeter Experiment, which provided competitive examinations for secondary school pupils from nearby schools. Within a year Oxford and Cambridge followed suit, each offering a revised form of Locals to secondary schools across the country. The targets of assessment were the pupils, but the information on marks and pass rates was also used as an index of a school's general quality, and particularly of the teachers' effort and effectiveness. From this beginning grew the British system of providing end-of-secondary-school examinations via university-dominated examination boards, with the minimum of governmental interference or regulation.

Limiting Curricular Differentiation. Compared to most of the other countries in this study, governmental control of the school curriculum in the United States and England and Wales has been extraordinarily weak, sometimes even absent. In the other countries, the government's control of the curriculum has been direct and extensive. Only in the decentralized systems of the United States and England/Wales have examinations served as a major instrument for limiting curriculum diversity.

Decentralization of school control has been even greater in the United States than in England/Wales, with a correspondingly greater differentiation of curricula and standards of grading. In order to establish a minimum set of curriculum standards and a modicum of interstudent comparability, the College Entrance Examination Board was formed in 1900 by a consortium of colleges. Its array of tests included the Scholastic Aptitude Test, the subject-based Achievement Tests (the so-called College Boards), and the Advanced Placement Examinations.[26]

Parallel motives were evident in England during the nineteenth century. As we have noted, secondary schooling expanded rapidly in the middle of the century, with little governmental inclination to regulate the schools. The English condemned central control as "the Continental approach." But *some* device had to be found to limit the extent of curricular differentiation from school to school. By 1917 the Local examinations of Oxford and Cambridge had grown into a widely recognized and prestigious set of School Certificate ("General" and "Higher") examinations, owned and operated by eight examining boards connected with different universities. The School Certificate examinations survived until 1951, when they were transformed into the General Certificate of Education ("Ordinary," "Advanced," and "Scholarship") examinations, or GCEs. In 1965 the GCE system was supplemented by the introduction of the Certificate of Secondary Education (CSE) examinations for less academically inclined students. The latest major restructuring in England and Wales has been unification of the Ordinary level of the GCE and the entire CSE into a new single, common examination, the General Certificate of Secondary Education.

While there were other reasons for the emphasis placed on these examinations in England/Wales, a major motive was to put in place some system of control over the curricula of a highly fragmented school system.[27] In the last few years, the British government has despaired of this decentralized system of indirect control of the curriculum via examinations and has taken the first steps toward direct governmental control along the lines of most other countries.

One consequence of the establishment of these examination systems was the building of a common mentality and even esprit de corps among the certificated elites in each country. This was particularly noticeable in Germany, France, and Japan, where the possession of educational credentials marked a major route to social status. The task of preparing for, taking, and passing nationally recognized examinations at the end of secondary school and higher education became the accepted initiation rite into the middle and upper levels of the social order. In Germany, indeed, another name for the Abitur is *Hochschulreife,* literally "readiness for higher education," and as we have noted, in Russia the term used is attestat zrelosti,

26. Frederick Rudolph, *The American College and University: A History* (New York: Alfred A. Knopf, 1962), pp. 436–437.

27. Montgomery, *Examinations.*

or "maturity certificate." Possession of a certificate earned via arduous study and examination implied admission to a superior civil status. When the numbers holding these certificates were still relatively small, the sense of being a member of an exclusive Fellowship could easily arise.

An "age of examinations" began in the nineteenth century, followed by the rapid, widespread, and ultimately firm establishment of these examinations. They were often highly competitive; they were usually public; individual candidates were typically unknown to the examiners/graders; and they were increasingly written, though oral examinations have survived.

The existence of examinations required that an organized body of knowledge be put down on paper and published, subject by subject, so it could be taught in the schools. Clearer objectives and more organized content in preparation for the examinations increased the apparent value of schooling. At the same time, the syllabus for the examinations tended to become the syllabus for the school, leading to the familiar complaint that curricula were dominated by the examinations.

Although, as we have seen, there were at least a half-dozen practical motives for the establishment and growth of examinations, there is also a certain ideological component to be noted. The nineteenth century was a time of belief in self-improvement through effort in education and success in examinations. Samuel Smiles's *Self-Help* and Frederic W. Farrar's *Eric; or, Little by Little* conveyed a powerful and easily accepted message along these lines. More sophisticated ideological support for examinations came from Herbert Spencer's thesis that social progress was promoted by "survival of the fittest." The logical leap was made to the proposition that competitive examinations could identify who were in fact the fittest, that appointments and promotions on the basis of examination results would not only promote social progress and national strength, but would also reward the fittest with deserved recognition of their innate talents and superior efforts. The widespread adoption and vigorous growth of examination systems can be regarded as a natural complement to belief in individual autonomy and responsibility and to faith in the justice of a society that rewarded each individual according to his or her measured deserts.

Comparative Study of Examinations: The Research Background

A vast literature deals with examinations in particular countries, spanning a range of topics: psychometrics, mechanics of examinations, standards of achievement, the effects of examinations on the rest of the education system, various kinds of bias (social, cultural, and gender), and to a lesser extent, the effects of examinations on social status, employment opportunities, individual life chances, and the like.[28] Reports about secondary school examinations in other nations appear from time to time in the popular press, typically describing outbreaks of student protest over examination practices or policies, or criticism by other special-interest groups.[29] By contrast, there is relatively little systematic, cross-national comparative work, and with only a few notable exceptions, the comparative study of examinations has been a largely neglected aspect of comparative education.

In the 1930s, Paul Monroe directed an international Examinations Inquiry at Teachers College, Columbia University, enlisting the talents of I. L. Kandel.[30] This project led to the publication of three volumes, plus many studies of individual countries by scholars associated with the project. In 1938 and again in 1969, *The Year Book of Education* and its successor publication, *The World Year Book of Education,* studied secondary school examinations from an international perspective.[31] Valuable descrip-

28. See Brereton, *Case for Examinations,* and Philip Hartog and E. C. Rhodes, *An Examination of Examinations* (London: Macmillan, 1935), for early discussions. A recent bibliography of mostly British items in J. C. Mathews, *Examinations: A Commentary* (London: George Allen and Unwin, 1985), lists about 250 titles. References to U.S.-published sources may be found in the end notes to Robert Klitgaard, *Choosing Elites* (New York: Basic Books, 1985). See also Montgomery, *Examinations;* R. A. C. Oliver, "Education and Selection," in Stephen Wiseman, ed., *Examinations and English Education* (Manchester: Manchester University Press, 1961); John Oxenham, "Employers, Jobs and Qualifications," in John Oxenham, ed., *Education versus Qualifications?* (London: George Allen and Unwin, 1984).

29. See, e.g., "Generation in Trouble: Spanish and Russians Find Their Young Alienated," *New York Times* (February 16, 1987): A6, which describes student unrest in Spain over university admission policies that are "based on a single examination, which many students see as an unfair throw of the dice." French student demonstrations against "la sélection," focussed on a *projet de loi* that would have permitted universities to exercise discretion in the use of baccalauréat results for admission, are described in "Class of '86 Takes to the Streets" and "Violence Mars Students' Victory," *Times Educational Supplement* (December 5 and 12, 1986), each on p. 17.

30. See the several volumes of the Teachers College International Institute Examinations Inquiry. This major project, under Paul Monroe's direction, was conducted in the 1930s, and was funded by the Carnegie Corporation and the Carnegie Foundation. Collaborators were drawn from the United States, England, Finland, France, Germany, Norway, Scotland, and Sweden. The work was summarized in three volumes reporting papers and discussion at three international conferences: Eastbourne, England (1931), Folkestone, England (1935); and Dinard, France (1938). See International Institute Examinations Enquiry, *Essays on Examinations* (London: Macmillan, 1936); Paul Monroe, ed., *Conference on Examinations* (New York: Bureau of Publications, Teachers College, Columbia University, 1936), and Paul Monroe, ed., *Conference on Examinations* (New York: Bureau of Publications, Teachers College, Columbia University, 1939). For a short description of the inquiry, see I. L. Kandel, "The International Examinations Inquiry," in *The Education Record* 17 (January 1936), pp. 50–69.

31. Harley V. Usill, ed., *The Year Book of Education* (London: Evans Brothers, 1938) described the nature of examinations in several countries of the British Commonwealth and

tive material and analysis were presented in these two volumes, particularly in the later publication.

Some elements of secondary-school-completion examinations in particular subjects have been incorporated into the specially devised achievement tests of the International Association for the Evaluation of Educational Achievement (IEA).[32] In both form and content, the IEA tests were required to be uniform and acceptable internationally to make comparison of levels of cognitive achievement across nations possible. In meeting this perfectly proper aim for an *international* tests of school achievement, however, IEA tests may omit important elements of the curriculum taught and examined in particular nations. Although some countries have added their own national items to the common international test, specifically national elements take second place to those with wider international currency. Moreover, since the IEA has not been concerned with the consequences and implications of examinations, it has ignored the dynamics of examination systems and their relation to school systems and societies. Similar priorities shape the activities of the Educational Testing Service in Princeton, New Jersey, which has initiated work on comparative achievement similar to that developed by IEA.

Other international projects have been devoted at least in part to the question of secondary school examinations. In the early 1960s an International Study of University Admissions was conducted under the joint auspices of the United Nations Educational, Scientific, and Cultural Organization and the International Association of Universities.[33] During the late 1960s, individuals representing institutions interested in the development of an International Baccalaureate examination met to examine national cur-

---

in other English-speaking nations, without attempting comparative analysis. In 1969 Joseph A. Lauwerys and David G. Scanlon, eds., *Examinations: The World Year Book of Education* (New York: Harcourt, Brace and World, 1969), covered a far wider range of countries, and the organization of the book offered a comprehensive framework for comparative study. Although proceeding mainly by juxtaposing descriptions of the purposes, organization, and structures of examinations in different countries, the 1969 study made use of a number of cross-national themes, e.g., the economic and social effects of examinations and the effects of examinations upon teachers and pupils. In addition, in the 1970s the Commonwealth Secretariat (London) engaged in a review of secondary school examinations in a number of Commonwealth Countries. See Commonwealth Secretariat, *Examinations at Secondary Level* (London: Commonwealth Secretariat, 1970) and *Public Examinations, Report of the Commonwealth Planning Seminar. Accra, March 1973,* in *Education in the Commonwealth* (London: Commonwealth Secretariat, 1973).

32. For overviews of IEA purposes and projects, see *Comparative Education Review* 18 (June 1974) and *Comparative Education Review* 31 (February 1987).

33. See International Study of University Admissions, *Access to Higher Education,* 2 vols. (Paris: UNESCO and the International Association of Universities, 1963, 1965).

ricula and examinations. Their goal was to provide a credential that would be acceptable to universities in many countries for purposes of matriculation. In the course of devising curricula and examinations for the International Baccalaureate, attention was given to the contents of the secondary-leaving examinations in a number of major European countries.[34] At about the same time, the Council of Europe considered the equivalence of school and university qualification among the European nations. But like the work of IEA, these efforts were concerned with the common elements of the several national examinations, and particularly with legal equivalents for the purpose of regulating university entrance, rather than with differences among them or with the effects and implications of those variations.[35]

More recently, the World Bank investigated examination practices in a number of industrialized and developing nations in order to promote the improvement of examination procedures, especially in the latter group of countries. Representatives of the World Bank have argued that it may not be a bad thing at all for teachers to "teach to the test" as long as the test is well constructed, covers material relevant to the candidates, and provides systematic feedback to the schools and to teachers on their candidates' performance.[36] The International Association for Educational Assessment has produced several volumes of conference proceedings concerning examinations around the world, the most recent in 1990.[37]

The current revival of interest in foreign examination practices on the part of many United States observers has been motivated by interest in what lessons may be learned. In 1991 the National Endowment for the Humanities published a brief report containing sample examination papers in humanities subjects from France, Germany, Britain, and Japan, contrasting those with the Scholastic Aptitude and American College tests in

34. See A. D. C. Peterson, *The International Baccalaureate: An Experiment in International Education* (London: George G. Harrap, 1972), and Martin Mayer, *Diploma: International Schools and University Entrance* (New York: Twentieth Century Fund, 1968), esp. chap. 9.

35. See E. Egger, ed., *Secondary School Leaving Examinations* (Strasbourg: Council for Cultural Co-operation, 1971, mimeographed); A. D. C. Peterson, *New Techniques in the Evaluation of School Work* (Strasbourg: Council of Europe, 1971); W. D. Halls, *International Equivalences in Access to Higher Education* (Paris: UNESCO, 1971); W. D. Halls, "School Examinations in the EEC," *Trends in Education* (autumn 1973); W. D. Halls, "The Oxford/Council of Europe Study for the Evaluation of the Curriculum and Examinations," *Education and Culture* (Spring 1974).

36. Stephen P. Heyneman and Ingemar Fägerlind, eds., *University Examinations and Standardized Testing* (Washington, D.C.: World Bank, 1988), pp. 11–12.

37. Anton J. M. Luitjen, ed., *Issues in Public Examinations: A Selection of Proceedings of the 1990 IAEA Conference* (Utrecht: Lemma, 1990).

the United States.[38] The Congressional Office of Technology Assessment has recently concluded an extensive study of examination systems abroad and has been conducting discussions on the implications of those practices for the United States.[39] Both efforts arise from current hope of using examinations to raise standards of student achievement.

Finally, the European Community has moved rapidly toward comparative study of credentials in member nations and the ways in which they are acquired, including study, work experience, and examinations. Such work has great practical value, stimulated as it is by the prospect of relatively unrestricted movement of qualified personnel across national frontiers and the need to work out a system of mutual recognition of credentials.[40]

The Significance of Examinations as a Subject for Comparative Research

The World Bank is not alone in suggesting that examinations can play a major role in raising educational standards.[41] Indeed, comparative study of examination systems finds its strongest justification when nations seek ways to bring about educational change, especially when the concern focuses on raising the level of school achievement, as is currently the case in a number of nations, including England/Wales, the United States, and China. Whether justified or not, occasionally a strong belief arises in the United

38. National Endowment for the Humanities, *National Tests: What Other Countries Expect Their Students to Know* (Washington, D.C.: National Endowment for the Humanities, 1991).

39. Office of Technology Assessment. *Testing in American Schools—Asking the Right Questions* (Washington, D.C.: Office of Technology Assessment, 1992).

40. See particularly the comparative publications of the European Centre for Development of Vocational Training, Berlin.

41. Thus, under a heading "Provide quality assurance in education," the Task Force on Education for Economic Growth of the Education Commission of the States recommends: "Student progress should be measured through periodic tests of general achievement and specific skills." *Action for Excellence* (Denver, Colo.: Education Commission of the States, 1983), p. 11. And in *A Nation At Risk,* the National Commission on Excellence in Education stressed the central role of examinations as follows: "Such expectations [of the level of knowledge required] are expressed to students in several different ways: .. .. . by the presence or absence of rigorous examinations requiring students to demonstrate their mastery of content and skill before receiving a diploma or a degree." National Commission on Excellence in Education, *A Nation at Risk: The Imperative for Educational Reform* (Washington, D.C.: U.S. Government Printing Office, 1983), p. 19. The commission went on to say: "Standardized tests of achievement .. .. . should be administered at major transition points .. .. . particularly from high school to college or work. The purposes of these tests would be to: (a) certify the student's credentials; (b) identify the need for remedial intervention; and (c) identify the opportunity for advanced or accelerated work. The tests should be administered as part of a nationwide (but not Federal) system of State and local standardized tests" (28).

States that certain foreign models merit close attention and possibly even emulation: for example, mathematics and science instruction in the Soviet Union in the 1960s, "open education" in Britain during the 1970s, and Japanese rigor in the 1990s. Foreign examination systems are often regarded as doing a better job of stimulating student achievement, defining the curriculum for teachers, preparing and selecting school graduates for subsequent education and work, and providing taxpayers and administrators with indicators of school quality.

While examinations exert a powerful influence on schooling arrangements, social and educational developments in turn affect examinations. In many nations of the world, the advent of mass education, especially at the secondary level, has profoundly altered the nature and purpose of secondary-school-completion examinations. From being almost exclusively directed at regulating credentials for entry into higher education and certain high-status occupations, they have become increasingly multipurpose, certifying completion of the upper secondary level of schooling and controlling access to a variety of further education and training opportunities far beyond the traditional institutions of higher education. If only because they now touch the lives of so many more young people, secondary-school-completion examinations fully merit close attention.

There are other, more general justifications for concern with these examinations in contemporary society. As economic and social life becomes more formalized and bureaucratized, schools are drawn to fit their procedures to the surrounding society. Certificates of completion of a course of study become valuable pieces of property, and examinations are a way to ensure that such certificates reflect degrees of learning rather than simply attendance. What each nation considers to be the most desirable opportunities after secondary school are necessarily limited relative to the demand for them. Thus, examinations are widely accepted as a politically and ethically defensible way of deciding which high school graduates to reward and which to deny.

From time to time, nations have tried to abandon examinations at the end of secondary school, but have then been moved to backtrack. China offers a contemporary example. During the Cultural Revolution, China broke with its well-established tradition of reliance on examinations to control admission to higher education and further training. Certification of political activism and "correctness" of social origin took their place. But one of the first changes made by the post-Mao regime was to return to using examination results for allocating university places. The Soviet Union also tried to do away with such examinations in the 1920s, but under Stalin they were reintroduced and became well entrenched in Soviet education.

Indeed, with the notable exception of the United States and Sweden, it is difficult to name a modernized or modernizing nation that does not rely on a national system of examinations to certify completion of secondary education, to allocate opportunities for further education or training, or to regulate hiring.

Alongside these manifest functions of examinations are some equally significant other functions. Examination results can be used to evaluate (with greater or lesser validity) the quality of a teacher or a school. They can be used to allocate money for salaries, buildings, materials, equipment, and the like. Examinations can serve to motivate teachers and students, stimulating teaching and learning by specifying in detail the system's expectations. In consequence, examination requirements can lead to undue concentration on the material to be examined. Indeed, examined subjects can drive unexamined subjects out of the school timetable entirely. Above all, examinations can serve as a way of legitimizing knowledge, signaling the acceptance of a new school subject. For these reasons, examinations are expected to be influential in implementing new school practices and educational reform programs.

Examination systems in particular countries demonstrate different ways of fulfilling these functions. They illustrate how changing social circumstances create pressures to change examinations either directly or indirectly. In addition, examination systems have a variety of intended and unintended effects on school systems.

The National Systems, and Why We Chose Them

Each of the eight national systems selected for study illustrates at least one important feature of the relationships among examinations, schooling, and society. All are committed to open access to public education, but all have well-established national patterns of organization, provision, and control. Most have introduced important changes over time, in some instances quite radical ones. Social and political contexts of the educational systems in these countries exhibit sharp differences: unitary national administrations and federal systems, richer and poorer nations, and large and diverse territories as well as small and quite homogeneous countries. The Soviet Union was until 1991 officially a Communist country. China remains Communist, but the others represent varieties of Western, industrialized, democratic systems. In Japan, France, and China, a central ministry of education exerts firm control over curriculum and other school matters, whereas in the other five countries, the central government shares power and responsibility with provincial and/or local authorities. Finally, the United States,

Sweden, the former Soviet Union, and Japan have long-standing commitments to open access to postcompulsory schooling and well-established secondary comprehensive school arrangements, whereas in the others a selective model of secondary and higher education remains influential.

Notwithstanding differences in size, level of development, administrative arrangements, and political system, secondary-school-completion examinations in these nations share a largely common set of functions. They differ substantially, however, in their control over various aspects of their educational and social systems and in how that influence is exercised.

Japan stands out as an examination-driven system par excellence, whereas Sweden, which once followed a standard European (Abitur-like) system, has rejected this approach. Sweden has gone further than the other nations we have considered in being willing to tailor curricula to suit individual choices, to relate them to employment, and to make fundamental reforms in its examination system. In both Germany and France, important changes have also been introduced into the systems, but examinations continue to operate as powerful mechanisms for qualifying students at the end of upper secondary education and for controlling access to higher education, Germany in a federal system and France in a unitary one. In England/Wales examinations have been an unofficial but powerful means of curriculum control in a hitherto decentralized system, but they have recently come under increasing government direction in concert with the move toward a national curriculum.

Examinations in China have a special and explicit role in controlling access to higher education and in shaping educational practice. In contrast to the developed, industrialized, democratic nations, China is committed to the idea of rational planning, in which examinations serve explicitly to shape the patterns of enrollment in higher education and to serve manpower requirements. Until recently, the same could be said of the Soviet Union, but the early 1990s witnessed the dismantling of the command economy that formed the basis for planned control of education.[42] The

42. "Prior to the Congress of Workers in Public Education [1989], the entire system [of education in the Soviet Union] functioned, in effect, as a system for training labor power to accomplish the targets of five-year plans; the Congress, however, for the first time since the 1920s said: 'Our goal is the development of the individual, the abilities of the individual, the upbringing of the individual and citizen—and, through this, the glory and power of the country and the future of the people. All this depends on the main thing: the development of the individual.' " G. A. Iagodin, "Only a Free School Will Educate a Free Person," *Soviet Education* 38, no. 7 (1991), pp. 26–27. (Iagodin was the chairman of the USSR State Committee for Public Education. Forced from office by right-wingers before the failed 1991 putsch, he was restored to his post immediately thereafter.)

likely effects of this change in ideology and practice upon the examination system are not yet clear.

The contrast offered by the United States with these more formally organized and regulated systems is striking. External examinations have virtually no role in high school graduation requirements and little direct effect on the curriculum. Instead, they are limited to informing the admission decisions of an extremely diversified higher education system.

Plan of the Book

Each chapter offers a particular focus on secondary school external examinations. The three chapters in part 1 present relevant background information and examine the range of variables relevant to examination systems. Chapters 2 and 3 describe the typical experience of two young persons in each country as they reach the end of their secondary school years. Both candidates, a young man and a young woman, are fairly good students, one rather better than the other, being prepared for the external examinations. Our purpose here is twofold: to describe the role of external examinations in their specific national contexts and to relate how, and to what degree, they control the lives and the education of students. In chapter 4 we describe and discuss the formal structures for administering examinations: who owns the examinations, how they are organized and controlled, and, among the several interests involved, the role of teachers in the external examinations.

Part 2 is devoted to the examinations themselves. In chapters 5 and 6 we describe and compare the examination papers in four subjects (language and literature, history, English as a foreign language, and mathematics), noting specifically their format, the style of the questions, and their content. We compare the national examination system in Chapter 7: what burdens are placed on students with respect to the quantity of work (number of subjects required, duration, question format) and its quality, that is, the degree of intellectual rigor required. Here we examine more closely the difficulty levels of questions in the common basic subjects of national language and literature and mathematics. Chapter 8 extends our consideration of how hard the examinations are by comparing rates of academic success across nations. This exercise brings up a series of related considerations and reveals that such international comparisons are by no means as straightforward as might be expected.

In part 3 we return to the broad issues suggested in this introduction. Chapter 9 covers the national debates in each country, reviewing recent and current expressions of concerns in both educational and noneducational realms and referring to current developments and trends. In this discussion, we stress the conflicts among different views, point to certain similarities across nations, and emphasize the essentially political nature of the debate. Finally, chapter 10 opens with a brief summary of the study's findings and discusses its implications. We conclude with an exploration of options, whether explicit or implicit, inevitably involved in adopting a particular form of examination system, and examine how these pose a number of dilemmas for educators, administrators, and politicians.

An appendix contains examples of examination papers in national language/literature and mathematics from the eight nations.

In addition, we direct readers' attention to a few major questions. Are the variety of examination practices and the changes currently taking place in the eight countries converging, forming a common model? In what circumstances do examinations serve as barriers or as levers to change? To what extent is it appropriate to regard different examination systems as compromises or trade-offs among variously desirable but mutually contradictory objectives? In what ways do the debates over examinations express different views of educational purposes, the functions of examinations, and efforts to assume control over these purposes and functions? And finally, how do examinations control education?

Part I

Description

Chapter 2

The Candidates and Their Schools:
The United States, Sweden, the Soviet Union,
and England/Wales

On each of us
Thy learning shed.
On calculus may we be fed.
And teach us, please,
To speak with ease
All languages,
Alive and dead!
—Chorus, *Utopia Limited,* act 1

As students approach the conclusion of secondary school, they have become accustomed to the conventional assessment practices of their schools:
formal and informal exercises to determine what they have learned and
periodic grading by their teachers. These practices, of course, vary considerably from the classrooms of one nation to another, even from one school
to another in the same country, but everywhere they testify to the persistent
and universal educational task of checking on what the students know and
can do. Everywhere, it will be acknowledged, educational assessments have
become steadily more important.

At this point in their lives, however, students face assessments of a
different nature, having longer-lasting significance. Hitherto test results have
been limited for the most part to the classroom or the school. But now the
examinations have significance for the world outside high school. Students
are at a transition point, about to leave school for advanced study, further
training, or work. They are poised at a critical point where their career
options are being shaped, if not finally determined, and where access to
the next phase of their formal education will depend, at least in part, on
their record of achievement so far. The more imminent the examinations,
the more powerful the influence (if not even the outright control) they exert
over the day-to-day activities of students and their schools. Frequently, the

lion's share of school time is devoted to examination preparation and rehearsals.

Whatever the formal curriculum might ordain, the "delivered" curriculum for at least one year, and often for two or three years before the examination, reflects the syllabus of the examination. Students' lives are also strongly affected, if not powerfully controlled, by the approaching examination: leisure activities give way to extra study hours, additional homework assignments, and quite frequently special tutoring and cram arrangements. In some countries the results of the examination will totally determine the students' subsequent work, studies, training, and careers as adults; in others, the examination results are not the be-all and end-all of everything, but will nevertheless exert a powerful influence on life chances. Students are now becoming involved with a large external examination system and the results will have significance extending well beyond the classrooms and the schools to a much wider world.

Of course, not all students will be approaching these final tests; some may have become discouraged, others may have been told that their academic records are too weak for examination entry. And even among those (usually a majority) who are being entered for the examinations, there may not be a uniformly positive response to the challenge. But teachers are busy grooming students for the event, with extra work, special drills, and rehearsal examinations. Some parents pay for special coaching courses and tutoring. The tempo of study, both during the school day and in after-school study, shows a marked acceleration. Family, friends, and schools all recognize the qualitatively different nature of these final examinations, and they do not hesitate to express deep interest in the outcome.

To illustrate the characteristic experience of these students as they complete secondary school and arrive at external examinations, we present two representative biographies from each of the eight countries. Both students aspire to take the examinations, but they have different interests, abilities, and backgrounds. The narratives describe school life as the students approach the final tests, take the examinations, and move on after the results become known. The stories also describe how the secondary schools in each nation are organized and how they bring students along to the challenge of final examinations. The order of presentation moves from those countries where external examinations exert relatively loose control over students' lives and school activities to those where the influence of examinations is great. In this chapter we begin with the United States and Sweden and move on to the Soviet Union and England/Wales where the impact of examinations is substantial. In the following chapter, we continue with

China, where final examinations are also important, and conclude with three countries, the Federal Republic of Germany, France, and Japan, where examinations dominate.

The United States

Peter and MaryLou are in the last month of twelfth grade, the final year of public secondary school. Though high school has been pleasant enough—busy, active, and varied—nevertheless they are looking forward to leaving the neighborhood comprehensive high school they have attended for four years. They live in Amherst, a suburb of Buffalo in New York State, and enjoy life, with its web of school lessons, extracurricular activities, sports, and social life. Schoolwork outside classes has not demanded much time or intellectual effort, and they have been able to follow individual interests, seek part-time employment, or just hang out. Although Buffalo was once a prosperous industrial center, it is now depressed. On the contrary, Amherst, the site of a major campus of the State University of New York (SUNY), has grown vigorously in the past fifteen years.

Publicly provided schools enroll over 90 percent of American schoolchildren, but substantial local variations are the norm. For example, Buffalo, together with its Erie County suburbs, has a large Catholic population, and church-related schools enroll about a third of the school-age population of the area. Because the provision of public schooling rests in the hands of locally elected school boards acting under powers delegated by each of the fifty state governments, local characteristics color many aspects of schooling in the United States. Tax revenue support per student varies greatly among the different local school boards from state to state, and even within states too. Federal powers in education are minimal, although federal influence, exercised via earmarked grants of money, can be considerable.

However, common features cut across local differences and lend a degree of uniformity to the country's system of public schooling. In most states, compulsory attendance extends from ages six to sixteen; a complete secondary education requires twelve years (grades), of which senior high school takes three or four; coeducation is standard practice in public schools; and federal (and often state) laws prohibit discrimination on grounds of race, religion, national origin, physical handicap, and the like. Other common characteristics stem from the nationwide activities of the textbook publishers, the professional associations and unions of teachers and school administrators, and, most important for the purposes of this book, from the work of nongovernmental testing agencies, especially the Educational Testing Service, (ETS) located in Princeton, New Jersey, and the American College Testing Program, in Iowa City, Iowa.

Peter's father is a self-employed medical technician in the relatively new technology of ultrasound imaging. His mother works as a secretary in a law office. The family moved around the country during Peter's younger years as his father completed his training and acquired experience in various hospitals and clinics in his specialty. However, at the beginning of Peter's seventh-grade year, the family moved to Amherst, and Peter enrolled in the local public junior high school, situated just across the road from their present school.

MaryLou has always lived in Amherst. Her father and mother were divorced when she was eight years old. Her father now lives in California and has a second family. MaryLou's mother has remarried, too, to a retail store manager. She is not employed, but volunteer activities on behalf of local associations concerned with environmental protection take a lot of her time.

MaryLou and Peter finished eighth grade in the junior high school and then moved across the street to their present senior high school. The school was built in the late 1930s in an impressively solid, monumental style to accommodate eighteen hundred students; its current enrollment is barely one thousand. Even though the total population in Amherst has been increasing steadily, the number of high-school-age children dropped precipitously in the late 1970s and 1980s. The school provides plenty of room for a wide array of academic and auxiliary activities and has funds for computers, projectors, television sets, a good school library, up-to-date textbooks, a fifteen-hundred-seat auditorium, a swimming pool, extensive sports fields, and so forth. An active Parent-Teacher Association (PTA) solicits money for many of these "extras." Because salaries and work conditions are good, the local school board is able to attract and keep well-qualified teachers. All this contrasts sharply with school conditions just across the city line in neighboring Buffalo, where tax money is scarce, buildings are not well maintained, and the poverty and cultural deprivation of many school-age children create special burdens for the city's school system.

During each of the four years of high school, Peter has been studying English and mathematics; this is his third year of French, second year of history, and first year of economics. In previous years, he has had a year each of biology, chemistry, and physics and two years of social studies (mostly history, but with a smattering of sociology and anthropology). In each of these courses, he has had to take frequent tests on the material covered in the past week or two. Usually, though not always, the teacher gave a final test covering the entire course. Indeed, Peter has experienced schooling largely as a process of studying discrete "units" of facts and procedures, on which he expects to be tested immediately before passing on to the next unit. There have also been classes in physical education, health, and driver education. He is registered in the school's "college track," along with about 60 percent of his fellow twelfth-graders. A further 20 percent are in the vocational track and the remainder in the general track. About 80 percent of Amherst high school graduates go on to some kind of postsecondary education, roughly half of these to four-year colleges and nearly 40 percent to community colleges for vocational courses lasting one to two years.

During this final year of school, Peter has five main subjects: English language and literature, French, mathematics, economics, and American history. His days are busy, filled with school-based but by no means exclusively academic activities. He is a valued member of the school's track team, and he is heavily engaged in helping to prepare the school yearbook and in stage-managing a series of drama productions (three of them during the year). Evidence of these extracurricular activities will be very important, he feels for applying to enter college. Studying often takes second place.

Unlike many of his school friends, Peter has no regular part-time job, but he does pick up a few dollars from time to time unloading, unpacking, and stacking stock in a nearby large hardware-supply warehouse. In addition, earlier in the school year Peter attended a private course to prepare for the Scholastic Aptitude Test (SAT) in mathematics and verbal skills. Many college admissions offices recommend, or even require, applicants to submit the results of this test (or of the broadly equivalent American College Test). The coaching, which cost his parents about five hundred dollars in fees, was intended to achieve two major objectives: to reduce test anxiety and to develop specific skills for answering multiple-choice tests. In addition, the instructors reviewed basic academic work in mathematics and language, especially vocabulary. The entire course comprised ten four-hour sessions and two intensive workshop sessions, given on Saturday mornings and some evenings, and Peter also made use of independent study materials in print form and on tapes available at the coaching center.

Peter is undecided about his career, but he does not feel pressured to make a decision "this early." Both he and his parents expect that during the four years of college following high school his ideas about a career will take more solid shape. His parents have told him that they cannot afford the tuition bill at a private college (the very cheapest would cost $6,000; the most expensive as much as $14,000 a year), but they have said that they are prepared to pay the much lower tuition costs (about $1,600 a year) at the publicly funded State University of New York system, and even for college residence away from home, which Peter earnestly desires. He plans therefore to apply for admission to three of the undergraduate colleges in the SUNY system—Albany, Binghamton, and Stony Brook. His college adviser told him also of a small, not too expensive, private college in North Carolina with an outstanding program in writing and theater arts, which attracts him a lot. Peter believes that if he works full-time over the summer after graduation and part-time during the school year, he can earn sufficient money to pay the added expenses of a private institution. He will apply for whatever student loans and tuition reductions may be available.

While Peter is content to leave his plans for a career largely unformed, MaryLou has very definite ideas about what she wants to do after high school: she would like to make a career in retailing. This decision has shaped her program of studies in high school. She has been enrolled in the general track, in which she has studied English for four years and has taken three years of various courses in social studies, but has had only two years of mathematics, only one year of science (biology), and no foreign language. She has passed an assortment of courses in typing, physical education, health, bookkeeping, and driver education, and has been active in extracurricular activities, particularly in girls' basketball and as a cheerleader for the football team. At the moment she has no plans to continue her formal education after high school, so she did not prepare to take the SAT.

She has been much influenced in her career decision by her stepfather, who will be able to smooth her entry into a trainee position in the company for which he works. However, like Peter, MaryLou is not overly concerned if it doesn't work out. She believes that there are plenty of opportunities for someone with her looks, personality, and willingness to work. Meanwhile, alongside her school attendance and a minimal attention to homework, she is devoting almost twenty-five hours a week to her part-time job as counter clerk in a nearby supermarket. Even though she spends a good deal of her earnings on music tapes, cosmetics, and clothes, she has managed to accumulate almost fifteen hundred dollars in her savings bank account.

Peter sat for the Scholastic Aptitude Test one Saturday morning in October of his final year. The test was given at the high school, and as it was composed entirely of multiple-choice questions, Peter was required to present himself equipped only with his official admission ticket, a couple of soft-lead pencils, and an eraser. The format of the test was very familiar, and the three hours went by quickly. In the mathematical portion of the test, the average time available to answer each question was sixty seconds, so Peter found himself working against the clock. Even the verbal portion, which contained fewer questions, provided significant time pressure.

Within a month, the mail brought Peter his results. They were certainly quite respectable, in the eighty-sixth percentile of all college-bound high school seniors for the mathematics portion and in the eighty-second percentile for the language portion. If he wished to strengthen an application to a selective college, he could make a second (or third) attempt in later months, perhaps after additional coaching by a private tutor. Peter is quite satisfied with his results, however, and has no plans to retake the SAT.

Because Peter did not want to attend the closest state college, he followed the standard practice of applying to several colleges of different academic standing. He hoped to be offered a place at more than one, but even if only one had responded positively, he would probably have settled quite happily for that one. If he had been seeking admission to the more prestigious and most academically selective colleges and universities, superior scores in the SAT would have enhanced his chances of being offered a place, though high scores alone do not guarantee admission. To bolster evidence of his academic prowess, he would no doubt have taken some Achievement Tests in school subjects, also offered by the ETS.

Early in April he received an offer of a place from one of his SUNY choices, Binghamton. He held off replying until he heard from the college in North Carolina. Its reply came later in April, and it was also positive. After long discussions with his parents, much of which was devoted to the financial aspects of attendance at a private versus a public college, the choice came down in favor of Binghamton.

With his college place in hand, Peter feels quite relaxed about the remaining two months of high school, even though there are still some examinations to take. To receive their high school graduation diplomas, both Peter and MaryLou must pass examinations in school subjects set by the state's education authority (the New York State Board of Regents), New York State being one of the few states to require such external, state-organized examinations for graduation. However, neither student expects too much difficulty in securing at least passing grades.

MaryLou is looking forward to having a real job and an income of her own. She has been assured that once her high school diploma is in hand, her stepfather's company will take her on as a trainee salesperson. Lengthy discussion with her academic counselor at school has persuaded her that some further education will be most helpful for her career plans, so, with-

out great enthusiasm, she intends to enroll in the local community college
and take courses in business and merchandising on a part-time basis. For
admission she need only show her high school diploma and pay the rather
minimal fees. A number of her friends are following a different route: they
will study full-time for two years to obtain associate degrees at the community college. By doing this, they hope perhaps to start on a higher rung
than MaryLou will be able to do, though whether they will be successful
in this remains to be seen.

So as the end of the school year approaches they are spared the severe
examination pressures experienced by many of their contemporaries in Japan, China, and France (and even by a few in the United States). Instead,
their lives are dominated by preparations for the whirl of ceremonies and
activities marking the graduation of their high school class—parties, the
senior prom, the formal ceremony of graduation ("commencement"), and
distribution of the illustrated yearbook.

Sweden

Sixten and Ingrid live in the northern outskirts of Stockholm, close to a
lake in the suburb of Stocksund, where almost everyone seems to have a
boat of some kind. Both students are in the final year of their upper secondary school courses, though Sixten's has been a long (four-year) course,
while Ingrid is finishing a two-year program.

They entered school at age seven (after two years spent in kindergarten)
and completed the compulsory, comprehensive, "basic" nine-year school
attended by all young Swedes. They then transferred to their present school,
a *Gymnasieskolan* (an integrated upper secondary school). Admission was
virtually automatic, taking place without entrance examinations or other
formalities. In the country as a whole, very few (only about 10 percent) of
the graduates from the basic school decide not to continue their education
into upper secondary school. In Stocksund the percentage of noncontinuing
students is minuscule. This is the point at which specialization begins in
the Swedish school system. There are twenty-five different upper secondary school "lines" to choose from, some academic and some vocational.
Courses last for two, three, or four years, according to the type of course.

Ingrid is eighteen years old. Even though her parents had higher hopes
for her career, she chose a relatively undemanding two-year line, nursing.
Her father, an official in the central government's National Board of Education, died when she was eight years old, leaving her mother to finish her
qualifications as a general medical practitioner while raising their only child.
In her early teenage years, Ingrid became very beauty- and fashion-con-

scious and spent long hours immersed in glossy magazines—Swedish, American, German, and French. Although this has given her a certain facility in foreign languages, she was left with little spare time for formal school study, and her grades suffered. If she had wanted to follow her mother's path into medicine, she would have needed to enroll in one of the three-year lines: natural sciences or perhaps liberal arts (classical variant). But with her interests and undistinguished school record, this did not seem realistic.

Ingrid is not especially interested in much of her schoolwork. She quite enjoys some of the romantic literature she has to read in Swedish and English language classes, as well as parts of her studies in biology, since she sees its relationship to her future in nursing. Other work in the standard common curriculum for all students includes continuing study in Swedish language and literature, English, history, mathematics, and physical education. The directly vocational portion of her course comprises theoretical courses in nursing and a practicum in the Karolinska hospital, which she thoroughly enjoys, except for the more mundane housekeeping chores she is asked to perform.

In contrast, Sixten is an academic high-flyer. Neither of his parents was ambitious for advanced education or social status for themselves—his mother drives a taxi and his father is a maintenance worker in Svenska Handelsbank—but both have marked his lively intelligence and encouraged him in his schoolwork. His grades in the basic school were superlative, and his ambition is large. On entry into the Gymnasieskolan he was undecided whether to apply for the four-year natural sciences line or the four-year technology line. In the end he opted for technology. By the end of his second year, he knew that he would specialize in the final two years in one of the most prestigious and difficult of all lines: chemical engineering.

For the first three years, Sixten continued with Swedish, English, mathematics, and physical education. He also took civics in the first year, and studied a second foreign language (German), history, basic chemistry, and technology for the first two years. In the third and fourth years, he added an array of chemistry courses (physical, organic, electrical engineering, biochemistry, chemical technology, technical chemistry), either for one year or both.[1] In addition, now, in his final year, he is preparing his special-

1. All students in upper secondary school continue the common curriculum—Swedish language and literature, English, history, mathematics, and physical education. The particulars of the curriculum will differ, however, depending on the course chosen. The longer programs allow for more advanced work and some specialization in the third and fourth years.

project paper on some of the chemical engineering problems to be faced as Sweden proceeds to deactivate its nuclear power reactors.

There are no final-leaving examinations at the end of secondary school for either Sixten or Ingrid. Instead, they have taken tests and examinations throughout their courses of study. For example, Ingrid has already taken tests set by the National Board of Education in Swedish language and literature in her final (second) year. The English-language achievement test is scheduled for March 15. Sixten took similar tests in English, German, and chemistry in his second year and in Swedish, mathematics, and physics during his third year. The tests are typically composed of a mixture of multiple-choice and extended-answer items, three hours for each subject. The dates for these tests are set for the entire country by the National Board of Education[2] and are spread over the academic year. This is done in order to make the testing process part of the ordinary school routine and to reduce the tension usually associated with a marathon period of testing crowded into one or two weeks at the end of the school career.

In addition to these "national" tests, a minimum number of other written tests in subjects is required, usually two or three a year. These may be set by the individual subject teacher alone or by all the teachers of that subject in a school, or occasionally for an entire school district. Grades are assigned on a five-point scale from a low of one to a high of five.

In this, the final year of school, all that remains is to complete the course of study. The award of a leaving certificate is made on the basis of satisfactory achievement over the entire course of study taken as a whole. Ingrid is making the grade, though not easily. She has improved her work since basic school and now has good hopes of finishing school with a respectable leaving certificate. This requires at least a three in all major subjects. Sixten, even with all his talent for study and exposition, is having a hard time keeping up with the enormous amount of work that is expected of him. He will soon be twenty, and he has been stretched academically for the past four years, ever since he left the relatively relaxed basic school. There he had grown used to getting fives without too much trouble. It was an effort to keep up his general education subjects for the first three years. If anything, his study load in this final year is even heavier, especially as he aims to submit an outstanding special-project report. But he is devoting all of his time to technical subjects where hoped-for high grades will be

2. As the decentralization of the Swedish school system continues, the authority of municipalities has increased while that of the board has been sharply reduced, though it retains an important coordination role. New arrangements for implementation of the new policy are currently under way.

important for his application to a university. His parents are justifiably proud of the grades their son is bringing home, a mixture of fours and fives.

Swedish government policy in education aims at equalizing access to postsecondary education, irrespective of the location of students' homes and schools. While parts of Sweden, especially in and around Stockholm, are highly urbanized and suburbanized, the country is large (one thousand miles from north to south) and mostly quite sparsely populated. Both students feel that living as they do in Stocksund, with its generally higher standards of income and education, they probably have to try harder in order to achieve the best marks in their schoolwork and their examinations than students from less favored parts of the country.

With all the undoubted importance of the tests, examinations, and marks, neither Sixten nor Ingrid feels the competitive urgency experienced by the Chinese and Japanese students we shall meet later. Their records have been accumulated over several years and include an exhaustive record of their experiences and accomplishments, grades on school, district, and national tests, and comments by teachers. They also include notes on periodic discussions about career preferences. Although Sixten particularly feels some anxiety about his immediate future, compared with typical secondary school completers in most other countries he and Ingrid are able to take matters very much in stride. The final year of school is important, but not absolutely critical to their futures.

They are confident that they will be able to pursue whatever careers they choose without too many hurdles placed in their way. They can always try a second time, and even a third, if their application for higher education or further training is turned down. There are ways of entering alternative career paths if they should change their minds later on.

Most important, perhaps, Ingrid and Sixten are not moved by much fear of unemployment after school. Ingrid is well aware that there is a severe shortage of nurses in Sweden and knows she will find a warm and ready welcome in a hospital once she graduates. She has had enough of being a full-time student, she feels, and has no intention of going on to a university, which is just as well, as her grades make it unlikely that she could be offered a place. Entry into hospital nursing will provide further training and a salary, outstanding working conditions, and a job she likes. However, if she changes her mind later in life, the door to higher education is not closed. Since autumn 1991, students who graduate from the upper secondary school with low grades have had an opportunity to take a proficiency test for university entrance to demonstrate their improved academic aptitude.

Sixten has his sights set on continuing his studies in chemical engineering at the university. But his leaving certificate will also confer on him the title of Certified Upper Secondary School Engineer. So if by remote chance he does not get a university place immediately, he expects to be able to find employment without difficulty (after doing his military service). In any event, as soon as he is twenty-five, he can apply again to enter the university under the 25-4 rule (minimum age twenty-five; minimum work/military service of four years), which reserves a number of places for people like himself. His prospects, he has every reason to believe, are very good.

These two young Swedes have been educated in a system that strives to provide wide educational opportunities to all. Tests and examinations continue to exist, but a deliberate effort is made to ease the psychological strain on students and to make the tests as nonthreatening as possible. The central government and the localities (municipalities) collaborate in providing the examinations, with the close involvement of teachers. A student who at first does not succeed can try again. The examination results are important, but do not virtually control an individual's future, as we shall see is only too frequent elsewhere.

The Soviet Union

Mikhail and Lara live in Zagorsk, a city of some hundred thousand persons, ninety miles northeast of Moscow, noted above all for its well-preserved (and functioning) Trinity–St. Sergius monastery. They are seventeen years old and in the eleventh grade, the final year of secondary school. They entered first grade when they were seven, after two years in kindergarten, and attended an eight-year (now nine-year) elementary/junior high school (so-called "incomplete secondary school").[3] They then transferred to their current "complete" secondary schools.

Mikhail attends a secondary vocational-technical school, offering grades nine, ten, and eleven; Lara is in the secondary general education school, offering grades ten and eleven. Though their school programs have diverged and they have very different ambitions, both students are shortly due to take examinations leading to the general education school-leaving diploma, the attestat zrelosti.

The examination for the attestat consists of a number of written and oral

3. A change to beginning compulsory school at age 6 instead of 7, was introduced in 1985 and met strong opposition from kindergarten teachers, who protested that children were not ready for the rigors of Soviet first grade at age six.

examinations, conducted and graded by a committee of examiners, including the director and teachers from their own schools and possibly someone from the district office. In addition, their course work has been regularly evaluated and the grades recorded on the five-point scale used throughout the Soviet school system. Together with the results of the written and oral examinations, course grades will form part of the final evaluation to determine whether they will be awarded the attestat and (more important) what grade will be attached to it. Three is considered a passing mark; "fives" are highly sought after.

Lara's eleventh-grade school timetable covers a broad range of subjects, as follows (the number of hours per week is given in parentheses): Russian language and literature (3); mathematics (4); physics (4); chemistry (2); biology (1); astronomy (1); English (1); social studies (2); history (3); physical education (2); premilitary training (2); labor and vocational training (4); obligatory socially useful and productive work (4); and electives (4).[4] Lara is doing her labor training and production practice in a local public library. She does not find the work of great interest, but she is content to do it because there are often quite periods when she can study and complete her heavy homework assignments.

Lara is very concerned about her grades. She has concentrated hard on her schoolwork, for she is planning to go to a university. Her parents have paid a retired teacher to give her private tutoring in mathematics and physics in his own apartment. In anticipation of the examinations, she goes over sample questions and takes seriously the careful comments made by her teachers and her tutor. She hopes that Moscow State University, one of the most prestigious in the country, will accept her. This is aiming high indeed, but it does not seem to her or to her family to be an unrealistic goal. She was deeply impressed by former President Gorbachev's thesis that the Soviet Union must become a society governed by law, instead of by arbitrary executive power, and this has reinforced her determination to apply for entry to the Faculty of Law.

Besides the attestat, Lara will have to take an entrance examination at Moscow State University, presenting her school records of accomplishment, including her attestat scores. There will be written tests in basic subjects (for example, Russian language and literature) and in one or two supplementary subjects (for example, history and social studies) related to her intended course of study.

Mikhail is far less concerned about his final examinations, though he

---

4. Recent changes have eliminated premilitary training, removed the compulsory nature of the work requirement, and given more time to foreign language.

also hopes to obtain the attestat zrelosti. In addition, he aims to receive a diploma attesting to his learning and skills in his occupational specialization. He is training to be a telephone repairman.

His curriculum seeks to provide a broad general education, as well as a broad, rather than narrowly occupational, set of courses in the technical fields. For example, he has taken courses in the fundamentals of electronics, mechanics, and technology, plus the organization of production and the economic principles underlying production techniques and choices. His class work occupies thirty-six hours a week, with about 60 percent given over to occupational courses and production training and 40 percent to general education.

Telephone repair and servicing promises to be outdoor work, which he wants. Although the training has been rather specialized, Mikhail believes it has given him sufficient general skills to enable him to move on to some other occupation, should he so wish, after the required three years of employment in his training specialty and his army service. What also attracts Mikhail is the knowledge that the three years of upper secondary vocational-technical education will count as work experience when he gets a job—with a corresponding increase in salary. He too will soon be taking written and oral examinations; in addition, there will be some practical tests.

Though they are at similar points in their school careers, the two students are quite a contrast in background, personality, and school record. These differences will probably affect directly their future job prospects, social standing, and level of living. Lara has a very lively, outgoing, positive personality. She eagerly embraces every opportunity for study and socializing in the school and the city. She was a member of the Young Pioneers and was hoping to be accepted into the Komsomol—before these Communist party organizations were abolished along with the party itself. She has had few difficulties in school and has long been a favorite of her teachers. That she has set her sights on a career in law is not unusual for a young woman coming from the Soviet professional classes. Both her parents are well educated, having attended higher education institutions. Her father was a Party member, holding a respected post as supervisor of production in a regional book publishing house, and her mother is an elementary school principal. Lara is their only child, on whom they have concentrated their love, attention, and parental hopes. She in turn has wholly accepted her parents' life-style and values and made them her own.

Mikhail's family is far less supportive of high-level educational and career ambitions. His father spent twenty years driving a heavy truck for a construction combine until alcoholism ruined both his driving record and his health. Two years ago he was transferred to night-watchman duties in the combine. His mother works as an assistant in a retail food store; the pay is low and the hours are long, but the opportunity to be first in line for goods in short supply is very valuable. In further contrast, Mikhail is more withdrawn and uncertain than Lara. Fears about his scholastic ability have affected his commitment to study. His grades are mediocre at best, and he is looking forward to the time when he will be finished with school and is out earning money. He is not a "joiner" and did not feel he needed to participate in officially sponsored activities of the Communist youth organizations. But he does socialize with a group of friends who collect and play video cassettes (mostly bootlegged copies) of Soviet and foreign films and TV shows. A substantial consumption of alcohol goes along with the group viewing sessions.

Toward the end of the school year, in May, the time for the examinations arrives. Written and oral examinations are required in mathematics and literature and oral examinations in history/social studies. Three other subjects must be selected from composition, mathematics, physics/astronomy, chemistry, and foreign language. Apart from the composition, these latter subjects are examined orally. For each oral examination subject, the Ministry of Education of the Russian Republic publishes an annual brochure setting out the topics from which the examiners may select their questions. Lara and Mikhail are quite familiar with the special procedures for the oral examinations. Candidates appear before the examining group, choose one from among a number of face-down cards, and are given about a quarter of an hour to prepare a response to the questions printed on it. After hearing the formal reply, the examiners will usually ask some follow-up questions. The whole procedure will last for no more than a half hour. Afterward, some candidates report that the experience was intimidating; others say that they felt quite relaxed during the oral and that their teacher-examiners provided them with friendly, helpful hints when they appeared to be hesitating or stuck for an answer.

Most students who stay in school till the end of eleventh grade are awarded the certificate. Lara, who had set her sights high, in fact does very well, obtaining the highest grades on her attestat. She has made an excellent start toward achieving her goal of entering Moscow State University. She now presents herself at the university to take the special entrance examinations in Russian language and literature (written) and in history and social studies (written and oral) and to have her interview.

Soviet doctrine regarding the advancement of young people was formally meritocratic, although alongside scholastic achievement, the official position took into account the "correctness" of a young person's socialist world outlook. Less publicized infringements on pure meritocratic selection criteria may be considerations of the candidate's ethnic and family origins, personality, political connections, and even the return of favors or the offer and acceptance of bribes. Lara's activities in the youth organizations, her personality, and her family connections all count greatly in her favor. Even were she a mediocre student, these things could translate into substantial help in securing a place at a good VUZ (higher education institution). But her excellent grades and good record of school and social participation, combined with the very positive impression she made at her interview when she discussed her reasons for wanting to embark on a career in law, make an irresistible case: she is accepted.

Mikhail's results turn out to be far less impressive, although somewhat to his and his parents' surprise and relief, he obtains the attestat. He achieved no better than a bare pass (three) on the written and oral examinations in the required academic subjects. He did little better in the theoretical parts of the vocationally related studies, such as electronics and technology. But he did reasonably well (four) in the practical examinations and has a creditable record of accomplishment in his shop work and production experience. His teachers and supervisors think well of his efforts and find him reliable and willing to cooperate with others.

Mikhail, however, has no plans to continue his formal education. He will be glad to be free of the demands of his teachers and the constraints of school, which he never particularly enjoyed, and do his stint in the army which, as he understands from older friends, is an opportunity to see other parts of the country but makes no great demands on one's energies or intellect. He will then return to civilian life where his prospects are good for a secure, if not generously paid, job with the state's telephone service. Because Mikhail is by no means as fortunate in his family origins and connections as Lara, his educational and occupational aspirations are perfectly realistic. Not only are telephone repairmen in demand, but Mikhail's knowledge and skills will probably provide ample opportunity to work *na levo* (sub rosa) on "private" telephone repair and installation in return for welcome extra income. Moreover, if he changes his mind about further study, there are many opportunities for part-time, evening, and correspondence study. Only a superior academic record like Lara's, however, will earn a full-time university place.

Their success in the examinations has meant different things for each: for Mikhail, certification of completion and blessed release from school; for Lara, it has opened a door, giving her the chance to sit for university entrance examinations and the possibility of joining a severely limited number of ambitious students in full-time higher education. Both students have also felt substantial, though not overwhelming, pressure to do well. Rather than the examinations at the end of schooling, it has been the state's official curricula and the pressure to get good grades in course work during their final two to three years in school that have been the major factors controlling their activities.

England/Wales

David and Jennifer are sixteen years old and are sitting for their first external, public examinations. From an international perspective, they are unusually young, for most other countries wait until their secondary school students are seventeen, eighteen, or even nineteen before submitting them to their first external, "national" examination. David and Jennifer live and go to school in Sutton, a busy town just south of London. David's father manages a large local food store; his mother works part-time in retailing. Jennifer's father works in the City of London where he is engaged in the stock exchange; her mother is employed at a large hospital as a pharmacist.

Both students are in the fifth year in their secondary school; the time is early June, toward the end of the school year. They are taking the examinations for the General Certificate of Secondary Education (GCSE) set by the Southern Examining Group, one of the five groups of GCSE examining boards in England and Wales. The GCSE is a new examination, first offered in 1988 to replace the Ordinary level of the General Certificate of Education (GCE, O level) and the Certificate of Secondary Education (CSE), and includes elements of both previous examination systems.[5] In some subjects there are papers geared to broadly different levels of ability, from more theoretical and academic to more practical and applied. Depending on the subject and level, assignments done in school are taken into account.

Today David and Jennifer are taking the examination in English. Seated well apart from one another, in a quiet room reserved for the purpose, they watch the proctor open a sealed envelope and distribute a question paper to each candidate. Instructions are read out. David and Jennifer duly inscribe their identification numbers on the answer booklet; then for the next

5. The GCE O-level examinations were intended to be tests of academic achievement, following traditional practices of preselection for university studies. The more innovative CSE, introduced in 1965, was designed for a larger proportion of sixteen-year-olds and, though covering the general education curriculum, aimed at a less formally academic level of performance. It also included some innovations: examination papers designed by local teacher groups teaching to their own syllabus and special student assignments done during the previous year, graded by their teachers, to be included with the examination and contributing to the total examination grade.

two hours they will ponder the questions and respond in writing to the best of their ability. At the end of the session, the answers will be collected, packed, sealed, and sent off to the examination board, which will then distribute them to part-time readers for grading. Some independent assignments they completed in school during the year may also be included in the packages and will be taken into account in assigning a final grade.

In the following two weeks, David and Jennifer will be taking other examinations, the exact number depending on their interests and previous performance. Jennifer's other subjects are history, French, and Spanish. Davis is a stronger candidate, so he will be taking history, geography, chemistry, and French, plus two mathematics examinations. Apart from the written papers, David's chemistry examination includes a practical assignment, laboratory work done a little earlier; the French and Spanish examinations contain an oral part.

This experience forms the climax of preparation that has been going on for some time. During the year leading to the examinations, while still studying new material, David and Jennifer have had to give increasing attention to reviewing and fixing in their minds what they will need to know and do on the examination days. Their teachers have increased the pressure, worked through old papers with them, and taken them through mock examination sessions following the procedures and using the kinds of questions asked in previous tests. During the two-week examination period, they are relieved of regular classes; their time is spent in postmortems with peers and teachers and in reviewing material for the remaining examinations. But when it is all over, they will have some respite while the other students are still involved in regular classes. The heavy load of homework, the interim tests, the constant repetitions, the pressure—all cease abruptly. David is fairly relaxed; he is confident that he has done well. For Jennifer there remains a good deal of anxiety about her results, which will be announced after about two months, toward the end of the summer vacation.

Like most students in state-supported education, David and Jennifer transferred from primary to secondary school at age twelve in the local comprehensive school. Local education authorities (LEAs) have wide discretion over how to provide secondary schooling for all, and practices may vary even among schools in a district. In a few LEAs, about 20 percent of eleven-to-twelve-year-olds will enter an academic grammar school, after selection based upon teachers' recommendations, test results, and parents' preference. Nearly 90 percent of all secondary school pupils attend LEA-provided schools; the remainder are in nonpublic, often church-related schools, most of which, however, receive public subsidies and are subject to some degree of public control and inspection.

On paper, David and Jennifer shared a common curriculum for the first two years or so. However, in a number of first-year classes, like French and mathematics, they found themselves together with others of similar ability based on previous school records. After the end of the term and the year, some further sorting took place, making some of their other classes more homogeneous academically. Grouping into forms (homerooms) on the basis of academic performance is quite usual in English schools. The practice of "setting"—grouping by academic ability for particular subjects (for example, mathematics and foreign languages)—is also common.

By the time David and Jennifer reached the fourth form (the third year of secondary school), they had passed through a sorting system that separated the more academically able from those less so. The pace and level of difficulty of work differed among the homogeneous groups, and certain subjects were added to or removed from the timetable of particular classes. Most pupils had, like them, begun to study a foreign language (most commonly French) at the beginning of secondary school, but while most continued with the language, some of the less academically able did not, in order to have more time for basic subjects such as English and mathematics. However, both David and Jennifer, in company with their more capable peers, added a second foreign language to their programs in the second year (David started German and Jennifer Spanish). David, who excels in mathematics, also took an advanced class in that subject.

Each secondary school, whether comprehensive or grammar, public, church-related, or private, must make a number of important decisions about its own curriculum to determine what subject choices the school will offer, at what levels of difficulty, when to introduce them, and which students can take them. In the absence of a national curriculum, these decisions were strongly influenced by the knowledge and preferences of the principal and teachers in each school, the size of the school, and the cultural and occupational priorities of the locality. However, variations among schools have been constrained by two forces: the traditional content of the general academic preparation that teachers and parents have themselves experienced and, above all, the published syllabi of the five external examining groups. These have been powerful determinants of curriculum, particularly for the 25 to 30 percent of the age group intending to take public examinations, and they have strongly affected the secondary education of the rest. Moreover, the recent establishment of a national curriculum covering about 40 percent of the schools' timetable, accompanied by evaluation of pupils' achievement in periodic national assessments, promises to reduce substantially regional and between-school variability.

In the fourth form, David and Jennifer's capabilities and future examination options were more or less settled by their daily school schedules. There might be some fine-tuning at the end of the year as they entered the preexamination fifth form, but, by this time, the distinctions between those taking the external examination and the rest, between those who would be sitting for a few subjects and those taking five or more, for example, and between those who would be tackling papers at higher and lower levels of difficulty, would all have become clear to their teachers, parents, and the students themselves.

All of the fifth-form students are studying a broad array of subjects, including English language and literature, mathematics, a foreign language or two, history, geography, and a science. They also have classes in religion, music and art, physical education, and sports. But they will not necessarily sit for examinations in all of these subjects. Because David has a rather better academic record than Jennifer, he will be taking the examinations in all of his seven subjects at the highest level of difficulty. In addition, he has been preparing for a more advanced examination in mathematics. Not so Jennifer, three of whose examinations (in English, history, and French) will be at the intermediate level of difficulty. However, since her marks have been very good in Spanish, her second foreign language, she will be taking this at the higher level of difficulty.

Toward the end of summer vacations, the results of the GCSE are announced. David has done very well, as expected. He has passed in all but one subject (his geography marks in the mock examinations the previous December had been borderline so, though disappointed, he was not surprised), and he was awarded superior ratings in his mathematics and chemistry papers. Jennifer's results are less impressive, however. She has passed in only three of the four subjects she had taken (English, French, and Spanish) with no superior grades.

Compulsory schooling ends at sixteen years, and since participation in the examinations for the GCSE is strongly encouraged, the qualification increasingly serves to certify completion of the first phase of secondary schooling. At this point, well over half the school population leaves full-time school to seek employment, sometimes combined with part-time further education. Various incentives by central and local government and by industry have increased the number who continue their schooling beyond sixteen. A growing number of students who first take the GCSE in just one or two subjects remain beyond age sixteen to study for the examination in one or two more subjects.

Just as important, the GCSE examination also serves as a preselection device for a second external examination two years later, the General Certificate of Education, Advanced level (GCE, A level). Success is necessary in order to enter universities, teacher-training programs, and certain other paths of professional preparation. Most full-time students between the ages of sixteen and eighteen will continue their studies in the sixth forms of their own grammar or comprehensive school. But a number (about 17 percent of this population) will leave to continue their studies in a local sixth-form college. Depending on GCSE results, individual talents, inclinations, and career plans, as well as what their school offers, students will now concentrate on the two or three subjects they plan to take in the GCE A level examinations at age eighteen.

These subjects are usually chosen from either mathematics and the sciences or the humanities and social sciences. Employers, parents, and many educators have criticized the high degree of specialization characterizing upper secondary education in England and Wales, particularly since the effects reach as far down as the second or third year of the secondary school curriculum. But resistance to change on the part of many university faculty and subject specialists continues to be strong. Nevertheless, there has been some movement toward broadening the limited range of subject opportunities and weakening the high degree of specialization. This has taken the form of a new examination option in many subjects, the Advanced-Supplementary level (GCE, AS level), which became available in 1989 and is intended to encourage students to broaden their sixth-form studies. The courses make intellectual demands on students similar to those of "regular" A levels, but require only half the study time. A "load" of two A level and two AS-level examinations (or three A levels and one AS level) would be considered quite normal, especially for students planning to continue into higher education, but lighter or heavier loads are common too.

Because her GCSE results were not very impressive, the question arises for Jennifer whether or not to remain in school, and, if so, which studies to follow. Having reached the age of sixteen, she could leave at this point like a number of her peers, but since she has no particular kind of work in mind and there is no financial urgency at home, she decides to remain in school.

Her school adviser encourages her and suggests an initial concentration on only two main subjects, leaving open the option of a third subject for later decision. So she is permitted to begin studying for A level in two of the subjects she has passed (English literature and Spanish), conditional on her passing her failed history examination during the coming year. Her parents are also advised by the school that she might benefit from private tutoring.

If she seeks a university place, she will need to pass in these two A-level subjects and at least one other—or better still, two—taken at the less demanding AS level. Furthermore, she could spread the course preparation and her examinations over two or even three years. Jennifer was advised that she had an alternative to remaining in the sixth form of her school with the high-flyers who achieved well in the GCSE the first time around. It might suit her better to transfer to a sixth-form college, where she would be in the company of slightly older students and in a more collegiate environment. She might be able to combine study with work related to her future career. Furthermore, sixth-form-college counseling services are better equipped to advise students and steer them toward programs in tertiary institutions more suitable than the standard academic options in the conventional university. But being hesitant to leave her familiar setting, she decides to remain in the comprehensive school, leaving future decisions to be shaped by the next set of examination results. So Jennifer devotes her first term in the sixth form to reviewing the history material she is going to repeat for the GCSE. Thereafter, if successful, she will concentrate on English literature and Spanish. She enjoys the literature she has been reading and likes the idea of traveling to foreign countries.

David chooses a different track entirely, selecting the science/math specialization. He has set his sights on entering a university to take a science degree. For both students, their Advanced-level school timetables have now become much lighter than their former GCSE class schedules. David is scheduled for classes in physics, pure and applied mathematics, and chemistry; Jennifer has her Spanish and English literature. In addition, since their school wishes them to retain some breadth in their studies, David has a general humanities class once a week with other students specializing in mathematics and science, and Jennifer takes a course in the history of science. These general courses will be required for the first year only, culminating in an internal school examination, but they will not be examined in the GCE. The classes themselves are now much different, too: the number of students in the specialized classes is small; the assignments are less directive, calling for more independent work and judgment; discussion is encouraged. It is all much more like a university seminar than the formal instruction typical in the lower school. In addition, both participate in sports on a voluntary basis. This leaves a generous amount of unscheduled time during the school day for private study in the library and for participation in the school organizations that interest them (as well as for socializing). They are now members of the school leadership, and though their class meetings are fewer, they are quite busy. Jennifer is active in the school's international club, which meets regularly with foreign students in the area and helps to arrange visits abroad. David continues to play soccer with the school team, but devotes most of his time to schoolwork.

Jennifer's second try at the GCSE history examination takes place toward the end of her first sixth-form semester. This time she is able to pass at a respectable level. The result, together with her steady progress in her two A-level subjects, led to a recommendation that she study for the AS level in French, which she begins to do at the start of her second sixth-form year.

Their A-level examinations are in fewer subjects than the previous GCSE examinations, but they are no less demanding. The level of work is significantly more advanced, and even more depends on the outcome. Without a doubt the mental strain is greater, and both candidates feel more nervous going into the examination room. They face many hours of physical strain, too, for each of the three-hour examinations requires them to cover sheets and sheets of paper with lengthy, handwritten answers. However, the room is familiar (it is, in fact, the school gymnasium), their proctors are their own teachers, and once again the immediate preexamination months have been used to prepare them intensively to answer the kinds of questions they see on the question papers. Nevertheless, David's practical tests in chemistry require fierce concentration and absolute precision, and the mathematics papers were challenging in the extreme. Jennifer's French oral requires her to talk about both Molière and her last school trip to France, but she is pleasantly surprised at the ease with which she understands the examiner and her fluency in reply, once the initial nervousness passed.

The examinations over, there are all the joys of celebrating the end of school, especially for David, who anticipates starting his university studies after the summer. He follows up his GCSE success by passing physics and pure mathematics and by achieving a superior grade in chemistry (he dropped applied mathematics after the first year). He anticipated good, solid results, though not necessarily brilliant ones. His teachers agreed with his assessment, and good, solid results were what he achieved. He knows that the door to higher education is open for him and that he will be able to "read" for the bachelor of science. In preparing his applications for university entrance, he was not inclined to try for either Oxford or Cambridge because of the competition and the cost. He also had the sense that the style of life would not suit him. So he applied to King's College of the University of London, which has a superior reputation in science, where his chemistry teacher had studied. He was interviewed and after the A-level results came in was accepted. He is now set to begin work for the honors degree, specializing for the next three years in chemistry, with some physics as a minor.

Jennifer is also gratified by her results, having obtained a pass in English literature and better still in French (at AS level). Her school experience over the past years has strengthened her self-confidence and ability to study, and her visits abroad have improved her language skill. During the summer vacation she is spending four weeks youth-hosteling in Spain, in the company of three of her school friends. Although she will definitely stay on for one term to polish her Spanish before taking the A level, any further plans for study are still very uncertain. She will have difficulty gaining entrance to a university, given her school record and examination marks, but she could get into a technical or commercial college. On the other hand, she rather likes the idea of getting a job that involves travel abroad. With her languages and experience, she is well qualified to start on a career in the travel business or with a firm doing business abroad in the European Economic Community.

In December of her third year in the sixth form Jennifer takes the A-level Spanish examination. By this time she is an experienced examination candidate, and the examination room holds few terrors and little nervousness for her. When she receives the results in February, awarding her a very respectable pass, she has already decided that she wants to begin a business career, and she is deeply involved in the search for her first job. Securing this will not be easy, because there is a high rate of unemployment among her age group in Britain. However, after three months of searching, applying, interviewing, and waiting she is accepted as a trainee travel clerk by Thomas Cook and Son, to begin on April 15. She, like David, is on her way.

The external examinations of the GCSE and the GCE A levels have been substantial determining elements in David and Jennifer's school lives. Indeed, their sixth-form years have been taken up largely (though not exclusively) with preparation for their A-level subjects. Yet there has been time for nonacademic activities, especially sports and hobbies, so that although the preparation for the examinations has been very important, it has not been all-consuming.

Chapter 3

The Candidates and Their Schools:
China, Germany, France, and Japan

We are three students, ma'am,
Three well-born maids of liberal estate,
Who wish to join this University.
—Hilarion, *Princess Ida,* act 2

As indicated in the preceding chapter, external end-of-secondary-school examinations everywhere affect students and schools. The influence may be fairly incidental, as in the United States and Sweden. It can be profound, as in France, Germany, and Japan, as we will show later in this chapter. Or it may be more pervasive for some students and some aspects of the school's functioning than for others, as in the Soviet Union and England/Wales and, as we shall now describe, in China.

China

Despite a commitment to universal schooling, China's historic educational underdevelopment and continuing lack of material resources have forced the government to adopt policies severely rationing schooling at the secondary and tertiary levels. Only 2 to 3 percent of those who enter the first year of primary school will reach the point of taking the university entrance examinations. Roughly one-third of primary pupils attend junior secondary schools, completion of which marks the end of compulsory schooling. About one-fifth of these continue to senior secondary schools, of whom fewer than 10 percent will be successful in gaining a university place. Wei-Lun and Mei-Ling are therefore exceptions among their peers, for they are among the few who are attending school full-time at age eighteen.

It is early July in the city of Wuhan, Hubei province, an industrial and river port metropolis of over three million inhabitants on the Yangtze in central China. On three days, for about two and a half hours each day in the morning and again in the afternoon, Wei-Lun and Mei-Ling are sitting for the university entrance examinations. Both are due to take examinations in Chinese, politics, and English, as well as mathematics (though there is an easier mathematics test for liberal arts candidates). Mei-Ling, who is interested in the humanities, will also be examined in history and geography; Wei-Lun, who aspires to a career in the sciences, will take tests in biology and physics.

Mei-Ling's parents are employed in one of the large textile factories situated in Wuhan, her father as a clerk in the personnel department and her mother on the looms. Wei-Lun's father is a provincial policeman; his mother works as storekeeper in the kitchen of a local hotel.

Mei-Ling and Wei-Lun are not new to the experience of taking school examinations. They are well aware that the results are likely to determine their entire futures. Both students, together with about a third of their peers, were selected as early as primary level for a "key-point school" on the basis of school performance. Their promotion in the school system has been based on academic records and examinations. The practices of the Cultural Revolution (1966 to 1976), when ideological commitment and worker or peasant family background were the determinants of school advancement, are long since gone. Examinations at the end of the nine-year period of compulsory schooling determine entrance to the various forms of upper secondary school (general academic, technical/vocational), and results on the university entrance examination largely determine who will continue into higher education. They know how fortunate they are to attend a key-point school with capable and motivated students, well-trained and experienced teachers, and adequate textbooks and other study materials. Most other students in Wuhan are not so well off. Selection for a key secondary school greatly improves chances of further promotion through the educational system and the probability of doing well in the examinations. Wei-Lun and Mei-Ling know, too, that if they do poorly, others are only too ready to take their place. They feel the pressure to excel exerted by their parents and their school, the latter whose reputation and continued key-point status depend on examination results.

Indeed, many of Wei-Lun's friends have dropped out of school, repelled by heavily academic and examination-oriented teaching, and deterred by poor grades. Some have had to drop out because they needed to support themselves or to supplement the family income.

Criticisms of the severe pressures imposed upon students and of the high degree of selectivity have led to official directives barring schools from giving too many examinations and homework assignments. New guidelines issued in 1988 provided for major high school examinations to be given only at the end or in the middle of each term and only in the main subjects. At the same time, it was announced, homework should not be given in first grade of primary school and should be limited to thirty minutes per day for second- and third-grade pupils.[1]

Whatever the official directives may have decreed, Wei-Lun and Mei-Ling still had to study long hours. To survive in the present system, meaning to become one of the 2.7 million candidates who actually sit for the examinations, required extraordinary dedication. Ultimate success—landing in the top 20 percent or so of candidates who are awarded a university place—will be solid proof that they have made a serious and unremitting effort in school. Both students have done their best and have taken schooling very seriously indeed. They have given careful attention to their teachers' lectures, taken detailed notes, and virtually committed their textbooks to memory. They have had little incentive to study anything that will not be on the examination paper. There is no time in their classes to explore questions that are unlikely to come up in the tests. Classes are devoted to lectures and recitations, and homework consists of reviewing notes and textbooks. Sometimes their science teachers may perform a demonstration, but materials and time are lacking for students to perform experiments. Science lessons, just as in the other subjects, are overwhelmingly "chalk and talk." During the school day there is little opportunity to explore interests or to participate in creative activities; these are pursued, if at all, in after-school centers, during vacations, and in programs organized by the youth clubs. Wei-Lun has joined an after-school group that builds and flies model airplanes; Mei-Ling has become very active in the Communist party's youth organization and is making a name for herself as an activist, organizing weekend projects to clean up derelict areas of Wuhan and to plant shrubs and flowers. For most high school youngsters almost any kind of extracurricular activity is a welcome relief from school and study. Besides, there is another major incentive for participation: it may be very important for the future, since a record of such activities must be included in the application for higher education.

During the past few weeks and months, Wei-Lun and Mei-Ling have been going over and over the material they have been taught. They have memorized lists of Chinese-language characters, names, places, dates, rules, and formulas and have made a habit of silently repeating them. They know that the examination questions will require them to know many facts and to respond with material that comes straight out of their textbooks and notes. There will be a mixture of short-answer, extended-answer, and multiple-choice questions. Their teachers have taken them through several examination rehearsals. But their anxiety level is still very high as they enter

1. *China Exchange News* 16 (September 1988): 19.

the large examination hall in the middle of the city to take the first test, which happens to be on Chinese language. This year, they have learned, the question papers have been prepared for the whole of China in the offices of the State Education Commission in Beijing. In the past, the provincial educational authorities had been given the power to prepare examinations, within national guidelines. No one is sure whether the change will make the tests harder or easier, so this is one more factor adding to the general anxiety. As it turns out, there is not much difference between the Chinese-language questions Mei-Ling and Wei-Lun must answer and those that they had rehearsed: comprehension questions, writing a six hundred-character essay on a given topic, and correcting errors in written characters in context. It turns out that the papers in the other subjects also contain few surprises. Both students are confident that they have done well. But have they done well enough to secure places at a university?

Their application files will contain not only marks on the examination papers, but also a medical certificate and recommendations from the school and from organizations and prominent individuals they have had contact with, especially those with political affiliations. These last considerations have become more important recently, after a period when marks carried the most weight in the university admission decision. In addition, applicants to the humanities and social science faculties are now being required to spend a year or two working in the countryside before being allowed to begin their studies.

After weeks of waiting, the results are announced. Two of their contemporaries obtain superior examination marks and are offered places in the top Beijing universities. Although his marks on the university entrance examination were not at all poor, Wei-Lun did not score well enough to be offered a place. He must now decide whether to try again. He can retake the examinations as often as he wishes until reaching the age of twenty-five. Many, however, do not take the opportunity, since the odds against success are great and young people of eighteen and nineteen usually feel they can no longer delay starting to earn an income. Besides, the daily grind and the long hours of study become wearisome. But Wei-Lun has retained his interest in the sciences, where career prospects are great, and he decides he will prepare to take the university entrance examinations perhaps one more time.

Mei-Ling has done very well. She has been offered a place at Shanghai Normal University and will be able to continue her studies in language and literature, with a view to obtaining a job as a middle school teacher in those subjects. The demand for teachers is great, though the pay is poor and the social status of teaching has been falling. Nevertheless, Mei-Ling believes that she will be very happy as a middle school teacher and jumps at the chance to go on to the university.

"Golden rice bowls," a secure and rosy future, await highly successful students if they study hard, avoid trouble, and manage to join the small, highly educated leadership cadre. The examination system in China is a strict, and perhaps rather crude, mechanism for distributing a severely limited number of opportunities among a vast number of aspirants. The technical problems associated with examining between two and three million candidates in six or seven school subjects all over the vast terrain of China in the space of three July days each year can only be imagined. But it does work to produce an ordered list of candidates and greatly reduces the risk of overt favoritism, influence-peddling, and corruption in the allocation of university places. In addition, although certain problems attached to being a university student have not vanished since the events of May to June 1989 in Tiananmen Square in Beijing, they are no longer so pronounced, especially if the student chooses engineering, physical science, or medicine and avoids such "less objective" subjects as humanities and social sciences.

The Federal Republic of Germany

Dieter and Irma live in the industrial town of Bochum, in the Ruhr area of West Germany, between Dortmund and Essen, original site of the famous Krupp iron and steel works. Forty-five years after the end of World War II, it is difficult for these nineteen-year-old Germans to imagine that their town once lay in ruins, shattered by continuous, systematic Allied bombing attacks. Today Bochum is a busy, tidy, reasonably prosperous German provincial town that boasts an important, twenty-five-year-old university and a thriving *Technische Hochschule* (technical university).

Dieter's father teaches history in a local Gymnasium (selective academic secondary school). His mother, once a nurse, gave up her career to stay at home when she became pregnant with Dieter's elder brother. Irma's parents run a small but prosperous hat shop in the center of Bochum, and the family lives in an apartment over the store.

Bochum is located in the *Land* (province) of Nordrhein-Westfalen, one of the eleven provinces of the original Federal Republic. Since mid-1990, the number has grown to sixteen by absorption of the former German Democratic Republic. Quite unlike the high degree of uniformity characteristic of France, school policies and administrative systems in the Federal Republic are totally at the discretion of each Land. Many major aspects of schooling in the city-states of Hamburg, Bremen, and Berlin, for example, differ substantially from those of the southern German Länder, Baden-Württemberg and Bavaria, reflecting different cultural, religious, and political traditions. The Nazi regime tried to do away with such regional differences in education, along with differences in other aspects of German society. In reaction to the Nazi policy of standardization (*Gleichschaltung*), postwar Germany insisted on the educational and cultural sovereignty of each Land, although the Länder ministers of education have formed a standing committee (the Kultus Minister Konferenz, or KMK) to discuss problems and policies of collective interest and to agree on guidelines for each Land to follow, more or less voluntarily. These guidelines are particularly important for upper secondary schooling.

Most Länder have some version of a tripartite system in which pupils reaching ten or eleven years of age are assigned to one of the three main types of school according to ability and parental wishes. The most academically able transfer to the Gymnasium, which offers a complete general academic secondary program, culminating for most eighteen- or nineteen-year-olds in the Abitur. Many in the middle range of ability and aspiration attend the Realschule. The latter provides general academic education for all as well as some prevocational classes. In the Realschule all students study a foreign language, some take more advanced work in such subjects as mathematics and science, and the more academically able may transfer to a Gymnasium at age sixteen via transitional classes, possibly added to their own school's offerings. The less able go on to the Hauptschule, which ends at grade nine or ten and, unlike the Realschule, makes no provision for general academic education beyond that point. Students completing the Hauptschule enter the work force, many of them via the apprenticeship system. This provides for continuing education in both part-time general education and on-the-job vocational training (the so-called dual system). There are a few comprehensive secondary schools in the original eleven Länder, located mostly in the three city-states, but they cater to less than 5 percent of the secondary school age group.[2]

Dieter and Irma have known each other since *Grundschule* (primary school) and have been good friends. At age ten they transferred together to the same secondary school, in their case a Gymnasium. Studies immediately became more serious than when they were in the Grundschule.

---

2. The German Democratic Republic (GDR) abandoned the tripartite system over forty years ago and instituted unified comprehensive secondary education along broadly Soviet lines. But the old debate over comprehensive versus tripartite secondary schooling has now been reopened, and private schools and Gymnasia are in the course of being established in some former GDR provinces. Wolfgang Mitter, "Educational Reform in West and East Germany in European Perspective," *Oxford Review of Education* 16, no.3 (1990): 333–341.

They began learning English, to which they added French in the second year. During the first two years of lower secondary schooling, they took the basics together: German, social studies (history, geography), mathematics, science (chemistry, biology, physics), music and art, religion, and physical education. But in the last two years of the lower secondary stage (grades nine and ten), each added a class in a specialty. Dieter chose art (drawing and painting), in which he had been showing some talent. Irma chose a social studies course. Other options were available in science, foreign languages, technology, the arts, and sports. Classes were formed around the different options, so that in the last two years, Irma and Dieter studied some of their subjects in the company of students who had chosen the same specialization.

They have enjoyed relatively short school days by European standards, but each class has been filled with serious work. They have had to learn to deal with the demands of the school day for thirty-nine to forty weeks per year. There has been little or no free time during the school day, and much homework to be done. Competition mounted as regular in-school tests followed one another, and Dieter and Irma both felt increasing anxiety as some classmates were left back at the end of the year to repeat an entire grade because of poor marks in even one subject.[3] Parents and many educators blame this system of continuous competitive assessment for the mounting levels of competition and anxiety among students.

Dieter and Irma completed the lower grades of the Gymnasium satisfactorily, however, and were promoted to the upper secondary level, where they have been following the three-year program of preparation for the Abitur. They have been reminded repeatedly that their school grades will contribute to the total Abitur marks and that the overall grade will determine which university will accept them.

The students' programs of study have been shaped according to their choice of Abitur subjects. Though, like their peers in other Länder, they are offering four subjects in the Abitur examinations (two subjects at the fundamental, "basic" [Grund] and two at the harder and more challenging "advanced" [Leistungs] level), their school required them to take a broader program with four additional basic subjects. Dieter's scores have not been as good as Irma's, despite the fact that he has selected what some think is an easier path. He has chosen to concentrate in the language–literary arts area, with an emphasis on German and foreign languages. But his schedule

3. The class grade is failed overall by four-hundred thousand students across the nation annually, who have to repeat the school year, while twice as many are on the borderline. *Times Educational Supplement* (May 27, 1988): A18.

until his final year included classes in science and mathematics, history and social science, and physical education. Irma, who has selected a physical science–mathematics concentration, similarly has had to study German, English, and French, along with music and art and physical education for at least the first two of the three years. Basic (minor) courses meet for about three hours a week, specialty option courses for as many as six. Thus both students had programs of 30 to 33 hours of class per week for the first two years, declining to about 27 during the final year or semester, the last stretch before the examinations.[4]

In order to meet national requirements, designed to ensure equivalence of the Abitur credential and reciprocity for entrance to higher education among the Länder, the examinations may be taken only after continuous work in at least two of the following subjects: German, a foreign language (one chosen before entering the upper secondary level), and mathematics. One of the subjects submitted for the Abitur may be tested orally instead of in writing, at the candidate's discretion. Irma is offering mathematics and physics at Leistungs level, English and chemistry at Grund level, with chemistry as her oral subject. Dieter is offering German and French at Leistungs level, mathematics and history at Grund level, with mathematics as his oral subject.

In 1972 the nationwide requirements for secondary graduation and university entrance were liberalized by reducing the number of subjects to be studied in depth for the Abitur and permitting students more options. However, revised regulations, came into force in 1989 and reversed the trend of the 1972 reforms. The changes grew out of concern over what some regarded as falling educational standards and were part of the retreat from the more liberal educational and social thinking of the previous decades. The new regulations are intended to strengthen students' basic and common knowledge: specifically, to prevent them from dropping ''difficult'' subjects and taking only ''easy'' ones in the examinations, to place limits on the system of options, and to reestablish the primacy of a certain common core of subjects. In addition, history and the natural sciences have been given more weight. Finally, new weightings of performance level are used: the scale of points for Grund courses has been raised and that for Leistung courses lowered.[5]

The overall grade on the Abitur is calculated using a complex formula

4. See ''Die Gymnasiale Oberstufe: Informationsschrift für Schüler 1988/89'' (Düsseldorf: Kultusminister des Landes Nordrhein-Westfalen, 1987), Nordrhein-Westfalen information sheet, for sample programs.

5. *Bildung und Wissenschaft* 1987, nos. 1–2: 13.

to weight and aggregate the raw scores obtained in the four examined subjects and the grades taken from the school record. Passing the Abitur is all that is needed for entry into a university, as entrance examinations are not given. For entrance into faculties where demand exceeds supply, however, local or federal restrictions (*numerus clausus*) apply. Applicants to enter medicine, dental surgery, and veterinary medicine must take a special test. Other restricted areas of study include architecture, business management, pharmacy, law, computer science, and surveying. The Central Office for the Allocation of Study Places in Dortmund selects those who will be admitted to study in courses subject to federal restrictions. The award of a study place is determined by a complex points system, taking account of Abitur marks, special test results (if applicable), and length of time on the waiting list. Some places are reserved for foreigners and hardship cases; about 10 percent of the medical, dental surgery, and veterinary places are awarded outright on the special test results alone. Even if a study place is awarded, the Central Office does not guarantee it will be at the candidate's institution of choice.[6] Competition for high marks is fierce, for the higher the grade, the more likely it is that an applicant will be accepted by a preferred university and in a preferred faculty or department.

Whereas his friend Irma has done well and is off to the university after the summer, Dieter will have to repeat the final year of school and take the examinations again. His aggregate grades did not reach a passing level. Under special circumstances, he could formally appeal to be reexamined in one subject shortly after the Abitur, but usually an unsuccessful candidate must take all four subjects again after spending another semester or year in the *Gymnasiale Oberstufe* (senior Gymnasium). Generally, only one repeat is permitted, but a second may sometimes be allowed.[7]

Although some students repeat the examinations to raise their marks and gain entrance into a more selective program or institution, Dieter's sights are set considerably lower. He simply hopes that by repeating the final stage of upper secondary school and the Abitur, he will have earned a second chance to enter higher education. On the downside, he realizes he will be twenty before he even enters the university, and at least twenty-five (and more likely twenty-seven) by the time he finishes. Added to which, graduates of the humanities disciplines have been experiencing difficulty in finding good jobs. Dieter is also considering a different path: bypassing

6. Inter Nationes, *Bildung und Wissenschaft*, 1990, no. 11/12(e). (Bonn: Inter Nationes, 1990): 18.

7. See, e.g., *Ausbildungs- und Prüfungsordnung mit Verwaltungsvorschriften APO-GOSt*, 4th ed. (Cologne: Kultusminister des Landes Nordrhein-Westfalen, 1984) no. 1101.

university studies entirely and sounding out one or two business firms to explore the prospect of entering an apprenticeship program. Fifteen years ago, it was virtually unheard-of for an *Abiturient* to sign on for an apprenticeship; now it is much more common. There is the added attraction that with the Abitur in hand, Dieter need spend only two years in apprentice status before taking his practical examinations, instead of the standard three years. Perhaps his training firm will offer him a regular job, but if not, he reckons that an Abiturient with an apprenticeship training in business skills is well placed to find a worthwhile position reasonably quickly.

Irma has a different, somewhat annoying, problem. She easily passed her examinations, and she is especially happy to have done well in science, since she wishes to specialize in mathematics and computing and go on to a career in industry or government. The problem is that she has been offered a place at Ruhr University in Bochum. She does not particularly want to attend her hometown university, especially as her boyfriend has been admitted to study law at the university in Munich. Her one hope is that she can find someone who has been admitted to Munich with results and academic preferences similar to her own who would be willing to trade places with her. The odds of success are long, but she has decided to invest 155 Deutschemarks for three successive personal advertisements in the *Frankfurter Allgemeine Zeitung,* for this purpose. At this point all she can do is to pray for the telephone call that might make it possible for her to study in Bavaria.

Upper secondary school in Germany is a serious business. The Abitur is normally taken at the end of thirteen years of education, a longer period than in most other countries. The level of knowledge demanded is high, and although only four subjects are normally offered for examination, students carry several other, nonexamined subjects during their upper secondary years. Moreover, the final score attached to the Abitur is a very important component of the aggregate score that will determine the offer of a study place at a university. Indeed, very small fractions of a point can make a big difference to an applicant's chance of admission. Preparation for the examinations therefore looms very large in the upper secondary student's life in Germany, leaving not much time for extracurricular activities.

France

Michel and Michelle are eighteen years of age. They live in Toulouse, a rapidly growing southern French city of some four hundred thousand inhabitants, less than two hours' drive from the Pyrenees mountains. Michel's father is an engineer at the area's large Airbus assembly plant; his mother works as a bookkeeper/accountant for a local real estate agent. Michelle's father, a farmer, died when she was ten. Her mother left the farm and moved into town, where she works in a factory producing office stationery.

Both students have attended state schools since they were six years old. After five years in primary school, they transferred to the *collège* (the lower secondary stage covering the age group eleven to fifteen). As they approached the end of compulsory schooling at age sixteen, about 20 percent of their classmates were assigned to two-year terminal vocational programs. Others left school entirely. Of the total 16-year-old age group, about 50 percent transferred to the *lycée* to take the three-year course of study (the "long" course) leading to the baccalauréat examinations. The grade in which Michel and Michelle entered the lycée is called the *seconde;* the middle year is the *première;* they are now in the *classe terminale,* the final year.

Even though Toulouse is 500 miles from Paris, and in an area of France that boasts a history and a culture quite distinct from that of the capital, public administration in France is so highly centralized that the same policies and organizational practices extend to the entire nation. Michel and Michelle have undergone and survived a sustained selection and sorting process to arrive at their present status as members of the classe terminale. Their school performance has been routinely tested each year to determine whether they will be promoted to the next grade. Promotion cannot be taken for granted, as each year about 7 percent of the students are required to repeat a grade. In the *troisième* (the final year of the collège), their adviser recommended both students for the lycée program. Michel had some difficulties in school earlier on and poor marks spoiled his record (though they were not low enough to require him to repeat), so that initially he had been referred to the vocationally oriented two-year program. However, after several serious talks at home and representations to the school by his parents, Michel was permitted to enroll in the longer, general academic program. He has settled down to steady work at school and at home, and his marks have improved greatly.

Students entering the three-year academic cycle must make several important curriculum decisions—which série to take, and within a given série, which elective subjects. Previous grades, personal preferences, and plans for further study and career all play a part in this decision. The guidance of their teacher-counselors becomes especially important, and parents usually heed the advice. Michel's father, having attended the lycée, knows well the importance of making the correct choices and is probably better equipped than most French parents to help his son make the "right" decision. The major séries available in the baccalauréat fall into three groups: (1) general education (A—philosophy, literature, languages, and arts, B—economics and social sciences, C, D, E—mathematics and sciences); (2) technology (F—mechanical and civil engineering, electronics, applied sciences, medical technology, applied arts, G—business studies, H—computers); and (3) professional/vocational studies. The options now comprise no fewer than thirty-eight alternative programs of study.[8] Each série requires some subjects common to all and several electives, but even in the subjects common to all, the scope of the syllabi and the level of difficulty may be different. Thus, programs of study become progressively differentiated in the lycée, as in successive years they must be tailored to the requirements of the different séries and options.

Michel and Michelle's programs of study in the seconde included required courses, required electives, and optional studies. Along with all their classmates they took a common core of classes in French, history and geography, a foreign language, mathematics, science (physics, chemistry, and biology), and physical education.

Required electives are necessary to meet the requirements of the séries and are additional to the common core subjects. For the séries in general education, in addition to an introduction to the social sciences, students select according to their planned specialization from a second foreign language (ancient or modern), computing, aesthetics, certain specialized sporting activities, automation, and business studies. For those aiming at the various technology credentials, required electives include industrial technology, medical science, biology, agronomy, laboratory science and technology, and applied arts.

Finally, there is room for a few additional options to complete their programs. Students may choose from a number of optional courses such as art or another language (classical, modern, and possibly regional) and from many of the choices in the required electives group. Even here, however, choices are constrained by the requirements of a particular baccalauréat. For example, A2 (literature and languages) requires three languages and B (economics/social sciences) only two. An "incorrect" choice of courses may bar a candidate from a particular baccalauréat program, and

8. Additional technical-vocational education programs are also available leading to the *brevet*. Possession of the brevet does not give the right to attend a university, but certifies completion of a technical-vocational course of study. Important forms of the qualification are: *brevet d'études professionnelles* (B.E.P.), *brevet de technicien* (B.T.), and *brevet de technicien supérieur* (B.T.S.).

students are enjoined to keep their options as open as possible by carefully choosing among the subjects available. Michelle and Michel recognized this as a good strategy: as they move through the final years of secondary school, they might change their minds about their baccalauréat target; their grades might drop in an important subject; or they could have a change of heart about future careers. But the price of following this advice was high, for it meant that they had to take on a heavy course load.

Michelle has an outstanding academic record so far, and is aiming high. She is preparing for the mathematics–physical science option (série C). In her final year she must take at least eight hours each of mathematics and physical and natural sciences per week, together with social studies, English, and philosophy. She took her written and oral baccalauréat examinations in French the previous year and has no further classes to attend in this subject. Michelle is still required to attend a class in physical education and has chosen to continue with her class in economics from the various electives in languages and social science available at her school.

Because Michel and his teachers think he will do well to pass a less rigorous course of study, he is preparing for série H, one of the new technical baccalauréats, with a specialization in *informatique* (computer science). His father agrees with this choice of study and is supporting Michel in what seems to be a practical program leading to a good career straight from school. In his penultimate school year (the *première*), Michel continued general studies in French, social science, English, mathematics, applied physics, and physical education. He also has courses related to his specialization in technology: economics, business methods, and a heavy concentration in computer science. Now in the terminale, he drops French and social science but has added philosophy (required by all in the final year), and retains the other general and specialty subjects.

In the first year of the three-year program leading to the *baccalauréat,* students have an official program of at least 25.5 class hours, with an additional two to three hours for optional subjects. In the première and terminale, class time may increase by one or more hours, depending on the specific program followed and whether additional options are taken. However, Michel and Michelle reckon that at least three hours a day of homework, and even more thereafter, are normal, thus adding between 21 and 28 hours to the weekly workload. Now that Michel has reached the final year in his technology option, he is taking 36 hours a week of class work, plus homework. The compulsory oral and written examinations in French language and literature (the *épreuve anticipée*) are the culmination of the première. The results will form part of the final baccalauréat grade and will be very important in confirming (or modifying) the original selection of série and specialization. Preparation for the épreuve anticipée required many hours of study and practice, not least because Michel and Michelle were also required to submit a dossier of all their literary studies in and out of school.

Despite the relief offered by having the épreuve anticipée behind them, and the dropping of some subjects in the final year, Michel and Michelle find their study load becomes heavier as they move closer to taking the baccalauréat examinations. They are attending school six days a week, starting at 8:15 A.M. and ending usually at 3:30 P.M. (though Wednesday and Saturday are half-days). They find that they often have to stay up late to complete their assignments. Michel frequently complains that he is exhausted, and even his parents agree that he looks pale and is overworked. Somewhat surprisingly, though, many students manage to find time for a private music lesson, an occasional visit to the movies, or a couple of hours with friends on a Sunday afternoon or evening.

To make matters worse, their timetables have become more complex and difficult to handle. On some days, there are classes from early morning till late, with hardly a moment to get a cup of coffee or lunch; on others, two or three hours may be unscheduled in the middle of the day, so that they must hang around in buildings containing only classrooms and offices, without space to accommodate them in free periods. Their school buildings date from the 1920s and are not only severely overcrowded, but also run-down from lack of maintenance during the past fifteen years. Both students resent what they feel is a lack of government concern for the quality of their education and were quite ready to join the lycéens' massive street demonstrations in November 1990, which quickly succeeded in extracting promises of more funds from the president of the Republic.

By the time of the examinations, the late evenings of work and rushed meals show in Michel's face: gaunt features, dark patches under the eyes, and nervous mannerisms. The written examinations are long, and several are scheduled close together, on successive days—a physical as well as a mental ordeal. Although Michel and Michelle are studying many subjects with the same label, they are covering quite different syllabi, their examination papers will be different, the grading standards applied will differ, and the weightings given to the marks in each subject when aggregating to obtain the overall score will also be quite different.

All candidates for the baccalauréat must take the written examination in philosophy. In addition, Michel has to take written examinations in mathematics, economics, business, and computer science, and oral examinations in English, physics, technology and computers, and economics and business studies (optional). Michelle has to take written examinations in her major areas of mathematics and physical science, and orals in English, history and geography, and natural science, as well as two more orals in the areas she has submitted written examinations. Nothing, she is convinced, exceeds the ordeal of the oral examinations. The long wait in line for her name to be called is bad enough, but as Michelle enters the room set aside for the oral sessions, she feels a profound sense of disorientation. She has to clasp her hands together to prevent them from trembling and betraying her near panic. And no wonder! The faces of a row of complete strangers seated behind a long table are terrifying, and for a moment, her mind seems incapable of thought. But then the mist clears, and she hears the question: "Compare French and U.S. policies in Vietnam in the post–World War II period, and explain the differences and the similarities." A few minutes are allowed her to prepare a response, after which Michelle is able to provide a well-organized and reasonably factual statement—just as she has been trained to do.

When the examinations are over, there is nothing to do but wait for the results. The maximum score for the entire examination is twenty, rarely if ever awarded. Scores bunch within the range of eleven and fourteen. A score below seven represents a "fail." A very few high-flyers will score seventeen, eighteen, and exceptionally nineteen. In July, Michel receives his results. He has been awarded a twelve, a clear pass, though by no means a brilliant one. The many late nights of study, the constant effort, have brought their reward. But after the results were published, as he stood in line to register at the University of Toulouse with the crowd of others who had been successful, he knew that he would have to work hard to pass the first set of examinations at the end of the second year. No longer is admission a ticket to remain a student for as long as he may wish, as it was in his father's day. The university is overcrowded and the competition will be strong. He will have to perform satisfactorily to complete university studies and is aware from his older friends and the newspapers that the failure rate is high, almost 50 percent.

On the other hand, Michelle has a difficult decision to make. The examinations were a highly stressful and exhausting experience for her, made worse by having to take an extra oral in mathematics, where her scores were on the margin. In the end, the jury did not award her a passing grade, so she must repeat the examinations in all subjects of her série after one year if she wishes to obtain the baccalauréat and attend a university. Michelle was fully aware when she selected série C that she had chosen the most difficult option. It was notoriously the most demanding and consequently the least popular, and, moreover, one taken by few girls. Her mother, proud of her accomplishments so far but worried about the effects on her health of long hours of study, is of two minds, but as the family discusses the future they leave the final decision in her hands. It is her life they are talking about, and she is the one who must exert the effort necessary to achieve what she wants. But she is firm in her desire to become a biochemist and enter a career in research. After a long conference with her school counselor, she decides to return to the lycée to repeat the terminale. Two of her friends are in the same situation, so it won't be too bad. Moreover, she is a little younger than her peers, so the delay need not worry her, especially since she knows that many university students do not make it through the first examinations and drop out, largely, it is said, because they are too immature to apply themselves to their studies on entering higher education. And she is encouraged by the fact that the success rate for those repeating the baccalauréat is high. An extra year of study will improve her chances of obtaining a high score, say a fifteen or better, which will help her gain admission to one of the specialist biochemistry university departments with limited enrollment.

Michel and Michelle have passed through a system in which external examinations have exerted a remarkable dominance over their lives and over the schooling they have received. In the eyes of their teachers and parents, and even in their own eyes too, preparation for the baccalauréat seems to justify the pressure they have felt for at least three years. In a singular manner the entire process carries a meaning beyond that of simply learning facts and techniques and then demonstrating that knowledge during the examination. Taking the baccalauréat for Michel and Michelle has been a culminating rite of passage, an entry into citizenship.

Japan

Kohji and Miyoko's teachers and parents have consistently held them to high standards of comportment, study, and work, and have encouraged them in an impressively competitive spirit of academic achievement. They live and go to school in Kyoto, one of Japan's most important cities. Kohji's father is an investment manager in Sumitomo, a Japanese bank. He has worked there ever since he graduated from his university twenty-five years ago, and he expects to remain with the firm till he retires. Miyoko's father runs a small automobile repair garage, employing four mechanics. In both families, the mothers are at home, even though Kohji's mother had completed four years of college in foreign languages (English and German).

The two youngsters are now in the final year of the *kotogakko* (senior high school, grades ten to twelve) in company with students much like themselves, with excellent school records and success in examinations. Each day, Kohji and Miyoko travel over an hour to the other side of town to get to their school, but they feel that the privilege of attending this institution is well worth the effort. Their school has an outstanding reputation based on its record of student success in the university entrance examinations.

Transfer from junior to senior high school is, as a rule, based in part on the results of achievement tests at the end of grade nine, and in part on high school entrance examinations. Miyoko and Kohji were admitted on the basis of their superior marks after three years in junior high school. Local educational authorities follow slightly different practices, but for some years now, most have tried to steer a middle course, trying to avoid the elitism that comes with strict selectivity when transferring students to senior high school and at the same time placing a limit on the extent of student heterogeneity within a school. Local policies thus make use of several criteria for transfer: examination results, parents' preferences, and the desired range and mix of student abilities in each school.

School attendance is not mandatory beyond grade nine and parents of high school students must pay fees. Nevertheless, the majority of sixteen-to-eighteen-year-olds are enrolled in the general, academic full-time course of study in a senior high school, and about 95 percent of the age group complete secondary schooling through grade twelve. A small number are part-time students and some are in technical schools.

If Kohji had not done well enough in the entrance examination to gain entrance to this more selective public school, his father would undoubtedly have made the effort to pay the substantial fees at a private school. There he would receive better preparation for the university entrance examinations than the other public secondary schools in town would provide. Miyoko's parents, however, would have given this a lower priority in the family budget, reasoning that girls do not need to have the same educational opportunities as boys.

The public school system in Japan is directed from Tokyo by the central Ministry of Education (popularly known as "Mombusho"), but which delegates administrative responsibilities to prefectures and towns. But major educational policies, such as curriculum structure and content, textbook approval, school organization and schedules, teachers' credentials and pay, are all determined and controlled by the ministry and are uniform across the nation. General policies are determined by national committees, discussed and voted upon by the Diet, and often questioned and vigorously opposed by the national teachers' union.

Kohji and Miyoko's curriculum for the first two years in senior high school differed little from everyone else's: Japanese, social studies (history, geography, and civics), mathematics, science, health and physical education, arts (music, art, calligraphy), and a foreign language (English). Miyoko, like all the girls, also takes home economics. Only in the final year have a few options become available, providing some opportunity for additional, more advanced work in either science and mathematics or the humanities, related perhaps to their target for the future. Miyoko chooses an elective social studies course, and Kohji takes additional mathematics at a more advanced level. These choices account for only 10 to 15 percent of their school timetable, however, and most of their classes are the same as all other students', using the standard textbooks and following the ministry's prescribed syllabi.

Kohji and Miyoko's memories of the more relaxed primary years, when school was fun, have faded. Junior high school had been something of a shock, with its increased pressure to perform, regular formal tests, and emphasis on preparation for the third-year examination. Some of their peers became demoralized by the change of climate, some even taking to such antisocial behavior as bullying their weaker classmates (*ijime*). Senior high school has intensified the pressure.

The thirty-five-week school year opens at the beginning of April, with classes running from eight to three, five days per week, plus a four-hour day on Saturdays. With six periods in a complete day, this provides for thirty-two classes a week of fifty minutes each, plus school clubs and activities. After school closes, Kohji and Miyoko, like more than half of their class, go directly to a juku. This is a private school where students may choose from an array of craft, aesthetic, and enriched study classes. But a major focus of this extracurricular system is intense instruction to reinforce what was taught in school and training in the techniques of taking the public examinations. The fees are high, but their parents do not begrudge the expense. Kohji arranges through his juku for his scores on practice tests to be sent to a company that specializes in predicting examination success. The company will also advise him about which universities he should apply to, given his scores and other personal details. Kohji attends the juku three afternoons during the week, Miyoko on Saturday afternoon. Only when they get home will there be time to sit down to their homework. They do not find this routine unusual since they have been attending such after-school classes since sixth grade: Miyoko attending music lessons, and Kohji classes in general school subjects. It is simply a part of the daily program and duties and the normal expectation among friends and family. Indeed, if they were not enrolled in juku, they would feel rather left out of things.

Much of the final year in high school has been directed at preparing for the entrance examinations for higher education. By now Kohji and Miyoko are accustomed to the daily grind, and they have become most efficient at the memorization and rote learning that characterize their schooling. The pace of work and intensity of study, which have been heavy all along, have become even greater—about sixteen hours a day.[9]—and there is less time for relaxation, for meals, and even for sleep. There has been no time for social activities for quite a while; now even chatting for a few minutes after school is seen as wasting time and provokes feelings of anxiety and guilt. They hear stories about classmates who have succumbed to physical and mental illness due to the pressures. The press adds to the stress by reports of student suicides—but they have no personal knowledge of anyone who has been that despairing.[10]

Kohji has been advised by the company that has analyzed his juku scores that he stands a chance of gaining admission to Tokyo University (Todai), a national, public university and one of the most highly regarded in the country. Miyoko also hopes to attend a public institution, though she recognizes that given her family's unwillingness to send a girl to a four-year degree-granting institution, she cannot aim very high. The first step is to register to sit for the Joint First Stage Achievement Test (JFSAT), organized by a special department of the Ministry of Education. The JFSAT is not needed for graduation from high school, nor do most private colleges and universities require it of applicants. But it is necessary as the first stage of application to the public institutions. So, halfway through the school year, in October, the two students submitted their application forms to sit for the JFSAT. Now, at the end of January, in common with about four hundred thousand of their peers across the nation, Miyoko and Kohji are taking the JFSAT at their school. Candidates take tests in six or seven subjects. There are some variations: for example, Kohji sits for a more advanced paper in mathematics, while Miyoko chooses a European History option.

The results of the JFSAT and the dates of the entrance examinations set by the universities are announced. Many of Kohji and Miyoke's contem-

9. John Greenlees, "Pupils Go Crackers over Study Aid," *Times Educational Supplement* (June 17, 1988): 15.

10. Thomas Rohlen notes that suicide rates are not higher for Japanese high school seniors facing examinations than for their counterparts in other nations, but that examination pressure as a *cause* of suicide is probably higher. Some of the yobiko (cram schools for repeaters) have their own clinics. Thomas P. Rohlen. *Japan's High Schools* (Berkeley: University of Berkeley Press, 1983), pp. 327–334.

poraries have obtained good results on the national examination. The Todai entrance examination will be conducted by the university in two months. Kohji signs up with a travel agency that is assembling a group of high school seniors to travel to Tokyo for the examinations and a few additional days in the capital. The tour package includes rail fare, hotel accommodation, meals, transportation from the hotel to the university's examination halls, and a sightseeing trip before the return home. The entrance examination will last two days, and applicants may choose to be tested in two or more subjects—some choose as many as five. Kohji will be examined in four subjects, including an advanced test in mathematics. Todai usually has about four applicants for every place offered, so this will be an exceptionally competitive examination, much harder than the JFSAT.

Miyoke takes only the JFSAT, for she does not expect to be able to apply to a college or university that requires a special entrance examination. For those who apply and are accepted, there is the prospect of four relatively relaxed years, beginning the social life they had little time for during the demanding years of secondary school. Now there should be time for dating, joining clubs, going to movies, and having fun, since the demands of college work are nothing compared with what they have endured in high school preparing for the entrance examinations. Moreover, for those who have been admitted to their chosen department in their chosen university, the future is already secure: they will have little difficulty obtaining a job that will earn them security and a good income.

Although Kohji did well in the JFSAT, he does not secure a place at Todai. He is utterly disappointed and ashamed. He feels he has let down his teachers, his school, and his family even though everyone knows how intense the competition is. Despite the hard work and late nights of study, he can only conclude that he did not make a sufficient effort. He resolves to try again and to study even harder. About a quarter of all candidates in the examination repeat it. To join the ranks of the repeating candidates (so-called *ronin*) is not dishonorable, and Kohji has been told, too, that almost half the applicants admitted to Todai and to medical colleges across the nation, which are in especially great demand, are ronin.[11] The chances of getting into a good university program are certainly enhanced by an improved second set of results. Driven by the desire to erase his failure and motivated by his interest in a math/computer science career, Kohji immediately enrols in the *yobiko* (a crammer solely for university entrance examinations) to prepare for another attempt a year hence.

11. U.S. Department of Education, *Japanese Education Today* (Washington, D.C.: U.S. Government Printing Office, 1987).

The yobiko fees and the cost of the study materials will be high, but Kohji's parents consider it well worthwhile. Good results mean entry to a top national university, where fees are low, quality of staff, facilities, and education are superior, prestige is high, and career opportunities are outstanding. Provincial universities do not offer these advantages, and set a clear limit on what careers will be available and the extent of advancement that may be expected in the future. Although some private universities have high status and thus offer better opportunities, they are very expensive; some of the others are viewed as second-rank or below.

If worst comes to worst and the results are not good enough for Kohji to be accepted in the course he wants, he may even take the examinations yet again, for there is no limit on repeating and students on a waiting list may apply for admission to a university as often as they wish until they succeed. However, though first-time repeaters are frequent, and second-time repeaters are common, few persist beyond that point.

For a young man, every effort must be expended to enhance the chances of entrance to the best university possible, for his whole future depends on it. But this is not so for daughters. In Miyoko's family, discussions over the examination results and her future are much briefer and take a different turn. While not outstanding, her marks are quite good and she has earned the praise of her family and friends. Though it is no longer rare for girls to continue their education, most still do so in junior colleges and in programs traditionally considered suitable for females: primary school teaching, nursing, business skills (secretarial work), and the "softer" subjects like the arts, humanities, and social sciences. Secretly, Miyoke had hoped to take a humanities degree in the provincial four-year college, and her marks are more than adequate for this. But her father insists that she attend the nearby junior college and study business skills, so that is where she will go for the next two years. If her marks are good, if her ambition and intentions remain strong, and if she can persuade her parents to give their permission, she may yet be able to attend the provincial university and obtain the degree.

The pressure exerted by examinations in Japan is extraordinarily high. They control the lives of students (and their parents) to a degree that is very rare in the other countries of this study. Indeed, it is not too much to say that education in Japan, particularly after sixth grade, is defined as preparation to take examinations. Secondary school students are provided with a very clear set of objectives, and they are expected to make the effort necessary to achieve them. Only lack of effort, not lack of ability, it is commonly accepted, stands in the way of their success. So, it is to study, more study, and yet more study for tests and examinations that Kohji and Miyoko have devoted themselves for more years than they can remember.

Conclusion

All of our students have submitted, with varying degrees of application, commitment, and seriousness, to an examination that they knew was important and which was to some extent an ordeal. All of them now stand at the beginning of a new stage in their lives, looking toward employment, training, or further education.

Although in these general terms they have been treated somewhat similarly by their societies and are at a similar stage, it would be a mistake to believe that for these students it doesn't really much matter whether they grew up to prepare for the baccalauréat, the General Certificate of Secondary Education, the Abitur, the attestat zrelosti, the Joint First Stage Aptitude Test—or the Scholastic Aptitude Test. It would be a mistake to believe that "a school is a school is a school" and that "an exam is an exam is an exam." However much they share substantial common elements, national examination systems at the end of secondary school differ markedly, and the differences carry important implications for societies, schools, and students.

In Japan and France, for example, examinations dominate students' lives vastly more than they do in, say, Sweden and the United States. In Germany and China, the examination is the culmination of a process of lengthy, specific, targeted instruction, whereas in the United States the most commonly taken examinations (the SAT and the ACT) are connected only loosely to the formal instruction given in the schools. In China, Japan, and the Soviet Union, examination candidates understand very clearly that they are in a highly competitive situation, whereas in Sweden and England/Wales, though competition may certainly exist, its presence is less obvious and controlling.

Even though all of the students whose experiences we have described have gone through a process of sorting and sifting, national differences are striking. Moreover, the differences in sorting procedures are closely related to the nature of the examination at the end of secondary school. In China and Germany, formal selection procedures separate students into schools that differ in curriculum, teacher background, and student orientation. Similarly, in Japan competitive entrance examinations to senior high school are well established and highly visible. By contrast, in the comprehensive schools of England/Wales, the sorting procedures are quite informal for the first two or three years up to age fourteen or so, but become much more overt once the results of the GCSE are in. Sweden postpones selection until the end of compulsory schooling, and even then students are not so much selected as given the opportunity to select themselves for one of the many lines of senior secondary school study.

The consequences of the particular grades and marks gained in the examinations also differ widely from nation to nation, even though for all students, options are gradually closed off so that after the results are in, opportunities become more limited. National systems differ, however, according to how critical the examination results are for a candidate's future. Thus, in China and Japan, high marks are very critical, although in both nations there is some opportunity to try again if the first try was not successful (perhaps more in Japan than in China). In the Soviet Union, high marks open the door to full-time, day study at university level, though places are quite limited, and those with good but less than excellent grades must be content with part-time and correspondence study. In England, advancement (whether in higher education or in later life) is possible, though not common, without good to excellent examination results. Meanwhile, in Sweden and the United States, poor performance or even failure to obtain the credential awarded at the end of secondary school does not necessarily exclude a young person from the prospect of advanced training or higher education. In Sweden, some university places are officially reserved for more mature persons with "life experience." In the United States and in England/Wales institutions have wide discretion over whom to accept and employ several criteria other than examination results for admission.

Where an "official" credential based on examination results is the main criterion for eligibility or admission, the consequences of failure are more serious and long-lasting. Although a small number of students may be admitted without formal qualifications on the basis of school recommendation (as in China and Japan), and a good record of community and school service counts for a lot (as in China and the Soviet Union), the examination results and possession of the requisite credential primarily determine the decision in France, Germany, Japan, China, and the Soviet Union.

Nations may thus be arranged on a scale ranging from those where the external examination systems are highly determining to those that are much more open, with many second chances and alternative opportunities for success. They may also be arranged according to those where the impending examinations dominate secondary school practices and the lives of students, and those where they are less central. In the first instances, the rewards of success are very great and the consequences of failure serious;

in the latter they are relatively less pronounced and conclusive. But even in the most selective systems, opportunities for making a second attempt are considerable and widely used. And even in those nations where examinations are not the be-all and end-all of schooling, they remain important.

Chapter 4

The Examiners: Organization and Control of Examination Systems

A complicated gentleman allow me to present,
Of all arts and faculties the terse embodiment,
He's a great Arithmetician who can demonstrate with ease
That two and two are three, or five, or anything you please;
An eminent Logician who can make clear to you
That black is white—when looked at from the proper point of view;
A marvellous Philologist who'll undertake to show
That "yes" is but another and a neater form of "no."
—Zara, *Utopia Limited,* act 1

Implementing a national examination system requires the involvement of different levels of authority and many interested parties, and may include both public and private agencies. The eight countries in this study represent a variety of administrative practices: highly centralized states, federal systems, and systems where power lies largely with regional and local agencies. They also illustrate the different powers, interests, and professional groups participating in the process of examining students as they reach the end of secondary schooling. We first describe the distribution of formal authority and responsibilities between central and regional or local government, and between public and private agencies. In several nations, the pattern appears to be well-entrenched and stable. However, we also describe several recent instances of changes in the locus of authority over examinations. We then review national differences in distributing responsibilities for specific aspects of examination practice, paying particular attention to the role of teachers. Finally, we draw attention to the interests of other parties frequently concerned with the operation of examination systems and show how they may participate informally in influencing examination policies, if not controlling them.

The chapter concludes with a discussion of the significance of various patterns of examination organization and control, the relation of these patterns to other aspects of educational control, and current trends.

Who's in Charge?

In France, Japan, and China, a central government agency is clearly in charge and in a real sense "owns" the examinations. For example, in France, the Ministry of Education issues detailed instructions concerning the syllabi for each subject. Each year it circulates a list of the topics to be addressed in the forthcoming examination papers. It sets the dates for examinations and announces procedures for administering them. The ministry formulates the rules for appointing local juries of examiners, describes their powers, their procedures, and the constraints upon them, and specifies the general criteria and technical aspects for evaluating answers and awarding marks (such as weighting scores on particular subjects according to the type of baccalauréat). The central authority gives limited discretion to the regional authorities (*académies*) and assigns certain administrative responsibilities to them under general ministry guidelines. However, the ministry retains control over the process through an inspectorate (Inspecteurs Pédagogiques régionaux). Members of the inspectorate are subject specialists in each region who work closely with the rector of the académie to appoint members of the juries supervising the examination (see below), to decide which questions will appear on the examination, and to determine grading criteria.

Japan's National Center for University Entrance Examinations, an agency of the Ministry of Education, is responsible for developing and administering the annual national examination (the Joint First Stage Achievement Test). Basic policies are formulated and reviewed by standing committees of the ministry and the National University Association and executed by the National Center, which manages the registration of applicants, testing centers, scoring of papers, record-keeping, reporting of scores, and so on. In addition, the National Center develops the examination papers, appointing committees to formulate the questions in each subject. About twenty working groups, with fifteen members each, are selected from the teaching staffs of the national universities; members serve for two years, half being replaced each year. All the costs of running the examination system are met by the ministry, though individuals must pay an application fee to take the tests. But, unlike France, no discretion is given to regional authorities to frame specific questions and to appoint local juries. Higher education institutions, whether singly or in small collaborative groups, design their own entrance examinations, offered after the JFSAT or, in some instances, in lieu of the national test.[1]

1. Katsuhiro Arai, "The Current Entrance Examination System on Higher Education in Japan" (unpublished paper, Deutsches Institut für Pädagogische Forschung, Frankfurt, Janu-

In China, too, since 1977 a specialized unit of the State Education Commission, the National Education Examinations Authority, has been in charge of the national university entrance examination. General policies, grading criteria, and cutoff points (passing standards) are set by central authorities, but in each province, municipality, and autonomous region a higher school enrollment committee takes care of local arrangements and prints and distributes the examination papers. The university entrance examination is centrally controlled in order to achieve a high degree of uniformity and comparability across the nation. Although central planning seeks to ensure that each province and municipality sets suitable targets for itself that fit national goals, the recent emergence of separate school graduation examinations set by the provincial authorities, discussed below, opens the door to greater local variations and authority.[2]

Thus, even when a national ministry of education has the dominant authority, certain responsibilities can be delegated to regional administrations. France exemplifies this practice: academic personnel and public officials in education participate in regional committees in each académie, though under strict national guidelines. The ministry exercises control through its regional inspectorate, which plays a key role in all appointments to such committees and in the procedures they follow. These regional agencies select topics from the national lists and frame the questions, though these will be reviewed before administration of the examination. The agencies monitor procedures at the local level, appoint juries to supervise the examinations, consider special appeals by students, rule on eligibility, and generally concern themselves with seeing that regulations are properly followed.

China's provincial authorities are responsible for monitoring and mark-

ary 1989); Tadashi Hidano, "Admission to Higher Education in Japan," in Stephen Heyneman and Ingemar Fägerlind, eds., *University Examinations and Standardized Testing: Principles, Experience and Policy Options* (Washington, D.C.: World Bank, 1988), pp. 9–25; U.S. Department of Education, *Japanese Education Today* (Washington, D.C.: U.S. Government Printing Office, 1987).

2. Keith Lewin and Wang Lu, "University Entrance Examinations in China: A Quiet Revolution," in Patricia Broadfoot et al., eds., *Changing Educational Assessment: International Perspectives and Trends* (London: Routledge, 1990), pp. 153–176; State Education Commission of the People's Republic of China, *A Brief Introduction of Higher School Enrollment Examinations in China* (Beijing: State Education Commission of the People's Republic of China, 1986); Lu Zhen, "A Brief Introduction to the System of Higher Enrollment Examinations in China," in Stephen P. Heyneman and Ingemar Fägerlind, eds., *University Examinations and Standardized Testing* (Washington, D.C.: World Bank, 1988), pp. 107–114; Lu Zhen, "An Introduction to China's High School Completion Tests and Higher Education Entrance Tests" (unpublished paper, Deutsches Institut für Pädagogische Forschung, Frankfurt, January 1989).

ing the examinations, though as in France, they must operate within narrowly drawn guidelines. However, no such latitude exists at the regional level in Japan, where the central authorities run the entire examination from start to finish.

In contrast to these more centralized nations, authority for external examinations in the Soviet Union, as well as in the United States and the Federal Republic of Germany, resides in regional governmental authorities. The locus of control and mode of operation may differ even among jurisdictions in the same nation. For example, in Germany, the Länder jealously guard their historic legal right to shape their own educational systems and manage their school affairs (so-called *Kulturhoheit*, that is, cultural sovereignty). In three of the jurisdictions the Abitur is uniform for all candidates, set by each respective ministry.[3] In other Länder, localities have some discretion to devise questions and procedures. Individual schools and groups of teachers formulate the questions and evaluate answers, subject to supervision by the Land ministry (as is also the case in the Soviet Union).[4] Nevertheless, in order to ensure national equivalence for the credential and in the entrance criteria for higher education, the Standing Conference of Ministers of Education (the KMK) has agreed on certain national guidelines for upper secondary schooling, conditions regarding entry to the *Abitur,* and procedures for grading. In this and other respects, the Länder have been willing to accept some constraints on their cultural sovereignty.

In each republic of the Soviet Union, local school-based committees of examiners (teachers and administrators) play an important part in setting questions and evaluating the answers, within the limits of official syllabi for each subject. As in Germany, these committees make their own local arrangements, conduct the examinations, and award grades to the candidates. However, the ministries of education of the several republics do exert a degree of control over schools in their respective domains. They publish guidelines for the conduct of examinations and set limits on the content of examination papers. In the Russian Republic, the central authority devises the written examination papers and distributes them to the schools. The papers are the same for all schools. Topics for the oral examinations are also formulated centrally. They consist of a fairly long list,

3. Bavaria, unlike the others, has not changed this practice since it was established in 1834. See Max Schmid, ''Die bayerische Form des Zentralabiturs,'' in *Die Höhere Schule* 38, no. 3 (1985): 86–88.

4. In reference to such differences *within* regions, the distinction is made between the more uniform practices in the ''Napoleonic'' Länder and the greater local autonomy in the Prussian Länder. See Wolfgang Mitter, ''Examinations in Germany'' (unpublished paper, Malaga, January 1988).

published well in advance of the examinations, from which specific questions are formulated at the local level.[5] Once students have passed these examinations and been awarded the attestat, if they wish to go on to higher education, they must usually then take the entrance examinations set by the particular institution to which they have applied.

Policy and practice concerning external examinations in the United States vary considerably from state to state, but, unlike Germany, without any coordination by Federal authorities. Although a few states set examinations as the basis for graduation from high school, the credential carries little weight outside its own territory. Since the early 1980s, many states have introduced new curricular requirements, reinforced by testing programs in the course of secondary schooling, and the number of state boards of education considering and introducing tests of minimum competency for high school graduation is growing. By 1990, twenty-three states used tests for promotion or graduation.[6] Nevertheless, at present, only two states (New York and California) offer achievement examinations for graduating high school seniors at a more advanced level. Instead, graduation from high school is typically based upon classroom performance: a combination of grades for homework, in-course tests, and end-of-course examinations.

In contrast to the other nations in this study, the only United States external examinations having national currency are owned and administered by private organizations: the related College Entrance Examination Board and the Educational Testing Service, in Princeton, New Jersey, and the American College Testing Program, Iowa City, Iowa. Their tests are available throughout the United States and abroad and the results are widely used by higher education institutions to assess the aptitude and/or achievement of their applicants. These organizations are private corporations answerable only to their boards of trustees and their customers, and are staffed by testing experts and subject specialists. They are not officially associated with school administrations at any level, though consultation and collaboration are widespread: they field test materials and consult with teachers and subject specialists from private and public school systems.

In response to public concern over declining educational standards and the persistence of gross disparities in educational provision and performance from region to region, both state and federal authorities have strengthened their activities in collecting educational achievement data. The National Assessment of Educational Progress (NAEP), initiated in 1969, is

5. Mikhail L. Levitskii, private communication, December 1989.

6. Educational Testing Service, *The Education Reform Decade.* Policy Information Report (Princeton, N.J.: Educational Testing Service, 1990), p. 6.

a federal project that annually reports on average student performance, based on tests in basic subjects given to representative national samples. These tests are deliberately not used for individual assessment or selection purposes. Until recently, state authorities limited NAEP activity on the ground that it was an intrusion upon states' rights in educational matters, but beginning in the late 1980s, governors and state education officers have responded more positively, even to the point of authorizing the results to be published in ways that permit interstate comparisons of achievement. Thus, the federal government, with considerable political support, has sought to stimulate improvement in levels of school achievement by arranging for regular and systematic tests of what students know and can do in various subject areas.

Changes in Patterns of Control

Once established, the locus of control of external examinations tends to remain fixed for a long time, so that recent changes in England/Wales are particularly noteworthy. For at least forty years, university and professional groups in that country successfully resisted central government efforts to become involved in the organization and administration of national examinations. The introduction of the new General Certificate of Secondary Education in 1988 represented a significant movement toward greater control by the central government. Until that time, eight regional, independent, university-associated boards had governed the general academic examinations (the General Certificate of Education, O and A levels), and several additional regional boards (comprising teachers and local education officials) ruled over the newer, less academic Certificate of Secondary Education. A revised framework was established for the GCSE, making five regional groups responsible.[7] This examination consolidates the former GCE O level and the CSE into a single examination aimed at a wide range of pupil abilities. It is devised so that in a given subject, there are examination papers for different syllabi at several levels of difficulty and marking scales to take care of these differences. Each examining group has representation from the former GCE and CSE boards; however, they now act "under the direction of the Minister" through the School Examinations and Assessment Council (SEAC), which is staffed by ministry nominees and thus operates under the administration of the Department of Education and

7. Four groups in England and one in Wales incorporate the former GCE and CSE boards. Colin Vickerman, "The Work of an Examining Group," in Keith Selkirk, ed., *Assessment at Sixteen* (London: Routledge, 1988), pp. 32–48, esp. p. 36.

Science. Some elements of each of the former examinations are retained and even fortified in the new consolidated GCSE, in which marks for school assignments contribute to the final examination grade in certain subjects. Paradoxically, an increase in central governmental control, intended to make the examination at once more uniform, more comparable across regions, and more comprehensive, has been accompanied by increased school-based participation in student assessment, at the expense of the more universal components.

University-associated regional examining groups continue to govern the GCE Advanced-level examinations. For eighteen-year olds completing the sixth form (upper secondary schooling), the GCE certificate serves as the major qualification for university entrance. At this level too, with government encouragement, certain reforms are being introduced. A new A-level supplementary examination (AS) has been devised for students who choose to take a subject at a lesser degree of specialization. The AS level became available in 1989. It remains highly controversial because it aims at reducing the degree of specialization that has been characteristic of the final two years of secondary schooling in England and Wales.

As part of a larger plan for educational reform, the Department of Education and Science has assumed an authority over external examinations it had not formerly possessed. Together with other provisions of the Education Reform Act of 1988, the reorganization of the GCSE was a means whereby the government sought to provide a general educational qualification to a larger proportion of sixteen-year-olds, to ensure a greater degree of uniformity in curriculum practice, and to establish more common standards of achievement among the many relatively autonomous local education authorities. It is one among several legislative and administrative moves designed to broaden and unify schooling, to reinforce establishment of a national curriculum for all pupils aged five to sixteen, and to reduce the degree of specialization in secondary schools. Full effects of the initiative will not be evident for a while. Already some of the original changes and plans have been amended, and there is reason to believe that further adjustments will be introduced as experience is gained. Pressure to change the A-level system has steadily mounted, but this has been adamantly resisted by the government, which has been disinclined to go beyond its support of the device of AS levels.

The Swedish system organizes national examination policy so that authority and responsibilities are shared among central and local authorities, and between government and such institutions as university-based educational research and training centers. Sweden's nationwide pattern of continuous assessment offers no regular external examinations until upper secondary school, and even at that point, individual schools, though required to conform to national guidelines, have considerable discretion in the choice of methods and materials to attain their educational targets. At the upper secondary school level, certain examinations are external, mandatory, and nationally uniform, while others are optional and locally determined.

Until 1977, passing the *studentexamen,* a national examination taken on completion of academic secondary school, was required for university entrance. Comparable to the Abitur, the examination served the purposes of an academically selective secondary school system that separated students as young as ten years old into academic and nonacademic tracks, preparing only those admitted to the former for entry to higher studies. The examination was centrally set and administered under the aegis of the National Board of Education (NBE) and the universities. However, the tracking system was abolished in 1964 as part of a series of radical educational changes instituted to increase secondary school enrollments, to liberalize school policies, and to provide open-access, comprehensive education through secondary school and on into higher education. Since 1977, when the Swedish Parliament approved new principles for university selection, admission of high school graduates is contingent on their completing one of the approved courses in the upper secondary, postcompulsory school, with a satisfactory school record. This record includes marks on national examinations set by central authorities, on school tests determined by local authorities, and on other school-based assessments of student work graded by teachers.[8]

The general pattern of assessment in Sweden is a national one, with policies enunciated and implemented by the NBE (equivalent to a ministry of education) at the direction of Parliament.[9] Construction, pilot-testing,

8. The number of nationally approved courses stood at twenty-seven in 1986, but the list has changed from time to time with as many as thirty at one time, reduced to twenty-two to twenty-four in 1989. With the disbanding of the National Board of Education (see note 9 below), local communities assumed the responsibility of defining program and graduation requirements, some retaining the former national criteria, others changing them. Since 1990, high school graduates may substitute their scores on the Swedish Scholastic Aptitude Test in place of their high school record when applying for admission. Special admission arrangements exist for mature students who are at least twenty-five years old and who have at least four years of work experience.

9. In December 1990, an act of the Swedish Parliament abolished the National Board of Education (NBE) and authorized the establishment of a new central authority as of July 1991. In place of the detailed regulations issued by the former NBE, the new authority will provide guidelines and overall targets, leaving municipal education authorities to adopt their own ways to attain them. Karin Rydberg, "A Redistribution of Responsibilities in the Swedish System" (Stockholm: Swedish National Board of Education, 1991). The full effect of the

and revision of the national secondary school examinations are delegated to an educational research institution, whereas the optional tests are left to local discretion. For both types of examination, grading schemes are based upon national criteria. The NBE issues rules and regulations for the required examinations and annual instructions concerning their development and administration. In addition, it appoints groups of experts in each subject to develop examinations (these comprise eight to nine people, chaired by an NBE staff member, and include subject specialists, active teachers, and an expert in testing). The required examinations may be revised from year to year.

The Swedish system is thus centralized and uniform in the sense that the same general assessment aims hold for all schools at the same level, based upon a set of generally required national syllabi. A complex system of weighting by school and community is used to maintain comparability and equivalence of assessment standards across the nation. However, the system also includes local, teacher-determined assessment based upon a school's own instructional practices. Therefore, in Sweden responsibilities for examinations are distributed among several authorities at different levels of administration. The one-shot, end-of-school, Abitur-like studentexamen has been replaced by an alternative: continuous assessment with both local and nationally determined components.

In summary, then, the examination systems of certain countries are highly centralized and separate from other kinds of student evaluation (as in Japan), whereas those of other nations allow various degrees of regional and local participation. In most instances, government agencies are in charge, but in the United States examination authorities include both independent private bodies and public agencies. In England/Wales, although examination boards are independent and private, in the sense that they are nongovernmental, they have official status and are increasingly subject to public regulation.

Recent developments in England/Wales and Sweden, in particular, show that although patterns of control over examination systems may remain fixed for a considerable time, important changes can take place. In England/Wales central government authority over examination policy has become firmly established after a century or more of control by relatively autonomous university examination boards; in Sweden, to the contrary, devolution and diversification have been introduced in place of central control. In both countries, changes in the locus of authority over examinations

---

new arrangements upon the number of approved courses for graduation and on the examination system is not yet clear.

have accompanied more extensive national educational reform. The two instances indicate convergence to positions characterized by shared responsibility and accommodation of the need for a national policy and the claims of regional differentiation and authority.

Distribution of Responsibilities in the Examination System

Although the kind of authority in charge of examinations is important—central or regional, public or independent—so too are the ways in which particular responsibilities for implementing the system are distributed. In fact, Lloyd Brereton considers it relatively unimportant whether the examinations are controlled by independent bodies, as in England, or by government authorities, as in other European nations.[10] What is critical, he believes, is the extent to which principals and teachers can share control over examinations and curriculum and whether subject teachers of the examined are involved in marking the papers. In this section we describe how the tasks of operating examination systems are distributed and, in particular, the different ways teachers are involved in external examinations.

National practices vary according to who is responsible for the particulars of the examination system and for such specific tasks as administering the examinations, test construction, monitoring procedures, setting grading standards, and awarding the certificates to successful candidates. In England/Wales, for example, all these tasks have hitherto been carried out by the several independent boards, comprised largely of educators (teachers and subject specialists) associated with various universities. After the CSE was introduced in the 1964–65 school year, local groups of teachers and school administrators were able to introduce topics related to their own syllabi and to include their own assessments of students' work assignments. Each of the reconstituted GCSE examining groups fulfils all the various tasks we have described but follows the guidelines set by the Department of Education and Science having to do with syllabus, levels of difficulty, and grading criteria. Equivalence among the boards is also maintained by interboard committees and through synchronizing examinations and adjusting marks within and across boards.

The range of syllabi offered by the five GCSE examining groups is somewhat constrained by the new national curriculum, a factor that has not yet directly affected the course of studies for sixteen-to-eighteen-year-olds. In-

10. Joseph Lloyd Brereton, *Exams: Where Next?* (Victoria, B.C.: Pacific Northwest Humanist Publications, 1965), pp. 15–16.

terboard collaboration among the A-level groups ensures a common core syllabus for each subject, thus restraining competition by mutual agreement. However, since the groups at both GCSE and A level are competing for business from the schools (which pay fees for their student candidates), market conditions ensure that each board offers an array of subjects with alternative syllabi in the more popular ones.

In France, the académies select topics for examination from a list published by the ministry and formulate the questions, all under ministry guidelines. Candidates register for the baccalauréat by applying to the rector of the appropriate académie, who later publishes the examination results as a representative of the minister of education. The diploma certifying the qualification is signed and sealed by the secretary-general of the académie. But the responsibility for administering written and oral examinations and for evaluating the candidates is assigned to local juries. These are charged with seeing that regulations and procedures are properly carried out.[11]

Each jury comprises at least five members, professors in higher education and/or qualified lycée teachers, usually with varying degrees of experience. They are appointed by the académie rector from a list of those eligible. The following rules are applied: juries should not include more than one member from a given lycée; members are not allowed to examine students from their own school; they should not be assigned to schools or cities where they operated the previous year. Juries evaluate student records, determine eligibility, grade papers, serve as examiners at orals, and adjudicate irregularities. They are responsible for resolving inconsistencies in grading—for example, between an individual's school and examination marks or between examiners. Juries decide on the final results for each candidate. A suitably qualified member (usually an *agrégé,* possessing an advanced degree as well as lengthy school experience) presides over the jury, which in the case of any disagreements among members makes its decisions by majority vote.[12]

In Germany too, though procedures may vary from one Land to another, local committees of teachers and school administrators take care of the examination process along broadly similar lines. They monitor the procedures and grading practices, award grades for written and oral examina-

11. "Le jury est souverain. Aucun recours n'est recevable contre les décisions qu'il a prises conformément aux textes réglementaires." *Baccalauréat de l'enseignement du second degré,* 17th. ed. (Paris: Programmes Vuibert, 1977), p. 58.

12. Ministère de l'Education Nationale, Direction des lyceés, *Baccalauréat de l'enseignement du second degré* (Paris: Centre National de Documentation Pédagogique, 1985), pp. 5, 8, 9, 10–13, passim.

tions, consider appeals, resolve inconsistencies between school and examination grades, and adjudicate disputes. Except in the few Länder where examination papers are set centrally by the Land ministry (for example, Bavaria, Baden-Württemberg), teachers propose the topics and questions in their own subjects, and the Land administration makes a selection for the schools to use. Then, in Nordrhein-Westfalen, for example, a subject teacher grades the answers, followed by a second opinion. In cases of disagreement, a third evaluation will be made. An examination committee of three or four members of the administration oversees the written Abitur procedures in a given school, and other committees are responsible for orals in their respective subjects. The latter usually have four members: the chairperson (usually an experienced teacher from that school or its director), the examiner (usually the candidate's teacher), a recording secretary, and another teacher from the school who acts as observer. Decisions on candidates' performance are made by vote, with all committee members required to participate.[13] Similar practices are followed in Hamburg and in Hesse.[14] In general, subject teachers and school administrators (principals, department heads, and student counselors) organize and administer the examinations in their own schools under guidelines from the ministry. The results and the diploma, however, are issued under the authority of the Land ministry of education.

Schools in the Soviet Union follow similar practices, the result of the persistent influence of the German model since the nineteenth century. Written and oral questions are derived from a list of topics developed at ministry level. But end-of-school examinations are conducted by school-based committees of administrators and teachers. Teachers pose the supplementary questions in orals, and the committees evaluate their own students.

In sharp contrast to France, Germany, and the Soviet Union, where committees of teachers and school administrators perform visible and important roles in the examinations, in England/Wales, Japan, China, and the United States virtually all the responsibilities for external examinations are conducted at some remove from the locality and the schools, though the New York State Regents examinations are graded by teachers.

The Japanese Ministry of Education's National Center for University

---

13. *Ausbildungs- und Prüfungsordnung mit Verwaltungsvorschriften APO-GOSt* (Cologne: Kultusminister des Landes Nordrhein-Westphalen, 1979).

14. Freie und Hansestadt Hamburg, *Ausbildungs- und Prüfungsordnung der gymnasialen Oberstufe vom 21.6.1983;* Hessische Kultusminister. *Gymnasiale Oberstufe: Gesetz und Verordnung vom 11.6.1982.* Wiesbaden.

Entrance Examinations rules over the JFSAT. While there is considerable liaison with other ministry agencies, with high schools, and with the universities, the latter have the dominant influence. A committee of experts numbering about 230 members develops the test questions, conducting their work in twenty subject committees. Committee members are selected from university faculty members nominated by their deans or presidents at national universities throughout the country. They are responsible, too, for following certain general principles such as conformity to the national curriculum, uniformity in the style and levels of questions, and consistency across subjects. Supervision of the actual examinations, scoring, and reporting results are all in the hands of the National Center. After the examinations, teachers from upper secondary schools meet with members of the test-setting committee to review the content, difficulty, and format of the questions in each subject, and representatives of national education associations submit their evaluations of the tests.

In China, a small core staff of the National Education Examinations Authority prepares items based on the official syllabus, and a subject-based writing group (usually made up of one or two core staff and five or six part-time subject experts) devises the examination itself. The subject specialists are identified through professional networks and recommendations by university presidents. Some sixty people from about twenty-five universities are involved in setting the examinations each year. Before 1988, examination-setters were held incommunicado for some two months, until the examinations had actually been taken, but this practice was discontinued when it became increasingly difficult to find suitable staff willing to forgo so much time. Over 100,000 people are required to proctor the examinations, which take place on July 7, 8, and 9 each year at approximately 53,000 centers across the nation. Marking is at the provincial level, where a further 100,000 persons are needed to grade the answer papers. In order to ensure uniform grading practices, the examiners, about 70 percent of whom are university faculty and 30 percent high school teachers, meet at regional centers for intensive preparation under the leadership of more experienced senior examiners, and their assessments of examination papers are routinely monitored and randomly rechecked to ensure consistency.

In developing achievement examinations for the College Entrance Examination Board in the United States, the Educational Testing Service also makes use of several review levels and expert groups. A development committee is appointed to review the curriculum in a given subject, to draft questions, conduct pilot tests, and evaluate and revise them before use. Committee members include college faculty, secondary school teachers, and testing experts on the staff of ETS. When a test is administered, it is likely to include experimental items or pilot sections (though these will not be included in a candidate's score) to be evaluated after the responses are in for possible subsequent use. Machine-grading is the usual practice, and even in the composition section, examiners conduct what is for the most part a mechanical exercise in which independent judgment is kept to a minimum through use of previously developed marking schemes.

The Abitur in Germany and the French baccalauréat have dual functions: they signify completion of secondary studies at a satisfactory level and qualify students for higher education. Nevertheless, the examination is in the hands of a single public authority. In Japan and the Soviet Union, the functions are split between two examinations, each under a different authority: the ministry responsible for public education, and the individual institutions of higher education. The first examination is more universal. It signifies school completion and serves as a qualification for taking the second-stage examination, the means of selection for a particular higher education institution.

In contrast, England/Wales has a two-tier system with stages set about two years apart. The first stage, the new GCSE, serves a largely retrospective purpose. It certifies that a student of about sixteen has completed a basic, universal course of study in a specified subject (or subjects). The second stage, the GCE A level, has a largely prospective function. It is the selection instrument for a smaller population of about age eighteen that has completed upper secondary education and may now be seeking university admission. Both examinations are run by similar independent boards, but they differ in their governing policies, their approaches to the syllabus, and particular aspects of form. In particular, several subject options in the GCSE take into account course work graded by teachers; A-level syllabi rarely do.

France also has examinations at two stages, similarly separated in time, though these occur at a more advanced level: The baccalauréat, provides the general entry qualification for universities. But the function of the second stage, the concours, is to select the crème de la crème for entry into the most prestigious, career-oriented institutions of higher education, the grandes écoles. As the Soviet Union and Japan, these examinations, taken after an additional year or two of study at the lycée and/or in private tutoring, are set by the respective higher institutions (whereas the first-stage baccalauréat examinations are devised by the académies under the close direction of the Ministry of Education).

Although China has offered a uniform university entrance examination since 1977, some cities and regions are currently instituting a preliminary first-stage examination serving to certify graduation from high school (the General High School Completion Test) and thereby confer eligibility for the university entrance examination. This, too, represents a differentiation of function and responsibilities similar to that cited above, and consequently a distinction in the authority exerting influence over the examination. The cities of Shanghai and Beijing and Zhejiang province were authorized to lead the way by experimenting with models and procedures for the high school graduation examinations, which could be adapted and emulated by other authorities. It is anticipated that metropolitan and provincial education officials and schoolteachers in other jurisdictions will follow suit, setting and administering their own graduation examinations aimed at the majority of students. These will be taken during the final years of secondary school as students complete the course of study in each of several required, basic subjects. At the end of the final year, students seeking admission to higher education will sit for the university entrance examinations, which will continue to be centrally developed and dominated by university faculty. The National Unified College Entrance Examination, first given in 1952, was abandoned during the Cultural Revolution and reinstated in 1977. The State Education Commission, through its National Education Examinations Authority, will retain its power to set broad policy on examinations and oversee implementation for the whole nation.

As we have shown, responsibilities involved in managing the examination system are assigned differently among the nations. Certain variations in responsibility at earlier stages of the examination process carry implications in particular for the role of teaching staff. The manner in which teachers are involved in the crucial matter of shaping the examination questions and evaluating the answers has important consequences for the nature of their authority in the classroom. The German tradition, also followed in the Soviet Union, is that subject teachers in a given school dominate the process of setting the examination questions and evaluating the examination performance of their own students. This is of course monitored through peer control and participation by district and local administrators. However, the oral component of the Abitur, which accounts for at least one of the four subject marks in the examination, and the evaluation of a student's school record are fully in the hands of teachers, though the final grade is determined by a local committee. In France, though local teachers participate as jury members and are influential in evaluating performance, they may not examine or grade students from their own lycée, and the written papers are graded anonymously by teachers who have not themselves taught the candidates. In Japan, the United States, England/Wales, and China, written papers are graded externally, and even when they are not centrally machine-scored and teachers perform this task, they do so anonymously and outside their school responsibilities. To the extent that the trend in England/Wales is to move toward incorporating more teacher-graded school work in the final examination grades, the balance changes from largely external evaluations toward the German practice of greater within-school teacher involvement. Swedish practice represents a mixture of some external assessment and a considerable amount of teacher assessment largely internal to the school. In short, although teachers are everywhere involved in setting examinations and evaluating the results, in England/Wales, China, France, Japan, and the United States, this is largely external to the schools, whereas in the USSR, Sweden, and Germany assessments are more internal.

The implication of these differences for the classroom role of teachers is profound. In those cases where they do not personally participate in the critical external examinations, as in Japan, China, the United States, France (except, perhaps, in orals), and until recently in England/Wales, teachers help their students to prepare for those examinations in a collaborative way. In Japan, it is noted, "the teacher becomes an ally who is trying to assist the student facing the examination." [15] Study aids in the United States not only include advice to students on how to prepare for the examinations but also on "how to beat the examinations." Teachers in England conventionally take their students through previous examination papers, alerting them to hazards and useful clues to the kinds of answers required, predicting the questions that will be asked, and generally contriving to stay ahead of the examiners. In short, under these circumstances, teachers form a common front with their students to overcome the challenges (even the traps) of the examining authorities. But where teachers are themselves the examiners, the nature of their authority is likely to differ, and in general the relationship with students will be more distant and oppositional than collaborative.

Interest Groups as Agents of Control in Examinations

So far, we have considered power and responsibilities within the formal systems of administrative control over examinations. In addition to the participants we have identified, however, a number of interest groups at different levels are involved in the process of shaping and implementing examination policies. The influence of interest groups is often informal in

15. E. F. Vogel, *Japan as Number One* (Cambridge: Harvard University Press, 1979), p. 165.

the sense that they do not necessarily participate in the responsible organizations. Yet they interact with the formal systems of examination control
in ways that may be highly influential, especially when it comes to changing policy and practices.

As assessment has become a matter of increased public interest, and as
government has become more accountable for its educational policies, such
groups have become more prominent in the control of examinations. They
may influence the distribution of power between central and regional authorities and/or between government and other agencies of control, and
they may limit the powers of the "formal" controllers of examination policy and practice. This section identifies some of these interest groups, notes
the roles they play, often as informal agents, in shaping and controlling
examinations, and provides background and an introduction to the subsequent analysis of particular issues and conflicts in chapter 9.

Interest groups are found within the educational system and in the broader
public arena where educational debate increasingly takes place. They serve
two contrasting functions. They can be constraining forces, setting limits
on action. But under other conditions, their role may be to push the formal
authorities in a particular direction. They can seek to maintain the status
quo in examinations or they can support changes, depending on their particular clientele or preferred purpose. In either event, such groups act as
control elements.

Within the formal education system, teachers, administrators, subject
specialists, and others are well represented in the agencies that control
examinations: advisory groups, boards of examiners, and the examiners
themselves. Each group has its own special interest in examinations, although within each group perceptions will differ over their utility and over
how they might be changed. For example, university professors and high
school teachers have a common basis of concern about academic work and
standards of achievement and about the subjects they teach, though they
may differ among themselves about approaches to the subject and the possible forms and content of examinations. Administrators are likely to be
interested primarily in administrative tidiness and convenience, accountability, justification, and cost. Technical experts, with a special concern for
such matters as examination validity, reliability, and objectivity, are an
especially strong interest group in Japan, Sweden, and the United States,
where objective testing has been popular. And many teachers give priority
to the diagnostic and instructional uses of examinations rather than to their
role as instruments of summative assessment and student selection.

Interest groups influencing examinations are not limited to educators.
As educational policy becomes a matter of greater public concern, the par-

ticipants in all manner of educational decisions, including those matters formerly regarded as purely for professionals to decide, proliferate and their interests become more diverse. Educational systems expanding in size and complexity now reach out to encompass the majority of a nation's population, so that parties outside the system as well as those within it develop their own special orientations.

Two groups are particularly prominent in having special concern about examinations: parents and employers. The former look to the future life chances of their children, whereas the latter are interested in the attributes possessed by their prospective employees. But both look for meaningful and reliable assessments of the skills necessary for working and living and heighten the debate over examination policies in significant ways. They gain attention through parents' organizations and federations of employers and workers, through the media, and through occasional policy statements and studies. In Germany, for example, employer and trade and craft union representatives figure prominently on the advisory and executive boards determining technical/vocational examinations, and even serve as examiners for formal qualifications, though not for the general academic Abitur. Organizations of workers, employers, and particular crafts are highly visible in debates over upper secondary schooling and credentials for those entering the labor force. In France, particularly since 1986 as the baccalauréat has expanded into many vocational areas, employer-supported on-the-job training and evaluation has been encouraged and has grown. Generally employers are favorably inclined toward cooperation with teachers in the vocational schools, though many are critical of the poor academic quality of the new *bacs-pros* (vocational baccalaureates). In response to growing numbers of candidates and passes in the baccalauréat, employers are demanding higher and additional qualifications from job applicants.[16] In debates over reform of the lycée, they periodically express dissatisfaction with the skills and attitudes of potential employees, claiming that school-based training is too narrow and based on redundant skills.[17]

In the United States, employers frequently criticize examination practices or the absence thereof and, increasingly in recent years, state what the school system needs and how it might be achieved in studies and reports by national and regional business and industry groups. The Committee for Economic Development, a business-academic partnership, has, like many employer groups, endorsed systematic testing of student achievement

16. *Le Monde de l'Education* (May 1991):49; *Times Educational Supplement* (June 28, 1991): 12.

17. *Times Educational Supplement* (April 27, 1990): A16.

and credentials.[18] The Secretary's Commission on Achieving Necessary Skills (SCANS), established by former U.S. Secretary of Labor Elizabeth Dole, identified specific educational targets for the schools and means of assessing them. Recent ad hoc panels such as the National Commission on the Skills of the American Workforce and the Business Coalition for Educational Reform have supported national standards of achievement and national assessment (though they are critical of current standardized testing methods)[19] and have encouraged employers to make greater use of test results and educational records in their employment practices (changes in regulations forbidding this practice are under consideration by the current federal administration).[20] Studies and reports by business leaders have fueled the public debate on education, focusing in particular on student assessment.

Business involvement in education and in examination policy in England/Wales has grown in recent years, strongly supported by the government. Activities similar to those in the United States have put the views of these special-interest groups before educational policymakers and have affected their deliberations. The influential Confederation of British Industry (CBI), comprising employers, and the Trades Union Congress (TUC) have repeatedly and severely criticized the dominant role of the A-level examination for its narrow academic specialization, neglect of work-relevant content, and irrelevance to most employers.[21] Both organizations are committed to the reform and rationalization of vocational qualifications and are represented on such bodies as the National Council for Vocational Qualifications, established in 1986 for this purpose.[22] Employers dominate the Training and Enterprise Councils and the Business and Technician Councils, charged with developing and extending study and training programs that lead to qualifications for sixteen-to-nineteen-year-olds.[23] They have expressed strong support for records of achievement and skill profiles (as defined by CBI in 1989) to supplement or serve as alternatives to examination-based qualifications.[24] The councils are active in efforts to break down the remaining barriers between academic and vocational qualifications.

18. Committee for Economic Development, *Investing in Our Children* (New York: Committee for Economic Development, 1985), pp. 24–26.

19. *Education Week* (June 20, 1990): 7.

20. *New York Times* (May 31, 1991): B6; *Education Week* (June 12, 1991): 20.

21. *Economist* (April 27 and May 18, 1991): 13, 64.

22. *Times Educational Supplement* (June 7, 1991): 4.

23. *Times Educational Supplement* (May 24, 1991): 14.

24. *Times Educational Supplement* (Jan. 26, 1990): 18.

In Japan, business interests tend to reinforce the policies of a well-entrenched national bureaucracy. They are represented on important national bodies such as the Central Council for Education, advisory to the Ministry of Education, and were prominent in Prime Minister Yasuhiro Nakasone's National Commission on Educational Reform. These bodies have repeatedly recommended examination reforms and called on universities to amend their procedures and broaden their admission criteria. Such proposals have not been implemented, however universities are at the pinnacle of a hierarchical system that selects and breeds the national power structure. Tokyo University leading all others, is said to be "virtually the sole gateway to the top positions in the country's powerful bureaucracy."[25] Employers attach great value to education credentials through their recruitment and employment practices,[26] and the multi-million-dollar examination-aids publishing industry, together with over 200 yobikos and 35,000 jukus, are an important sector of the domestic economy.

Similarly, the entrenched bureaucratic network of the Soviet Union dominates educational policies and practices. Since 1984, however, reform efforts have emphasized the role of teachers in innovations and have sought to empower parent committees and school councils (comprising students, parents, trade union, and Communist party representatives). But party and bureaucracy tend to reinforce one another, so that despite the growth of public interest and the expression of opinion, the sponsorship of special schools, and other signs of liberalization, a picture emerges of well-meaning reforms sabotaged by entrenched interests. Significant practices such as examination policy are not addressed.[27] One of the leading agencies in determining educational policy and practice has hitherto been the Academy of Pedagogical Sciences. This body has recently been blamed by critics from various quarters for many of the ills of Soviet education. Elections in 1989 to fill 31 vacancies in the 123-member academy afforded the opportunity for substantial change and gained considerable public attention. But the results have been criticized from several quarters, including teachers and parents. "Public opinion has been entirely ignored," wrote *Pravda*. "This sharply contradicts the principles of *perestroika*. The time of anon-

25. *New York Times* (May 24, 1991): 10.

26. U.S. Department of Education, *Japanese Education Today*, p. 60.

27. Wolfgang Mitter, "The Teacher and the Bureaucracy: Some Considerations Concluded from the Soviet case," *Compare* 17, no. 1 (1987): 47–60; Gerald Read, "Education in the Soviet Union: Has Perestroika Met Its Match?" *Phi Delta Kappan* 70 (April 1989): 606–613; review of James Muckle, *A Guide to the Soviet Curriculum: What the Russian Child Is Taught in School,* in *Times Educational Supplement* (Jan. 2, 1991).

ymous decisions has passed. It will be interesting to know who is personally responsible for contradicting the public stand."[28]

In the United States, parent associations are prominent at both local and national levels, and have long been acknowledged, indeed powerfully sanctioned, as groups with legitimate interests in educational policy determination. On the specific matter of examinations, the National Parent-Teacher Association has endorsed the need for national standards and means to assess and implement them, though it has gone on record against several practices: a school curriculum driven by test-makers, "top down" reforms dictated by national authorities, and multiple-choice examinations.[29] A recent Gallup poll revealed that most Americans do in fact want national standards, achievement tests, and a national curriculum.[30] And in England, the Educational Reform Act of 1986 gave parents, as well as employers, an increased voice in the management of schools, which was, according to observers, a further means of reducing the powers of local and independent education authorities.[31]

Even in those nations where parent organizations have not been prominent and active in educational policies, they have achieved increasing recognition. For example, the French *Fédération des parents d'élèves de l'enseignement public* (PEEP) has grown in size and visibility, pressing for reform in the content and structure of the baccalauréat. The Federation has been strongly encouraged by recent ministers of education, perhaps as a way of enlisting public support for changes in the system resisted by the powerful teachers' unions. In 1990, Minister of Education Lionel Jospin, in an open letter to parents, encouraged the activities of parent associations, underlined provisions of the new education laws (including payment of expenses to parents attending meetings and training for national education councils), and called for a broader role for parents in school councils and in orientation conferences that determined students' lines of study and baccalauréat targets (hitherto dominated by teachers). A teacher's response was not untypical: a letter to the editor of *Le Monde de l'Education* deplored parental dominance over school decisions from preschool to lower secondary school, citing the intervention of parents in such professional

28. Cited in *Times Educational Supplement* (March 31, 1989): 11.

29. *Education Week* (April 7, 1990): 23.

30. See the twenty-first annual Gallup poll on the public's attitudes toward the public schools in *Phi Delta Kappan* 71 (Sept. 1989): 41–54; *Times Educational Supplement* (Sept. 8, 1989): 21.

31. "Power Drains Away to the Centre," *Times Educational Supplement* (May 5, 1989): A15.

matters as promotion from the third to the second class and speculating that their influence will soon extend to the second class, to the detriment of French education.[32]

Political interest groups seek to ensure that their constituencies are not disadvantaged by the examination system and by proposed changes to it. They are concerned with "fairness," consistency, and standards, though the perceptions of the different groups as to what justifies the examinations, the criteria by which they should be judged, and how they should be improved may differ sharply. They are likely to draw attention to results that appear to discriminate against particular economic or ethnic groups and may challenge the examination on grounds of bias. Disputes about such matters are likely to be rooted in the special interests of a particular segment of the population.

The United States presents a striking example of the formation of an organization to represent a particular broad social concern. FairTest is a consumer group, an offshoot of public watchdog organizations involved with truth in advertising, devoting itself solely to the specific educational activity of testing. It is financed by several nonprofit foundations, including the Rockefeller Family Fund and the Ford Foundation, and by individual contributors. FairTest presses for full disclosure of examination questions and answers, grading criteria, and weighting practices. It seeks legislation and political and legal action in matters of ethnic discrimination and unwarranted claims for the predictive value of examination results. It is highly critical of multiple-choice testing programs (and currently favors performance testing), accuses the test of cultural bias and of denying opportunities to minority groups, and lobbies for greater public accountability by testing agencies and educational administrations.[33]

As "accountability" has become a watchword among public education authorities, examinations have been supported as a way to measure the quantity and quality of the output of schools. Some groups support the extension of tests and examinations on the ground that they produce solid evidence of the value of schooling and can thus act as guides to determining the level of resources that should be assigned to education. This approach is, however, strongly opposed by those who object to an essentially industrial ("input-output") model of schooling and the use of testing and examination systems to measure output.

32. *Le Monde de l'Education* (June 1991): 6; *Times Educational Supplement* (June 16, 1989, and April 27, 1990): 15, A16.

33. See *FairTest Examiner,* periodical of the National Center for Fair and Open Testing, Cambridge, Massachusetts.

Thus in Japan, teacher opposition to the Ministry of Education's national university examinations is part of the running battle between these two interests over control and autonomy in educational matters. Teachers criticize the exaggerated importance given to the examination and its stultifying effects upon students, the curriculum, and their own teaching. It renders them powerless, some argue, to introduce necessary innovation into the classroom. But, as indicated above, government and business regard ministerial control of the first-stage university entrance examination as an essential guarantee of secondary school standards and efficiency and as the necessary means to maintain the conditions for effective recruitment to higher education.

In sharp contrast, Sweden has for some decades been engaged in restructuring its education system and, in particular, its ways of assessing students. While centralized in the sense that Parliament continues to determine national policies and standards and to exert a significant supervisory role over practices, devolution of examination practice is extensive. Formal and informal assessments prevail. Policy is unitary but not uniform. Educational reforms continue to be dominated by concepts of formal justice and public control so that the participants in educational discussions at all levels are drawn from all sectors of society: parents, employers, trade unions, professional groups.

When a government-sponsored assessment effort is mounted for the first time, it may well arouse suspicion in various quarters. In the United States and in England/Wales, two agencies (the National Assessment of Educational Progress and the Assessment of Performance Unit, respectively) were established with government support to develop achievement tests and use them to assess the condition of education. Both of these initiatives were prompted by similar concerns: the absence of reliable national benchmarks for student achievement; fears that local autonomy had allowed schools to become excessively heterogeneous in matters of curriculum and standards of performance; and a growing sense that standards in education were unsatisfactory. In both nations, however, teacher groups have expressed the fear that national test results would be used as a means to limit teacher professional autonomy and as a device to assess teacher competency. Some have warned that such practices would lead to invidious comparisons among schools, school systems, and regions, with dire results, both educational and economic. Such fears may have been allayed somewhat in England but are not totally stilled.[34]

34. Caroline Gipps, "A Critique of the APU," in Desmond L. Nuttall, ed., *Assessing Educational Achievement* (London: Falmer Press, 1986), pp. 99–113.

Testing of this kind, initiated by central government to assess the nation's educational condition, is a challenge to the traditional pattern of control over examinations. It may be seen as an improper extension of the uses of examinations from assessing students to shaping educational policies and even to making personnel decisions (through revival of the old policy of "payment by results"). Interested parties in both of these two nations regard this development as a "takeover bid" by the central government to assume powers hitherto exercised by regional or independent authorities.

From time to time, tension may develop between a central authority's efforts to control, unify, and standardize diverse practices across the country and its acknowledgement that accommodation may need to be made to the different circumstances of particular regions. All the nations we have discussed show signs of such tension from time to time and may alter the distribution of authority in order to meet changing conditions. In China, for example, the size, wealth, educational level, and general power of Shanghai and Beijing particularly have enabled these cities to assume greater control over their own examination practices, which in other locations are directed entirely by national or provincial authorities. High school graduation examinations not only certify school completion but also preselect candidates for the university entrance examination, thus limiting the number of applicants and, at the same time, allowing closer control over the proportions of the university population from more and less developed regions of the nation.

In France, regional language/culture groups have pressed the government to add examination subjects or special conditions for their respective populations. In the United States, England/Wales, and Germany, political and social action groups have pointed to the poor examination performance of recent immigrants and ethnic minorities and have sought ways to remedy the situation by applying pressure from within and outside educational systems.

In short, various interest groups serve as supplementary agents of control over the examination system. Those from within the education system, professionals of various kinds and interests, but especially teachers, are usually well represented in the administration and management of examinations. Others in the broader social arena outside the field of education itself, such as employers, unions, parents, and public policy groups, may not participate formally in these matters. However, this is not to say that they do not participate in public debate. Though their roles may be informal, nonetheless they can be influential either in promoting or hindering changes in the patterns of examination control.

Summary and Discussion

Differences in the ways examination systems are organized, administered, and controlled have significance because of their relation to the control of the education system, to the involvement of different groups, and to the overall legitimacy of the examination process. National examination systems differ according to the location of authority and responsibility. This depends, in the first instance, upon the overall administrative precedents and traditions of the respective nations and the way they govern education. Arrangements for external examinations follow national patterns of educational control and administration. They tend to reflect and reinforce the distribution of authority over school governance in general, especially over school curricula and syllabi. We may expect, therefore, that in nations where the school system is directed from the center, external examinations will most likely also be centrally directed, and in those nations where regional and local authorities enjoy greater autonomy, they will exert more control over examinations.

As shown in figure 1, in France, Japan, China, and, until fairly recently, Sweden, the central government establishes the procedures and retains a dominant role in providing end-of-secondary-school examinations. But in Germany, the Soviet Union, the United States, and, until very recently, England/Wales, in examinations as in other educational matters, administrative decentralization has been the rule, and regional or other authorities have been able to resist centralization and to dominate the examination process. Only in the United States and England/Wales are arrangements for nationwide, external examinations in the hands of agencies that are independent and/or private, again consistent with the national traditions of educational devolution.

Even in the more centralized systems, however, some degree of devolution of important parts of the examining process is the rule. Regional or local decisions are critical in the choice of questions (France, the Soviet Union) and assessment of papers (China, Germany, the Soviet Union), and even to giving weight in the final grade to teacher evaluation of student work done in school prior to the actual examination time (Germany, England/Wales).

Educational systems can be controlled directly by legislation and regulation by a central agency or indirectly by financial and other means, including examinations. Thus, in Germany, Japan, France, and China, the ministry "owns" the examinations and controls the curriculum directly. But in Sweden and the Soviet Union, although there is direct central control over curriculum, examinations are less important as a device to rein-

Figure 1. Control of External Examination Systems

	England/Wales	France	Germany	Japan	China	Sweden[a]	United States[b]	Soviet Union
Locus of Control								
Central	✓ ←	✓		✓	✓	✓ →	✓ ✓	✓
Regional			✓			✓ ✓	✓	✓
Kind of Control								
Government	✓	✓	✓	✓	✓	✓ ✓	✓	✓
Quango							✓	
Private								
Formal role of Teachers						*a* *b*		
Devise Exams	✓	✓	✓	✓	✓	✓ ✓	✓	✓
Examine/Grade own students	–	–	✓ ✓	–	–	– ✓	–	✓ ✓
others' students	–	✓	✓	–	–	– ✓	–	✓
anonymously	✓	✓	–	✓	✓	✓ –	✓	–
Moderate Results	✓	✓	✓	✓	✓	✓ ✓	✓	✓

Notes:

a. In Sweden, *a* refers to national exams, *b* to subnational.

b. In the United States, reference is to both national (privately owned) and state examinations.

Arrows point in the direction of recent/current changes in locus of control of examinations.

force that curriculum control. In the absence of any organized determination of curriculum by a central authority, examinations can serve as an important means of shaping curriculum. This has been so in England/Wales, where a considerable degree of curriculum standardization has been achieved through consensus among the examining boards. Current trends in the United States indicate that this nation too is seeking some degree of curriculum control and standardization via examinations.

Once in place, patterns of control tend to remain stable for long periods. Changes are likely to be related to changes in the control of the school system at large, whether as cause or effect, which in turn affect the roles and powers of the different participants in the examination process. Sweden and England/Wales provide examples of recent sharp change in the locus of control over examinations (as indicated by the vertical arrows in figure 1). The causes of such changes and of the preoccupation of government agencies with control of examinations are complex and bound up with changes in overall national policies.

Though rooted in the administrative traditions of a given nation, control of examinations is challenged by swings in political power and conflicts among educational ideas (for further discussion of this theme, see chapter 9). At times of rapid change and stress, challenges to the status quo call for reconsideration and often redistribution of power and authority. The examples cited above, of England/Wales, Germany, Sweden, China, and the United States, illustrate ways in which change in political power is reflected in educational policies and specifically in influences upon examinations. Japan and, up to this point, the Soviet Union show how the absence of such change is accompanied by great stability in the examinations and their controllers. In England/Wales, in dramatic contrast to precedent, central government has asserted a strong, direct role in examination policy as part of a larger effort at educational reform, a response to concern about excessive local variation in school practice and poor and inconsistent standards of student achievement. Similar considerations in the United States have led to a strengthening of the role of state departments of education, at some cost to the traditional autonomy of local school districts. When national needs are pressing, central government direction may be enhanced, as in China, where resources are severely limited and examinations are used strictly to control the flow of students from secondary to higher education. On the other hand, among the traditionally centralized nations, France and Sweden have in different ways proceeded in the direction of delegation to regional authorities. In France this has resulted in substantial broadening of the scope of the examination system and an increased role for the subnational administrative units; in Sweden, although central government continues to be important, its role in examinations has been greatly reduced, and decisions and practices in examination matters are distributed among a number of different authorities and government levels.

In all cases, however, whether the direction of change in controlling the examinations is toward or away from the center, in the direction of greater or lesser diversity, governments have often been forced to acknowledge regional and private interests and to share responsibilities with the interested parties and levels of organization.

Three major factors explain why national public authorities concern themselves with examinations and why these authorities become or remain involved in the management of examinations.

First, national examinations serve as a means to limit excessive variability in a large nation where regional diversity and a history of administrative autonomy challenges central governance and uniformity (China, the Soviet Union); or to designate standards in educational provision and performance (England/Wales, Japan, Germany, the United States); or to document and address such issues as regional disparities, fairness, reliability, and objectivity in educational achievement. In England/Wales, for example, although teachers have apparently enjoyed great discretion in matters of syllabus and curriculum, in practice their freedom of choice has been limited by the constraints of external examinations. On the other hand, in Germany and the Soviet Union, teachers are permitted great autonomy in final assessments, constrained though they are by official syllabi and curricula.[35]

Second, examinations are a means to move educational policy in a given direction. A new examination policy provides a way to deal with new and sometimes contradictory functions. In China, examinations were reintroduced after the Cultural Revolution in order to change national policy for higher education selection. In an attempt to achieve both efficiency and equity, the Chinese permitted criteria of political reliability to give way to those of expertise. France, Germany, and Sweden have all amended, even reformed, their examination practices in response to growing upper-secondary-level enrollment and the need to diversify. England/Wales changed the structure of its "sixteen-plus" examinations (now the GCSE) to increase opportunity, to establish more consistent national standards in education, and to limit local autonomy and curriculum diversity. The United States is

35. See also Stewart Ransom et al., "Examinations in Context: Values and Power in Educational Accountability," (p. 94) in Nuttall, ed., *Assessing Educational Achievement*, pp. 81–98.

under pressure to institute some form of national assessment to achieve similar goals and to raise overall educational standards. All of the above instances illustrate efforts at reform that involve changes or attempts to change the national practice in and through examinations.

Third, examinations can control the flow of students during and after secondary school in the nation's social and economic interest. This consideration is crucial when resources for postsecondary education and training are severely limited, as in China and the Soviet Union, or when government seeks to develop or change a national economic plan.

One consequence of the central role of examinations is that a variety of different groups have an interest in examinations and seek to exert influence over them in both formal and informal ways. These groups include governmental and nongovernmental authorities at national and subnational levels, educational professionals, parent groups, and employers. As the complexity and importance of examinations increase, the special interests of the participating groups may lead to a tug-of-war over control. For example, complementing general concern over the broad links between education and the national economic interest, governments may have an interest in examinations that is linked as much to costs and efficiency as to educational achievement. To this end, they may seek an assessment system more useful for evaluating institutions than students. (See chapter 9 for further discussion of the issues involved here.)

Professional educators, in particular, secondary school teachers, who can serve as both instructors and evaluators, are a special-interest group of considerable significance. The role of educators depends in important ways on how the examination process is conducted, on the agencies responsible for controlling teachers, and on the tasks instructors are expected to perform. In all countries, educators participate in setting the questions and determining the criteria by which answers will be judged (see figure 1). French, German, Soviet, and Swedish teachers play a more important role than others in judging student performance in the examinations, even of those students they have themselves taught. They have substantial discretion in practice over how they may act in oral examinations and may even have a hand in selecting questions for written tests taken by their own students, and in evaluating them. In other places, teachers are expressly excluded from evaluating their own students' work and all activities that could expose them to the charge of conflict of interest.

Such differences in teacher role account for some of the differences among nations in what is considered to be appropriate behavior, and also the ambiguities that face the teacher. The extent to which and the ways in which teachers participate in the examination process determine whether the student sees the teacher as an adversary or an ally in the examination, and changes in the arrangements may require both parties to make adjustments.

Progress toward universal, comprehensive schooling enlarges the student population at upper secondary levels and the scope of education, and increases public interest and debate over educational policies. This creates problems of authority, influence, and control over external examinations. The dilemmas are being resolved in several ways. In those instances where control of examinations rested largely in the hands of regional, private, or relatively independent interests, public authorities have assumed a larger role, including the control of external examinations. A common development over the years has been the erosion of academic, university-based influence and control over examinations, as public authorities assume what may be a new role as brokers among different interests. By the same token, public national-examination authorities that enjoyed virtual official autonomy have recognized special interests such as the claims of distinct regions and those of the non-college-bound student population. Thus external examinations are being reshaped if not completely reconstructed, and different interests forced to confront and accommodate one another in order to meet different purposes. This suggests a degree of convergence among different nations away from the poles of centralized government control and regional/local autonomy, toward greater degrees of reciprocity and shared authority.

Part 2

Comparison

Chapter 5

The Examinations: National Language and Literature

I've information vegetable, animal, and mineral,
I know the kings of England, and I quote the fights historical,
From Marathon to Waterloo, in order categorical . . .
—Major-General Stanley, *The Pirates of Penzance,* act 1

What kinds of knowledge and skill are candidates expected to demonstrate in their examinations? Both the shape and the substance of examination papers help to answer this question, as they indicate some of the actual learning objectives of schooling. This chapter opens with a review of the various formats that examinations take in the eight nations of our study. We then detail the kinds of knowledge characteristically tested in one basic school subject, common to all countries, national language and literature. In the following chapter, we review two more subjects in the humanities/ social science curriculum—history (sometimes as part of social studies) and English as a foreign language—and conclude with mathematics. Our purpose in these two chapters is to show how question papers in four common subjects of the secondary school curriculum demonstrate learning objectives.

Some nations may tend to stress a particular kind of task or knowledge above others. Most countries typically use several approaches in testing their students, as reflected in the format and the types of questions asked. And in some countries, important changes have occurred or are in progress. Each of these points is covered in the following discussion.

Format

The most common setting for examinations, familiar to students everywhere, is the large room in which the candidates assemble and, sitting at separate desks, carry out instructions provided at the beginning of a printed question paper they now see for the first time. However, there are ways in which candidates may be examined other than the conventional pen-or-pencil-written responses: examinations can be based on oral questions and replies, practical performance tests, and assessments of previously assigned schoolwork done outside the examination room.

Written examinations are common to all nations, though the specific formats differ widely and several kinds of written responses may be called for in a given test paper. While orals are probably the oldest form of public examination, they are rare nowadays in external, national examinations, except for foreign languages, where they serve as adjuncts to the written tests. A very few nations have retained oral examinations for other subjects. Similarly, practical performance tests are rare in general achievement examinations, except for some papers in science and technical subjects where candidates may be required to handle materials and perform an experiment. In history and literature, candidates may be presented with a set of documents and asked to sort, analyze, and interpret them. But such exercises are likely to be evaluated at the end of school as part of the record of schoolwork during the preceding year. In some instances, marks for schoolwork over a previous period or for specific assignments may be added to the examination proper and those marks included in the final examination grade.

As a rule, written examinations call for more or less extended student responses (essays, whether short or long; step-by-step computations; or explanations including diagrams, formulas, and the like) or short-answer replies. Lengthy essays and shorter composed responses are the usual forms candidates are expected to use in France, Germany, and England/Wales. Less common among the nations are the so-called objective, multiple-choice, machine-scorable tests. While they are the norm in Japan and the United States and are increasingly used in China, they are seen rarely elsewhere.

In Germany, France, and the Soviet Union, oral examinations have comprised a significant part of the examinations in all subjects. This practice has been waning in Germany, where students are now required to take an oral examination in only one of the four subjects offered in the Abitur. Special circumstances may call for an oral when a candidate has already completed the written examination in that subject. This occurs when the examiners find a discrepancy between a candidate's marks on the written examination and on schoolwork or cannot agree in their judgment of a student's performance.

In France, the specific requirements for oral examinations vary according to the série; candidates write examinations in five or six subjects and take orals in two to four subjects. In French language and literature, an oral is required of all students in addition to the written examination. Candidates for series A or B take orals only in their second or third foreign language; those in C, D, or E take an oral instead of a written examination in their (usually one) foreign language. Students must also submit to a supplementary oral examination, an *épreuve de controle,* in two subjects for which they have taken a written examination.[1] The purpose of the oral, like that of the written examination, is to determine the adequacy of the candidate's knowledge in a major subject.

The oral tradition remains even stronger in the Soviet Union's secondary school graduation examinations for the attestat zrelosti. The student appears before a small group of examiners and chooses from a number of face-down question cards. A little time is allowed for the candidate to prepare an appropriate answer. After the oral presentation, supplementary questions are posed by the panel of examiners.

In contrast, oral examinations are required only for foreign languages in England/Wales, Sweden, and the Advanced Placement examinations in the United States. In China, Japan, and the other United States examinations, orals are not required at all.

In some examination systems, previous work outside the examination room accounts for a portion of the total examination result, either by including an average for schoolwork performed in the given subject over, say, the preceding year or by taking into account grades earned for specific previous assignments. For example, in Germany, the final mark for each Abitur subject includes both the last semester's grade and the examination marks, weighted 1:4. In England/Wales the newer examinations in both the GCSE and GCE A level may include school assignments graded by teachers as part of the final score in specified subjects, as well as "performance" questions requiring candidates to "treat" materials distributed especially for the examination in, for example, science, English, and history. In Sweden, too, considerable weight is attached to the candidate's average performance in courses over a given period, to performance in specified assignments, and to the results of written in-class examinations. But even with all of these exceptions and recent changes, final results are still predominantly decided on the basis of the quality of written answers submitted in the final examinations.

Examinations may be concentrated in a short period or may be staged over a longer period. For example, plans for the new provincial secondary school graduation examinations in China call for students to take examinations in individual subjects at different times during their final and penultimate years. In similar fashion, in Sweden, whatever examinations are required nationally in upper secondary school are spaced over the final years to avoid placing excessive pressure upon students. The French language and literature examination is taken a year before the remaining sub-

1. For further details, see Ministère de l'Education Nationale, *Baccalauréat de l'enseignement du second degré*, 1985, in particular Circulaire no. 70-214 du 5 mai 1970.

jects in the baccalauréat, and in England/Wales candidates may take Advanced level examinations just one subject at a time, at intervals of six months or a year. In the United States, too, the SAT and ACT are quite separate from College Board Achievement Tests and Advanced Placement examinations. Students can take the latter subject by subject, one by one, with months, if not years, in between. In addition, we have noted that in France, Japan, the Soviet Union, and England/Wales, the important external examinations occur in two stages: typically, the first is a completion or qualifying examination and the second an entrance examination.

The ways questions are posed, and the words characteristically used to introduce them, represent a code that students must learn in order to perform satisfactorily. Preparation may account for considerable instructional time during the year(s) leading up to external examinations. This is particularly well illustrated by questions in national language and literature papers. For example, in England/Wales, questions often begin with the words "Illustrate" or "Discuss" or "Compare and contrast." In France, "Write a résumé" calls for a condensed version one-quarter of the length of the text provided (give or take 10 percent), whereas seemingly open-ended essay questions, "Write a *commentaire composé*," and the more personal literary essay must each have a particular content and be constructed in a specified way. In Germany, the instructions *"Analysieren Sie"* (analyze), *"Erläutern Sie"* (explain or comment on), and *"Vergleichen Sie"* (compare) call upon candidates to focus upon the literary methods, the content, and the context of texts in the national language and literature examination. The composition question in a Chinese paper often takes up a moral theme, and candidates are expected to include positive comments on the ideal and practical examples of how it might be realized. These are examples of questions that call upon the candidate to respond personally and creatively but to do so within a prescribed form, following certain rules, using particular kinds of illustrations, and demonstrating a characteristic logic, rationale, and way of thinking. In contrast, questions beginning with the words "Complete the sentence," "Fill in the blank," or "Select the most appropriate answer" represent a quite different approach and assumption about what is to be learned: candidates are presented with a number of more or less suitable and/or correct possibilities and must select the one that is closest to the truth, most accurate, or most reasonable.

Content

End-of-secondary-school examinations reflect the academic knowledge and skills considered of most worth for a particular age group in a particular nation. Examination authorities publish subject-by-subject syllabi listing the range of knowledge and/or skills candidates are supposed to master, even though it is not expected that the questions on any given paper will cover the entire syllabus as published. For this reason, the content of past examination papers, rather than the lists of topics published by the examiners, is perhaps the more accurate guide to what knowledge is considered of most worth.

The following descriptions are based on representative examination papers administered to students in the course of externally regulated examinations taken at the end of senior secondary school. These papers cover four subjects common to the curricula of the eight nations of this study: national language and literature, history or social studies, English as a foreign language, and mathematics.

But first, a methodological note. In countries without a central examining authority, different question papers will be set for the same subject. For example, the six GCE examining groups in England/Wales and the eleven Länder in Germany each produce their own examinations in all the basic subjects. Furthermore, in Germany and elsewhere, the examination papers can differ according to the syllabus chosen in a given subject, which may be taken as a specialty (major) or as a basic (minor) course or may concentrate upon a choice of topics or materials for close study. For some countries we therefore had to make selections from the many alternatives available. Where this was necessary, we gave closest attention to the papers containing the most representative questions, while providing examples from papers geared to the different levels of performance. In all instances, however, the examination papers are those usually taken by eighteen- or nineteen-year-olds completing upper secondary education, dating from the most recent years available.[2]

National Language and Literature

England/Wales. Two kinds of English language and literature examination papers are offered in the General Certificate of Education: Advanced and Advanced Supplementary levels. The latter is for candidates who offer the subject as a minor and who have studied the subject for approximately half the time devoted by A-level candidates. AS levels were available for the first time in 1989. They were based on examples that had been published

---

2. See Appendix. We have therefore omitted from consideration the GCSE in England/ Wales, since it is usually taken at the end of compulsory schooling at about age sixteen, prior to the upper secondary phase.

by examination boards in some subjects. The AS level cannot yet be considered an established alternative to the A level. A and AS levels differ somewhat among the examining boards, but most are based upon an interboard common core and contain common elements of content and approach. All have some required portions and several options. Two or three separate papers must be taken in a subject. Answers are written in the form of long or short essays, and some examinations incorporate schoolwork.

At least one of the literature papers deals with particular works ("set books") selected from the examining boards' lists by individual schools as the basis of their sixth-form studies. Examining boards announce the syllabi and their various options (set books, genres, literary periods) well in advance and schools submit their candidates for particular examinations. Usually, these tests cover the major categories of poetry, prose, and drama. Literature questions are directed at plot and character analysis, literary style, and personal responses to authors' works. Language questions test comprehension and powers of expression and explore knowledge of the characteristics of the spoken and written word and various uses of language. A previously unseen text is often the basis of a group of questions about content, style, and form.

The A-level examinations clearly require a specialized knowledge of specific literary works as well as a general grasp of various periods and genres. Furthermore, candidates are expected to express themselves in correct and appropriate language. A vigorous professional debate continues in England over the nature of the syllabus and the examinations in English, however. The arguments focus on at least three dimensions: the balance of attention given to the classics as opposed to more contemporary literature; the move toward the personal response and away from the traditional style of literary criticism; and the integration of language and literature into a single course of study and culminating examination. The development of a national curriculum for pupils in compulsory schooling (up to age sixteen) has been controversial and threatens to touch the course syllabi preparing students for the specialized A-level examinations. Though changes have been quite marked in the GCSE examinations, A levels in language and literature have retained their traditional content and approach. "The set-text lists of the past twenty years . . . have changed little. . . . The Brontës, Austen, Shakespeare and Hardy rule" states one observer in response to criticism that the contemporary and the personal have swamped the classics.[3] However, no less a notable than Prince Charles recently de-

3. Roy Blatchford, "All That Glisters Is Not Old," *Times Educational Supplement* (March 1, 1991): 20.

plored the fact that it is now possible for a student in English literature not to be examined in Shakespeare.[4] This is no doubt due to the proliferation of alternative approaches and syllabi in language/literature courses for the increasing school population preparing for GCSE examinations.[5]

France. The language and literature examination in France exemplifies more than any other educational practice the view expressed by the historian Fernand Braudel: *La France, c'est d'abord la langue française* (France is first of all the French language). A common examination in language and literature is required of all *baccalauréat* candidates, regardless of specialization, though the results are weighted differently in the final grade according to série. The examination is taken one year before all other examined subjects, at the end of the première, and is thus referred to as an épreuve anticipée. Students whose marks are inadequate will be advised to postpone entry to the full examination and repeat their studies. Thus in France, the language/literature examination serves in fact as a qualifying test for all other subjects in the baccalauréat.

The examination in French is above all an examination of the candidate's literary culture: knowledge of French literature; ability to discern different uses of language and literary styles and to relate these to the themes treated by writers; and ability to present and discuss these in an organized and properly expressed written text. A national list of broad questions, themes, and authors approved for the written test is published annually in advance by the Ministry of Education. The académies construct their own examination questions on the basis of this list, and local examiners have some choice within this, but all must follow the national guidelines concerning the scope of topics, how questions are to be formulated, and the grading criteria. Everywhere the premium is on precision and organization, as well as on knowledge of literature, style and form, and on the social and philosophical themes handled in literary works. The candidates are evaluated on mastery of a specific, reasoned, analytical approach—a set procedure explicitly taught and practiced in school—and on the extent of their personal literary culture.

The examination offers candidates three alternatives: exercises in language usage, a literary critique, or an essay on literary works previously read. The first consists mainly of writing a précis of a short text, but also calls for responses to short comprehension exercises and a brief essay on

4. *Manchester Guardian Weekly* (April 28, 1991): 3.
5. *Times Educational Supplement* (Jan. 3, 1991): 6; and "Special Report—English" (May 24, 1991): 33–44.

a theme from the text. The second requires the candidate to write a commentaire composé, a formal analysis and critique of a literary text. And
the third requires a literary essay on works read in class and on one's own
in which candidates must demonstrate their personal responses to literature. The candidate chooses one alternative and is allowed four hours in
which to complete the written examination.

In addition, all candidates take a short oral examination. Described as
un dialog ouvert, it is an open-ended conversation between examiner and
candidate in which the latter is called upon to show his or her knowledge
and personal appreciation of French literary culture. The candidate must
present a dossier listing works previously read, in school and privately.
The examiner poses two questions based on these works and the candidate
then has about twenty minutes to prepare an oral response. The first question is intended to be rather broad, on a whole work or group of works,
asking about plot, characters, ideas, structure, period, and artistic qualities. The second is more precise: the candidate is asked to read aloud about
fifteen lines of prose or poetry, examine the extract methodically, and give
a personal appreciation of the work.

Both written and oral tests are intended to assess comprehension of written texts and the clarity and precision of the candidates' expression appropriate to the subject and context of communication. They must demonstrate
literary knowledge through familiarity with authors and schools of thought
from the Middle Ages to the present and awareness of the relationships
between such works and their historical and social contexts. In addition,
candidates must link authors and common themes across time and show
their relevance to the present. Finally, candidates must discuss literary works
by presenting different positions and arguments on a theme, using illustrations from the author(s) and constructing a logical argument of their own.
Thus "beyond the acquisition of extensive knowledge in the field of French
literature and the evolution of ideas, the student is expected to develop
techniques which will allow him to structure his thoughts, be able to express himself with clarity and nuance, understand the thoughts of others,
develop his critical thinking and his ability to reflect and expand his taste." [6]

Germany. The Abitur examinations are offered at two levels in each subject: the Grundkurs, or basic level, and the Leistungskurs for candidates

6. "Organization of the French Educational System Leading to the Baccalaureat" (French
Embassy, Washington, D.C., Service des Examens, July 1987, Mimeographed); see also
Baccalauréat de l'enseignement du second degré, 17th ed. (Paris: Programmes Vuibert, 1977);
Bacs: Mode d'Emploi (Paris: Hatier, 1984).

who have elected to study the subject more intensively. The tests at the Leistungs level are longer (generally five hours rather than four) and more demanding. At both Grund and Leistungs level, all the questions require short or extended essays and are directed at character, plot, and content analysis as well as literary, poetic, and dramatic form and style. Leistungs-level candidates are expected to show greater knowledge of the social and historical context of a literary work and to analyze critically its literary and other value.

Since syllabi are set by the respective Land ministry of education, the specific literary texts studied in preparation for the Abitur will vary. Though most students will have read key works from German literary classics and be familiar with modern authors, the choice of works and the balance between classic and modern writers depend on where candidates go to school and, where there is no uniform regional examination, on the preferences of their teachers.[7]

Candidates have wide choice in the specific topics and questions they answer. In Nordrhein-Westfalen, both examinations test candidates on their knowledge of language and literature, their ability to apply methods of critical analysis to given texts, and their capacity to discuss problems and make informed judgements. They must analyze extracts from fiction (a novel, play, short story) and from a nonfiction work (an essay on a contemporary issue, a newspaper article), showing understanding of the main and subsidiary themes, the conceptual structure of the works, and the author's use of language. Leistungs-level candidates are asked to provide a comparative analysis of two pieces in each literary genre to demonstrate comprehension, grasp of form and style, and knowledge of literary and linguistic theory. In similar fashion, the centrally set Abitur paper in Bavaria requires students who have taken the Grund course to describe the conceptual structure of a given extract, to consider aspects of its literary form, and to evaluate it. They are graded on their use of language, ability to apply the analytical approaches taught in school, and knowledge and comprehension of literature. For the Leistungskurs candidate, the questions also include an open-ended discussion on a literary theme, including analysis and comparison of literary works.[8]

7. *Times Educational Supplement* (May 10, 1991): 6.

8. *Richtlinien für die gymnasiale Oberstufe in Nordrhein-Westfalen: Deutsch* (Düsseldorf: Kultusminister des Landes Nordrhein-Westfalen, 1981), esp. sections 1 and 2, and pp. 147ff.; *Grundkurs Deutsch-Leistungskurs Deutsch-Abiturprüfungsafgaben Gymnasium*-Bayern, (Freising: Stark, 1988).

Japan. The language and literature examination in Japanese is a hundred-minute multiple-choice test of thirty-eight items (some with subquestions) and is required of all students. Students are given extracts from modern and classical prose and poetry and from a Chinese classic, among them a long poem, several pages from a novel, and briefer portions from a Japanese and a Chinese classic work, and must answer questions about each on grammar and word usage, literary style, and character motivation. Comprehension questions figure prominently in the test paper. Candidates are asked to select the best of several alternatives to replace a written character or phrase, to choose the best explanation of the meaning of an expression, or to provide the best description of a character's motivation. In addition, candidates must characterize the feelings or mood of a character or situation and select the most appropriate literary judgment from several cited. Some questions ask for the names of writers and styles and periods of literary work.

Candidates are tested on their knowledge of Chinese as well as Japanese written characters and literature, on grammar and syntax, and on literary moods, themes, and styles, all in a form dictated by the constraints of the short-answer format. They are nowhere required to compose answers of their own nor to write in their own words about their appreciation of literature, their feelings, or their responses. They are, however, extensively questioned about literary expression, proper language usage, and different ways of observing, thinking, and feeling.

China. The university entrance examination in Chinese lasts for two and a half hours, fifty minutes longer than examinations in other required subjects. In the examination given in 1988, questions on a passage from an ancient historian tested knowledge of classical prose; others addressed stylistic problems in ninth-century Tang poetry. Candidates were asked to unscramble phrases from a famous line of twentieth-century poetry, testing subtleties of comprehension. The final assignment was to write an essay of six hundred characters on the subject of "Habits."[9]

The format and the content of the examination in Chinese, as in other subjects, are changing: short-answer questions have been introduced to complement essay answers, and the proportion of multiple-choice questions has grown quickly, from 12 percent in 1985 to 70 percent in 1987.[10]

9. Described in *New York Times* (July 12, 1988): 2.
10. Duomei Wang, "Admission Examinations in China vs. Scholastic Aptitude Test in the United States," in *The Third National Symposium on the Reform of Examinations and Recruitment of College Students by Ordinary Higher Education Institutions* (Beijing: Higher

In addition, the traditional emphasis on formal, literary questions has shifted to more contemporary applications of language.

Nowadays, the examination is divided into two sections. The first tests basic knowledge and skills in phonetics, grammar, words and phrases, reading and comprehension. Furthermore, it evaluates knowledge of classical and modern writers and literature, literary techniques and style. The questions are of various types: filling-in-the-blanks, multiple-choice, short-answer, structured-answer. Candidates are required to correct written errors, to identify particular literary usages (metaphors, styles of speech, language structures), and to explain meanings of words and phrases. While some items test comprehension, many more require no more than recognition of terms and categories and are tests of memory. The second section assesses writing ability through an essay of seven hundred characters, to which about a quarter of the total examination time is assigned. Candidates may be asked to write on an open-ended theme, to compose a report based on information provided, or to discuss a position paper.[11]

Sweden. Compared with the practices of other nations, the centrally administered, required examination in Swedish language takes a somewhat unusual form. One week before the date of the examination, candidates receive a printed pamphlet from the National Board of Education. It contains an array of different materials on a single broad theme. In 1988 the theme was "Children" and the material consisted of nine short stories; in 1990 the topic was "Travel" and materials included a contemporary poem, prose and poetry extracts by various authors, practical advice on how to plan a trip, and travel data presented in text, statistical tables, and charts. The pamphlet concluded with a list of nine essay topics, with notes on what might be covered in each.

On the day of the examination, candidates have five hours to write an extended essay on one of the themes. Particular questions on the texts provided are not asked, but instructions note that essays will be evaluated on a number of specific criteria. The syllabus that Swedish students will have followed emphasizes proper language usage in different circumstances, such as social and work situations, and comprehension of the purposes of language, from conveying information to influencing opinion and

---

Education Press, 1989), pp. 72–76 (a collection of papers edited by the Administrative Center for Examinations, State Education Commission).

11. Keith Lewin and Wang Lu, "University Entrance Examinations in China: A Quiet Revolution" in Patricia Broadfoot et al., *Changing Educational Assessment: International Perspectives and Trends* (London: Routledge, 1990), pp. 153–176.

facilitating creative self-expression. Grammar and word usage are taught as aids to communication and literature as a doorway to knowledge of different times and peoples, as well as to common and persisting human themes.

Therefore, evaluation criteria will include understanding and use of the materials provided in the National Board's pamphlet; demonstrating the use of language for purposes of persuasion and reasoning, including the ability to integrate ideas and information into a coherent whole; and linguistic and stylistic skill in using the Swedish language. In addition, candidates will be graded on the personal, creative, and original qualities of their essay. However, teachers grading the essays are enjoined to adapt criteria and tailor evaluations to the school programs students are completing and plans for future study and work.

The United States. Two English papers are included in the Scholastic Aptitude Test, verbal ability and standard written English, each lasting one half hour. The first consists of antonym and analogy questions, sentence-completion exercises, and reading-comprehension questions. The test of written English presents a series of multiple-choice questions on language usage. Some questions call for identification of errors and others for corrections of improper usage. The candidate is not required to compose anything. The main target of the SAT in English is comprehension; no attention is given to either the literary aspects of language or a candidate's ability to use it, beyond the simple comprehension of the questions posed.

The claim for the SAT is that it does not attempt to measure what the candidate has learned in school nor the applications of that knowledge. Rather it measures verbal and other reasoning ability without emphasis on memorized information.

The English examination offered by the American College Testing Program differs somewhat from the SAT, but is similarly a multiple-choice test of English usage, of forty-five minutes' duration and containing seventy-five items. It tests ability to recognize errors of diction, punctuation, sentence structure, grammar, and logic or organization. Candidates are given short prose passages and asked if certain words and phrases are correctly written or, if not, which of four choices supplies the best replacement.

The College Board Achievement Test in English language comes in two versions. The first is a one-hour examination with twenty minutes for a short essay on an open-ended theme (no choices of topic allowed) and forty minutes of multiple-choice questions, which require the candidate to identify and correct errors of grammar and usage. The second alternative consists entirely of ninety multiple-choice questions, which in addition to identification and correction of errors include rephrasing specified sentences. These questions address common writing problems such as consistency in tenses, noun, pronoun, and subject-verb agreement, and clarity and precision of expression. The essays test the candidates' ability to write English correctly and to construct an organized presentation, demonstrating some literary quality.

The College Board Literature Achievement Test assesses candidates' skill in reading literature, rather than their knowledge of literary background, periods, or authors or their critical views of particular works. Questions concern six to eight short prose and poetry texts from English and American literature (roughly 55 to 65 percent and 35 to 45 percent of the questions posed respectively, with a small number, 5 to 10 percent, on other texts). The questions test comprehension as well knowledge of structure and form, voice and tone. They inquire about characters and their traits, the uses of literary forms such as imagery and figures of speech, and the meanings and connotations of words and phrases. There are no prescribed texts or suggested reading lists for this test, and candidates are not expected to have read or studied any of the poems or passages that appear on it.

In contrast to these examinations, the Advanced Placement examination in Literature and Composition lasts three hours and comprises both multiple-choice questions and three or four short essays. The former are based upon several passages of prose and poetry; the essays are directed at contrasting the themes in a poem, writing about a literary work of the candidate's own choice, and discussing an author's use of stylistic devices and the tone and content of the work.

A recent study reports the results of a survey of assessment programs in literature in the United States. The authors reviewed tests in commercial anthologies, batteries of achievement tests, and college placement and admissions tests. They conclude that the majority of test items deal with comprehension rather than with literary aspects. Essay examination assignments ask for "more complex cognitive strategies than do objective measures, but these are limited to a few tests for specialized students or to anthologies where they are often supplementary to objective measures." Only university placement examinations contain a high number of items calling for knowledge of literature and literary skills.[12]

12. See abstract from Pamela Brody, Carol DeMilo, and Alan C. Purves, *The Current State of Assessment in Literature* (Albany, N.Y.: Center for the Learning and Teaching of Literature, University at Albany, State University of New York, April 1989).

The Soviet Union. Russian language and literature is one of the three compulsory subjects in the school-leaving examinations. Russian and mathematics are the only subjects with written and oral components. The six-hour written examination in Russian consists of an extended composition on a given theme.

By the final two years of school, instruction in Russian language (grammar and orthography) has been virtually completed, and students are engaged largely in the study of literature. Examination topics and essay titles are published by the republic ministry of education well ahead of the examination date, and are normally available for sale in local bookstores and newsstands. The course of study for the final years includes classical Russian literature, some foreign classics such as Goethe, Shakespeare, and Balzac, and more recent Soviet literature. Questions address language, literary history, style, and criticism as well as moral and ideological themes: the moral outlook of the worker, Lenin on party organization and literature, civic motives in poetry. Since the topics are known in advance, students spend considerable time preparing and rehearsing their responses. Grades rest on skills in using language, but also on "the pupils' moral ideals, aesthetic taste, and [on] their ability to understand and evaluate works of artistic literature." [13]

The oral examination in literature is conducted as in other subjects. Candidates choose from a number of face-down cards. Each contains two questions based on the previously published topics, and the candidate has a short time to prepare oral responses to each. The topics assigned in the Russian Republic in 1988 included works by such authors as Pushkin, Gorky, Mayakovski, and Sholokhov, their literary styles and qualities, and their treatment of such broad themes as "nature," "revolution," "the Great Patriotic War," and "family relations."

Similarities and Differences. Viewed comparatively, examinations in national language and literature are all directed, though to varying extents, at knowledge of the nation's literary heritage and of the formal structure of language. Most require candidates to demonstrate writing ability and, again, to varying extents, to apply their language skill to particular situations and occasions.

Some nations question students on formal grammar, language structures, and correct/incorrect usage (China, Japan, and the United States), either in language examinations or in combined language and literature papers. Others assume such knowledge and expect examination candidates

13. Leonid Novikov, personal communication, March 12, 1990.

to follow proper usage, requiring them to demonstrate their language skill in integrated examinations containing essays on literary or other subjects (China, England/Wales, France, Germany, Sweden, and the Soviet Union).

By the same token, different kinds and degrees of attention are devoted to literary appreciation, history, and criticism. Literature is treated as part of a nation's heritage, as a product of human civilization extending beyond a nation's borders, and as a form of creative expression to which individuals respond personally. All countries stress the cultural value of literature and its significance as part of the national heritage, but they differ in the extent to which they test candidates' knowledge of the literary heritage of other cultures, their personal responses to literature, and their own literary, creative abilities.

Examination papers reveal the differences between the practice of teaching language as a formal structure of rules and practices, with emphasis upon grammar, and teaching it as basic communication skill; and between teaching literature as "high culture," as national inheritance, and as something to be used for personal expression and appreciation.

In England/Wales GCE A levels have so far remained largely fixed on the more traditional, literature-based approaches. The English practice of relatively early specialization explains the close attention to specified set books. The Swedish examination is representative of the integrated, instrumental, individual approach. The external examinations usually taken in the United States (apart from the Advanced Placement tests and the optional ACT English Composition Test with short essay) emphasize recognition of incorrect language forms and comprehension, but do not evaluate candidates' own use of language.

Unique cultural and historical circumstances explain certain outstanding differences. The examination in Japan gives considerable attention to its Chinese literary and linguistic antecedents, though there is pressure to reduce this component. The Russian-language examination is especially important for non-Russian speakers, and in both China and the Soviet Union ideological content and criticism are a prominent feature of literary analysis and comment.

Chapter 6

The Examinations: History, Social Studies, English, and Mathematics

I'm very well acquainted too with matters mathematical,
I understand equations, both simple and quadratical,
About binomial theorem I'm teeming with a lot o' news—
With many cheerful facts about the square on the hypotenuse.
—Major-General Stanley, *The Pirates of Penzance,* act 1

In this chapter, we continue to review the content of examination questions and to extend understanding of the actual learning objectives of schooling as revealed in external examination papers.

History and Social Studies

England/Wales. History examinations at A and AS level offer a bewildering array of alternatives. Characteristically, candidates are asked to write, say, four essay answers in three papers on particular periods of British, European, or world history. These will be of the order of: "Explain how Prussia benefited from the reign of Frederick the Great," "Why were the French defeated in the Franco-Prussian War?" and "Compare and contrast the foreign policies of Castlereagh and Canning, in the twelve years after the Congress of Vienna." Specific, detailed facts must be presented in historical context to explain, verify, or justify a particular position. Although there is a wide choice among periods and questions, specialized knowledge is demanded.

The variety of papers is in part due to the recent upheaval in the history syllabus, most evident in the debate over the national curriculum. While all papers include British and European history, there are many options for specialization in British, European, and world history, and in particular periods of ancient, medieval, and modern history. Options exist, too, in approaches to history, for example, social, institutional, or military. Increasingly, as a result of new developments in the organization of the history syllabus, thematic approaches are becoming common in some of the examinations at GCSE level, so that questions may be formulated around common basic issues and trends rather than around chronological events.

Other new directions in history affecting the content of examination papers is concern over students' "capacity for empathy" with persons and peoples from the past. Additional alternatives in the format of history examinations for the GCSE, and now for A-level work, include the use of archival material, calling on students to interpret and analyze documents, and the incorporation of schoolwork, such as individual research projects. As a rule, the school determines the kind and scope of the syllabus it wishes to provide, and chooses the suitable examination for its students.

Some view these developments with alarm, fearing that the new national curriculum in history will mean "the end of traditional history teaching in schools. Children should learn facts and should not be asked to form opinions about them," as one critic observes.[1] As in English language and literature, changes are marked in the GCSE examinations. But they are much less controversial at A level, where students are expected to interpret historical events in their open-ended essay responses, not merely to report them. At this stage students have concentrated upon selected periods and types of history. The variety of examination options faithfully reflects that high degree of specialization.

France. A combined examination in history and geography is required of all students taking the baccalauréat. Half of the three-and-a-half-hour examination is devoted to each subject, the content being the same for all séries. Examiners are reminded, however, that mathematics and science students (C and D) will have devoted less time than other students to these subjects, and the grade is more heavily weighted in the aggregate final score of students in séries A and B, humanities and social sciences, than for those in C and D, by a coefficient of 3 compared to 2.

Prior to 1990, candidates in history could choose one of three types of assignments, each on a specified theme or topic, and respond to a question or group of questions on it: the first, an extended essay, required organized presentation of knowledge on a given topic; the second called for interpretation and commentary on documents such as texts, maps, diagrams, and statistical facts; and a third called for reorganization and synthesis of previously acquired knowledge. Since June 1990, only the first two types of questions have been given. Examples of essay topics include:

---

1. Dr. Sheila Lawlor (deputy director of the Center for Policy Studies), quoted in "History Proposals Criticised," *Times Educational Supplement* (Feb. 22, 1991): 9.

The 1970s in the world: economic development and international relations. [Candidates are provided a chronology of about ten dates and events to guide them in constructing their answers.]

Using your own examples, analyze how liberal democracy works in the Western world.

Relations among the major powers, the role of political parties, other forces such as the media and public opinion.

Domestic and foreign policy in France, 1962 to 1969.

Decolonization: why were the European nations unable to maintain their colonial empires in the aftermath of World War II? What were the major phases of the process of decolonization? [Candidates are given a list of new members of the United Nations, 1946 to 1975.]

United States foreign policy from Yalta to Camp David.[2]

For a document-based assignment, candidates are provided with several documents on a broad topic, such as Soviet society: for example, they receive a table containing demographic data, a biographical account by a Soviet worker, and a cartoon. They are asked to respond to leading questions on ethnic diversity, daily life, and cleavages and tensions in society.[3]

In addition, students may opt for an oral examination in which three questions are posed, and they are allowed fifteen minutes to prepare an answer to one of them. The response may be followed by supplementary questions.

Germany. Each Land has its own history syllabus, and examination papers differ accordingly. As in England, examinations show signs of recent upheavals in the subject. Reforms have sought to integrate history, geography, and civic education into a single syllabus of social studies; to devote greater attention to mid-twentieth-century history; and to move from chronological to thematic organization of subject matter, and from political and military history to social history. More traditional syllabi are found in Bavaria, while some of the more progressive administrations, such as Nordrhein-Westfalen and Hesse, have incorporated newer approaches. Characteristically, examination papers consist of several extended essay questions and contain pointers on several aspects of the question that should be addressed. A short text will introduce a period, an event, or a theme, and the candidate selects two of several options on which to write. The questions test the ability to assemble and organize knowledge on the

---

2. *Annales Corrigées du Bac: Histoire & Geographie* (Paris: Vuibert, 1990): 13ff.
3. Ibid., p. 36.

given subject. The examination for the basic (*Grund*) course lasts three or four hours; that for the advanced (*Leistungs*) course contains more complicated questions and usually lasts five hours. In Bavaria's *Grundkurs* in history, the ministry sets six questions and the history department head teacher in each school selects four of these for his students, who then choose two.

Japan. Questions on Japanese and world history form about half of the social studies examination required of all students taking the JFSAT. The remainder of the hundred-minute paper is devoted to geography, philosophy, politics, and economics. History covers a broad time span from the dawn of Japanese culture to the mid-twentieth century, and the approach is encyclopedic. World history traces the development of East and West Asia and Europe as "cultural zones" and focuses on major events and trends in the nineteenth and twentieth centuries and the growing involvement of Japan in international affairs. Students are tested on their knowledge of the chronology of events and historical periods and the relation of persons and actions at a particular time. They are asked to select the correct explanation for an event or historical development from several options and to identify an incorrect generalization or interpretation of a historical event or personage from a number of statements offered. The examination stresses factual content rather than interpretation of historical events.

China. The history examination given in 1988 was a two-hour paper largely devoted to recognition and recall of names, events, and places in Chinese and world history. An essay question gave students the opportunity to select, organize, and interpret historical facts.

Questions were varied and included filling in the blanks, multiple-choice, matching, map-reading, and listing names, as well as the essay. Two-thirds of the content was directed toward Chinese history and the remainder to world history. The shorter answers were nearly all recall of events, dates, places, and people. Only questions in the essay portion gave candidates an opportunity to put facts together, to interpret them, and to express their own ideas. But even here, the marking scheme rewards reference to specific facts, not the quality of argument or originality. Recall questions dominate testing in history, with no room for analysis and judgment.

Candidates must also take an examination in politics. As in the history examination, the test paper contains short-answer, filling-in-the-blanks, multiple-choice, and essay questions. The content includes current affairs, philosophy, politics, and economics. Here, too, emphasis is on recall of facts.[4]

The United States. The College Board Achievement Tests offer two alternatives: American history and social studies, and European history and world cultures.[5] Both are one-hour multiple-choice tests and examine recall of facts and terms as well as reasoning through determining the relation between concepts and facts. The American history examination emphasizes political history, to which about one-third of the questions are devoted. About one-fifth of the questions concern social history and foreign policy, a little less (about 17 percent) economic history, and some 10 percent are on intellectual and cultural history. While the time span is wide, covering the period 1763 to the present, modern history from 1900 to the present receives the most attention (40 percent).

The Achievement Test in European history and world cultures has a broader geographical scope, but also emphasizes political history and the modern period, to which almost half the questions are directed. The history of North America and Western Europe dominates, and questions deal with historical facts and terms and their relation to generalizations. In both papers, candidates are asked to select the best answer or completion to such items as: "During his term as President, Andrew Jackson did all of the following except . . ."; "Which of the following wars of the United States would fit the description of a war neither lost nor won?" or, "Which of the following was immediately responsible for precipitating the French Revolution?"

The American College Testing Program offers a reading and comprehension test (thirty-five minutes, forty items), a quarter of which is devoted to social studies. The candidate must read passages on several social studies topics and interpret the information contained in them.

The Soviet Union. History/social studies is one of the three required subjects in the leaving examination. It covers Russian history since the decline of czarism and world history, mainly since the mid-nineteenth century, touching on West European nations, the United States, and Japan. Each of the republics includes elements of its own history in its curriculum. The topics

4. Keith Lewin and Wang Lu, "University Entrance Examinations in China: A Quiet Revolution," in Patricia Broadfoot et al., *Changing Educational Assessment: International Perspectives and Trends* (London: Routledge, 1990).

5. College Entrance Examination Board, *The College Board Achievement Tests: Fourteen Tests in Thirteen Subjects* (New York: College Entrance Examination Board, 1986), pp. 189–245.

are published in advance and are usually examined orally. Students are tested on knowledge of important historical events and personages and their significance, and on the role of the Soviet Union in history. They are also asked about Marxist-Leninist ideology and the role of the party.[6]

The history examination was canceled in 1988 as a result of Mikhail Gorbachev's demand for a more "candid approach to history." Schools were instructed to substitute discussions of current events in place of formal lessons and to award no grades in the subject, pending revision of the curriculum and rewriting of the textbooks.[7] At the time of writing (March 1992), external history examinations have not yet been reinstituted.[8]

Similarities and Differences. Some examinations in history and social studies emphasize recall of commonly accepted facts about the past, others ask candidates to use information to explain events or to comment upon an interpretation. Some examinations define history quite narrowly, others include geography or other social sciences. The extent to which world history enters into the scope of the final examinations varies according to a nation's involvement with other nations.

"History Is Politics" runs the headline over a review of a recent collection of articles dealing with history in the new national curriculum in England/Wales,[9] thus emphasizing that history as a school subject, like national language and literature, is an instrument for instilling in students a sense of national and personal identity, a view of their nation's place in the world, past and present. So-called historical facts and their interpretation vary from country to country and from time to time. A nation's history curriculum is subject to reinterpretation as a result of new research, but changes, as well as controversial or sensitive topics and approaches, are often slow to become incorporated into the examination syllabus. However, the content of the history examinations is often quickly affected by swings in "official" political ideology, especially when governments sponsor efforts to revise the content of school history programs.

6. James Muckle, *A Guide to the Soviet Curriculum: What the Russian Child Is Taught in School* (London: Croom Helm, 1988), pp. 67–69.

7. *New York Times* (May 31, 1988): 1.

8. Social studies examinations in Sweden are at the discretion of schools and municipalities. They are therefore omitted from this review.

9. "History Is Politics," *Times Educational Supplement* (April 19, 1991): 28 (review of Richard Aldrich, ed., *History in the National Curriculum* [London: Kogan Page, 1991]).

English as a Foreign Language

France. Students in the humanities and social sciences (séries A and B) must take written and oral examinations in at least one foreign language. Those in mathematics and the sciences (séries C and D) need take only an oral in one language. The format and regulations for the written English examination are the same as for other modern foreign languages. Comprehension is assessed through questions on a previously unseen text. The quality of personal expression in the language is demonstrated in two short compositions, and general language competence and cultural knowledge are tested by an array of short questions. Similarly, the oral is a test of the candidates' comprehension and communication skill in the foreign language. In a fifteen-minute period, after a similar allowance of time for preparation, the candidate must present and discuss a work previously studied. He or she must also read aloud a short, previously unseen text, present a response to it, and engage in a dialogue with the examiner by answering leading questions.

Directions to the examiners stress the importance of savoir faire and culture, and specifically reject evaluation of theoretical knowledge, grammatical facts, and the history of literature and civilization. The candidate is to be evaluated on intelligibility, accuracy of expression, use of the language, conversational skill, and appropriateness of his responses to the examiner's comments and questions.

Germany. Abitur examinations in English test comprehension and the ability to write and/or speak correctly and coherently. Candidates are expected to be able to interpret an unseen text, to recognize stylistic devices, and to refer to its literary, social, and historical contexts. They must show some knowledge of English literature. In both written and oral examinations, the candidate is presented with an essay on a literary theme or an extract from a literary work and must respond in English to several questions about it and related themes.

The English examinations taken at the basic and advanced levels differ, as in the courses of study leading up to them, in duration and scope: the examination for the advanced level is usually an hour longer (five or four, instead of four or three hours), presents a more complex English extract, and calls for more extensive knowledge of literature and literary theory.

China. The English-language examination in China consists of several groups of short questions in multiple-choice format, comprising altogether some ninety to a hundred items. One set of five to ten exercises tests knowledge of phonics: an English word is given and candidates are required to select one of the, say, four words provided whose vowel sound matches it. A set of completion exercises asks for selection of a missing word or phrase from several offered, testing word choice and knowledge of correct grammar. Comprehension is examined through word definitions and questions on the meaning of phrases in a brief piece of English prose. The premium throughout is to select the correct sounds, definitions, proper word usage, and grammatical forms from several options provided. The examination paper may also include a few questions requiring the candidate to fill in short blanks in his own words.

Japan. Although listening, speaking, reading, and writing are all defined as the goals of the English syllabus in Japan, the examination itself, like language exams in many other countries, provides no opportunity for the first two objectives. In similar fashion to the English examination in China, several groups of multiple-choice questions are directed at testing sound recognition (phonics), proper word and grammatical usage, and comprehension. A few short fill-in questions are included.

Sweden. The Swedish examination in English comprises a vocabulary test, consisting of multiple-choice and sentence-completion questions (thirty-five minutes); reading comprehension, in which candidates must answer short questions on a previously unseen text (forty minutes); and listening comprehension, in which candidates answer multiple-choice and open-ended questions testing comprehension, vocabulary, and grammar (thirty-five minutes) after hearing a tape recording. An oral of about ten minutes' duration may follow for selected students.[10]

The Soviet Union. English as a foreign language is an optional subject in the school-leaving examination. It is an oral test, the basic format of which is the same for all foreign languages: the candidate is asked to read aloud a short English text, translate it into Russian (with or without a dictionary), and answer a number of questions about it. It is a test of comprehension and of the student's ability to respond in the foreign language.[11]

Similarities and Differences. Examinations in English as a foreign language generally address similar aspects of learning, but the balance between the

10. *Instruktionshafte för centrala prov i moderna sprak ak 2–3 och 2–4.* (Stockholm: Skoloverstyrelsen, 1988).
11. Nellie Apanasewicz, *Final Examinations in the Russian Ten-Year School* (Washington, D.C.: U.S. Department of Health, Education, and Welfare, 1966).

more formal and literary (grammar, reading and writing, accuracy in use, intellectual and aesthetic content) and the uses of language for interpersonal communication (emphasis on speaking, clarity, informal language use) differs from one nation to another. Even in the study of literature, a distinction may be observed between the more traditional and formal literary criticism representing "high culture," for example, in Germany and France, and a more personal and individual approach rooted in general themes as in Sweden. In Japan and China, there is no oral; in Germany and France, the candidate's choice of subjects and specialization usually determines whether there is an oral; in the Soviet Union an oral examination only is required; and, unlike the other instances, the English examination in Sweden includes an aural test of comprehension. The presence of an oral or aural component in the examination, whether required or optional, is indicative: it represents an emphasis on the importance of "live communication" as a substitute for or counterweight to formal academic knowledge of the language.

Mathematics

Along with national language/literature, mathematics is the most frequently required subject in the secondary-school-leaving examinations of the eight nations.

England/Wales. Advanced-level mathematics examinations are taken by candidates who have selected the subject and who have devoted two years of specialized study to it. The syllabi cover a broad array of topics, typically testing numerical, graphic, algebraic, and problem-solving skills and abilities, as well as the ability to construct and interpret mathematical models.

Each examining board offers tests covering pure and applied mathematics. The boards have agreed on an "Inter-Board Common Core" of topics to be included in the syllabus of each. The existence of this common core is important for limiting curriculum diversity and increasing the comparability of candidates' results across the different boards.[12]

Boards continue to offer different assortments of syllabi and examination papers, however. For example, the Associated Examining Board or AEB (serving primarily the south and west of England) offers no fewer than seven syllabi, no doubt reflecting the board's desire to accommodate the

12. Associated Examining Board, *1990 Syllabi. Section 3: Mathematics and Computing* (Bristol: Associated Examining Board, n.d.), p. 91.

demands of schools having different emphases in their mathematics teaching. By comparison, the Oxford and Cambridge Schools Examination Board offers just two syllabi (or "stages"), Mathematics and Further Mathematics.

Candidates (or their schools) may choose among the different examining boards, and may choose within boards among alternative syllabi and tests in pure and applied mathematics at varied levels, including or omitting the specialized topic of statistics. All the papers, however, characteristically present markedly difficult material, spanning a wide range of topics.

The AEB offers two tests in each of the following: mathematics, pure mathematics, applied mathematics, and statistics. In addition, candidates can take an "S" (Special) test containing questions "of a more searching nature" in any one of these subjects.[13] To satisfy the requirements of a particular syllabus (for example, either the single subject areas listed above or some combination, such as pure and applied mathematics, pure mathematics and statistics, and applied mathematics and statistics), schools and candidates may "mix and match" papers. All syllabi call for two written examinations of three hours each. The S paper is a single three-hour test.

Oxford and Cambridge follow the same pattern of requiring two three-hour tests for each syllabus and providing an optional Special test, with harder questions. "The chief aim will be to test ability in using mathematics, but not always in familiar ways."[14]

A candidate taking Pure Mathematics 1 in the Southern Universities' Joint Board examination has three hours to answer seven compulsory questions in section A and four questions (chosen from a further seven) in section B. In 1987, section A of the question paper covered simultaneous equations, geometrical progressions, inequalities, differential calculus, curve-sketching, analytic geometry, and trigonometry.

A typical paper in applied mathematics offers twenty questions and instructs the candidate to answer not more than seven. Answering any of the questions requires substantial mathematical knowledge and skill in solving complex problems requiring long chains of reasoning. S papers emphasize proofs and present questions that require a good deal of ingenuity and mathematical dexterity for their solution.

France. Mathematics is a required examination for students in all séries. But for candidates in séries A2 and A3 (languages and arts), it is an oral,

13. Ibid., p. 90.

14. Oxford and Cambridge Schools Examination Board. *Regulations for Certificate Examinations for the Year 1989* (Oxford: Oxford and Cambridge Schools Examination Board, n.d.), p. 76.

the mark for which receives relatively little weight in the combined final score for all subjects. Candidates must respond to two questions, one, common to all, on basic mathematical knowledge; a second chosen from a list of topics studied in class, including number theory and simple equations, real-valued functions, and arithmetic and geometric sequences. Candidates in série A1, which emphasizes philosophy and mathematics, are tested in basic concepts and the theoretical uses of mathematics, based on a more extensive syllabus that includes number theory and equations, sequences and series, algebraic functions, logarithmic and exponential functions, differential and integral calculus, complex number theory, and probability and statistics. Candidates in série B (economics and social sciences) will have concentrated on statistics, curve-sketching and applications, and linear algebra. The examination consists of two exercises and a problem on different topics, all of them obligatory.

Candidates in séries C and E must demonstrate knowledge in depth, be able to solve difficult problems, and reason with abstract concepts. They will be examined on such topics as numeric sequences; differential calculus and differential equations; algebraic, logarithmic, and exponential functions; integral calculus and complex-number theory and their applications; probability and statistics; vectors and linear algebra; linear equations; and plane and solid geometry. Like the mathematics examination for candidates in série D (emphasizing mathematics with biology, physics, and chemistry), the test requires extensive knowledge and demonstration of higher-order cognitive skills, though série D candidates cover a more limited range of topics. Less theoretical knowledge is required of candidates in série D than série C. The written examination in mathematics is more heavily weighted for candidates in séries C and E and lasts four hours, compared with three hours for candidates in humanities and social science.

Groups of académies set papers with different content, but of comparable difficulty. In general, the papers for série B contain more applied mathematics, focusing more on probability, than do the papers for série A.

Germany. As in England/Wales, mathematics is an optional examination subject. In Germany, however, the Abitur syllabus demands three years of advanced study, compared with the two years in England/Wales for A level. As with other subjects, mathematics can be offered at either basic (*Grund*) or advanced (*Leistungs*) level. Oral as well as written examinations are available, students choosing which to take. Each Land defines its own syllabi within guidelines agreed via the Kultus Minister Konferenz.

Thus, despite certain differences, there is a high degree of overlap of subject matter across the Länder.

Statements made in the guidelines for Hesse exemplify the difference between the Grund and Leistungs courses of study. Grund courses are to use simple examples to illustrate important concepts and techniques, and comprehensive treatment of the material is not the aim. Within these limits, however, the mathematical material and skills are developed so that students have practice in problem-solving and in the transfer of concepts from one problem to another.

According to the guidelines, Leistungs-level courses treat the material in a more comprehensive and complete manner. Students are expected to formulate mathematical expressions using an orderly, deductive approach. They must demonstrate insight into the development of mathematics and show skills in using mathematics in complex situations. At the Leistungs level, examination questions are significantly more difficult.

Candidates in mathematics whether in Grund or Leistungs courses are expected to be familiar with three different areas: analysis (calculus, infinitesimal and integral), linear algebra, and probability and statistics. Among the Länder, there are variations: Hesse, for example, provides for a fourth area—either to deepen knowledge in one of the three standard areas or to introduce a new area.[15]

The written examination usually lasts three hours. In Bavaria it is based on three questions, one from each of the three main areas just mentioned. The Bavarian Ministry of Education and Culture sends a sealed list of approved questions for the year's examination to each Gymnasium. Early on the morning of the examination, which is scheduled for the same day for all Gymnasien, the envelope is opened in the presence of the mathematics faculty of each school. The faculty then choose one question from each of the three areas, and all candidates at that school attempt those questions. Members of the school mathematics faculty grade the answer papers of their students, using the evaluation guidelines supplied by the ministry. In this way, even in those Länder where central control of the Abitur is long-standing, important elements of local school discretion are sustained.

Candidates choosing to take an oral rather than a written examination in mathematics are presented with a written problem and are given up to thirty minutes to prepare an answer, or even up to an hour if use of a

15. Kursstrukturpläne—Gymnasiale Oberstufe—Aufgabenfeld III-1. Mathematik (Wiesbaden: Hessische Kulturminister, n.d.), p. 7.

calculator is required.[16] The examination is normally conducted by the student's current teacher in the presence of three others (a recorder, another mathematics teacher, and a chairperson) and lasts for at least twenty, and at most thirty, minutes. Regulations in Nordrhein-Westfalen expressly forbid an oral examination in the form of a series of disconnected questions. Instead, it focuses on the candidate's ability to present a coherent, reasoned solution to the problem set in the first part of the examination. The second part can then contain questions related to the problem and its solution. As far as topics are concerned, little distinction is made between questions for Grund- and Leistungs-level candidates, though the complexity of the questions and the depth of knowledge is expected to be significantly lower in questions asked of Grund-level candidates.[17]

Overall, the Abitur examinations in mathematics call for a thorough grounding in standard mathematical techniques and are characterized by straightforward problems and tests of the candidates' ability to apply textbook procedures.

Japan. All candidates for the JFSAT must take mathematics, though there are different tests for candidates with different specializations, for example, mathematics with bookkeeping/accounting, applied mathematics/physics, and general mathematics. Each of these tests lasts for one hour and forty minutes and has two parts. Part 1 contains three compulsory questions; part 2 offers three questions, of which the candidate chooses two. The questions are multipart and are all worth the same number of points.

Some of the compulsory part 1 questions are identical from one specialization to another, but irrespective of specialization the pattern is to give one question on finding the roots of one or more quadratic equations, another on understanding the equation and/or graph of a parabola, and a third on using trigonometry.

Part 2 of each test represents the particular specialization. For general mathematics, there are three questions: in geometry, coordinate geometry, and probability. For the bookkeeping/accounting option, the questions involve accounts to be drawn up and reconciled and profit and loss margins to be calculated. The applied mathematics/physics option offers questions

16. See *Leistungskurs Mathematik: Abitur Prüfüngsaufgaben Gymnasium-Bayern*, 11th ed. (Freising: Stark, 1988).

17. Kultusminister des Landes Nordrhein-Westfalen, *Gymnasiale Oberstufe: Richtlinien Mathematik*, (Düsseldorf: Kultusminister des Landes Nordrhein-Westfalen, 1981), pp. 139–140.

about mechanics and dynamics, electricity, and volumes and pressures. All of these papers present a mixture of tests of formal, textbook knowledge, analytic ability, and "practical" problem-solving. The bookkeeping/accounting test is the least difficult; the applied mathematics/physics is far and away the most difficult; the plain mathematics examination lies in between.

China. Mathematics is an obligatory subject for candidates taking the university entrance examination, though, as in Japan, different requirements govern candidates in the humanities or behavioral sciences and those specializing in science, engineering, and medicine. When the examination was reintroduced in 1977, humanities candidates had to answer fewer questions on a common mathematics paper that stressed computation and factual recall in geometry, algebra, and trigonometry. Since 1979, however, separate tests have been set for each group. The examination for humanities and behavioral sciences students is shorter and less rigorous than that for science majors. An analysis of examination papers offered in 1980 found that the content remained largely "classical," reflecting little of the mathematics reforms of the past twenty years. Emphasis was placed on geometric problems based on deductive reasoning; few if any problems called for the use of statistical inference, modeling techniques, or matrix algebra. Since then, modernizing reforms have influenced the Chinese mathematics curriculum and are making their way slowly into the examinations,[18] which have begun to include an occasional practical or applied problem.

Specific questions vary from province to province, but the format of the papers is standard for the country. Typically, there are four compulsory multipart questions for a total of eighty points and two optional, extra-credit questions for a further twenty points. Roughly half the paper consists of short-answer and multiple-choice items.

The mathematics examination in China continues to be characterized by formal, textbook material, especially proofs. Calculus is absent, and the level of knowledge required is in some cases elementary, and at most intermediate (except for the extra-credit questions).

Sweden. Students in their final years of secondary school take an array of tests in mathematics, at least one of which is sent from the central government's education department in Stockholm, the rest being locally produced and graded. The central tests are not end-of-year examinations, but are given during the course of the school year. Sweden, like France and China, provides different mathematics examinations for students in the different "lines" of study at the upper secondary level: for example, a test stressing business mathematics for those studying the social sciences and economics, and a more difficult one for those in the natural sciences/technology lines. The first deals with such practical problems as compound interest, present value, and descriptive statistics. The second contains some elementary calculus and coordinate geometry. Questions are a mixture of formal, textbook material and tests of comprehension. Somewhat curiously, there is a marked absence of practical problems to be solved.

The United States. Four external mathematics tests are nationally available in the United States: the Scholastic Aptitude Test, the American College Test, College Board Achievement Tests, and College Board Advanced Placement tests.

The mathematics section of the SAT attempts to measure candidates' ability in mathematical reasoning. The questions are primarily devoted to elementary algebra and plane geometry. There is no coordinate geometry, no trigonometry, and no calculus. There are some questions about elementary number theory and mathematical-logical reasoning. Questions rarely if ever refer to formal, textbook material; instead, they test ability to comprehend the question quickly and choose the correct answer from the four or five options given. A frequently used style of question asks the candidate to decide if two quantities are equal, or which is the greater, or whether the information given is not sufficient to make a determination.

The mathematics part of the American College Test resembles that of the SAT: its format is multiple-choice; the emphasis is on speedy comprehension and decision; and sixty questions are to be answered in sixty minutes. The ACT distinguishes itself from the SAT, however, by explicitly acknowledging, "The ACT measures the knowledge, understanding and skills that you have acquired throughout your education." [19] Four major areas of mathematics are covered: pre- and elementary algebra (40 percent of the items), intermediate algebra and coordinate geometry (30 percent), plane geometry (23 percent), and trigonometry (7 percent).[20]

The College Board Achievement Test in mathematics has two levels.

19. *Preparing for the ACT Assessment* (Iowa City, Iowa: American College Testing Program, 1989), p. 3.
20. *The Enhanced ACT Assessment* (Iowa City, Iowa: American College Testing Program, 1989), p. 8.

Level 1 provides questions at an elementary to intermediate level; level 2 is more solidly and uniformly intermediate and is designed for students who have taken college preparatory mathematics. Both levels include algebra, solid and coordinate geometry, trigonometry, and functions. Level 2 omits the plane geometry that occupies about one-fifth of the level 1 paper and reduces the algebra content in favor of more trigonometry and questions referring to functions, while adding some probability/statistics.

Each examination is a one-hour multiple-choice test covering similar areas of study and includes questions involving computation, completion, and some problem-solving. The major areas covered and the percentages of questions directed at each area in each paper (level 1 first) are as follows: algebra (30 percent, 18 percent), plane geometry (20 percent, none), solid geometry (6 percent, 8 percent), coordinate geometry (12 percent, 12 percent), trigonometry (8 percent, 20 percent), elementary functions (12 percent, 24 percent), other topics (12 percent, 18 percent).

Relatively few students take the Advanced Placement test in mathematics (only some sixty-six thousand in 1988). Mathematics here is quite limited in scope: either calculus and trigonometry or calculus and functions is offered, plus some algebra and geometry. Despite the narrow scope, questions demand a much deeper knowledge of mathematics than in the three other U.S. examinations. In addition, the examination takes three hours, and only half is in multiple-choice format; the other half, consisting of six questions to be answered in ninety minutes, requires open-ended answers.

The Soviet Union. As in Japan, the mathematics test is compulsory for all prospective graduates,[21] with a written examination lasting four hours. Because of the discretion afforded to each republic in establishing its own written mathematics examination paper, we base our judgment on evidence from the Russian Republic. Algebra, geometry, trigonometry, and calculus are represented (probability/statistics is absent); questions on the written examination can be quite difficult, especially for more advanced students. For the more basic mathematics courses, however, trigonometry and calculus do not typically reach above the elementary level; and questions in algebra and coordinate geometry are presented at an intermediate level. Papers tend to stress formal, textbook material rather than problem-solving.

21. Leonid Novikov, "Characteristics of the School Leaving Examinations in the Secondary Area of the Soviet Educational System" (unpublished paper, Deutsches Institut für Pädagogische Forschung, Frankfurt, January 1989).

Similarities and Differences. Mathematics is widely regarded as the hardest school subject of all, though it is also considered to be one of the most important. The subject is required in most nations (France, Japan, China, Sweden, the United States (on the SAT and ACT), and the Soviet Union), but it is optional in England/Wales, Germany, and in the Achievement and Advanced Placement tests in United States. This means that very different proportions of upper secondary school students take mathematics in their final year(s). Furthermore, in most nations candidates can choose between more and less advanced tests and among different specialized topics. Consequently, examinations in mathematics represent very different levels of complexity and difficulty.

Across all the eight countries, the mathematics curricula generally cover the same broad areas: arithmetic functions, algebra, coordinate and plane geometry, trigonometry, differential and integral calculus, and probability and statistics. However, examination papers do not cover all topics to the same extent. Some topics are omitted in some countries. Perhaps half of the material is common to all nations. Moreover, differences do exist between traditional mathematics and more modern forms. The former tends to emphasize calculations, recognition of symbols and formulas, and reproduction of proofs, whereas the newer syllabi give greater attention to open-ended problem-solving and "mathematico-logical elaboration" and also include set theory and calculus.[22]

Conclusion

We have noted some major common and divergent features of the examination papers in four subjects. Taken together, they point to curriculum characteristics and issues that transcend single subjects and national boundaries.

Examination papers indicate some of the contrasts between older, more traditional views of knowledge and newer approaches: detailed, encyclopedic information versus knowledge structured on the basis of concepts or themes, theoretical, academic versus practical and applied; subject- and discipline-based knowledge versus knowledge based on an integrative, multidisciplinary organization, cultural versus skill-related learning, specialized versus general knowledge, elitist versus popular knowledge, and

22. S. J. Prais and Karin Wagner, "Schooling Standards in England and Germany: Some Summary Comparisons Bearing on Economic Performance," *Compare* 16, no. 1 (1986): 5–36; S. J. Prais, "Education for Productivity: Comparisons of Japanese and English Schooling and Vocational Preparation," *Compare* 16, no. 2 (1986): 121–148.

high versus mass culture. All of these contrasts are reflected in the curriculum at large, in particular subjects, and in the examinations.

Examinations validate the work of teachers and legitimate the knowledge they purvey.[23] Their content and format define and reflect the curriculum. Some examinations place a premium on the ability to recall discrete items of information or to reproduce sets of related facts. Others favor interpretation and analysis of various kinds or problem-solving approaches. Thus, in the process of assessing knowledge and skills, examination papers reveal a preferred cast of mind, way of thinking, or critical approach to knowledge, which presumably has been fostered in school during the preceding years. While examinations do not by any means cover the total school curriculum, they do identify the knowledge and skills considered to be important.

National language/literature is a general, basic subject for all students to take, though it is not an obligatory examination subject in those nations where a measure of specialization exists and where the required subjects are few. Some nations offer choices among different examination syllabi, but they are choices among different approaches, study materials, and periods, not necessarily between greater and lesser levels of difficulty.

Mathematics, too, is a subject that all must take in some countries, with accommodation for more and less advanced studies. In others, it is differentiated according to specializations in the subject, all at an advanced level, whereas in yet other countries it may not be required at all. Substantial differences among countries in the knowledge required of candidates in history or literature are to be expected: political and cultural differences among nations are obviously likely to affect content in the humanities and social sciences. What may be more surprising are the substantial differences in the material required in mathematics.

The international comparisons point to the inseparability of format and content, and it is a commonplace that the format of examinations strongly influences both the content and style of teaching. As a consequence, the format of examinations, as much as their content, is a target of the debate over the proper objectives of instruction and over what teachers and schools are supposed to do. The United States and Japan continue to rely heavily on multiple-choice formats. In China as well, in response to the large num-

---

23. Nevertheless, in spite of the undoubted power of examinations to influence teaching, they may be somewhat paradoxically at odds with what many teachers actually do. See, e.g., Hans-Werner Eroms, "Teaching the Mother-Tongue Curriculum in Germany," in W. Tulasiewicz and A. Adams, eds., *Teacher Expectations and Teaching Reality* (London: Routledge, 1989), pp. 133–150; and Karl-Wilhelm Eigenbrodt, "Freedom and Constraint in Teaching German Literature," in the same work, pp. 151–168.

ber of candidates, the high cost of university entrance examinations, and concern about their reliability and objectivity, the examination authorities are increasingly substituting short-answer and multiple-choice questions for the traditional extended-answer format. Concern for reliability and validity thus influences choice of format, which in turn influences the content selected for examination, which in turn influences the content and style of classroom instruction. Under these no-longer-new approaches to testing, questions may meet stringent technical requirements, while skirting those aspects of learning that are more complex and ambiguous and hence more difficult to measure. This tendency stands in opposition to the current view of curriculum, which seeks to foster individual, divergent, and creative thinking and an appreciation of cultural diversity. Instead, what is encouraged is an emphasis on such examination-taking skills as speed of response and elimination of clearly incorrect or absurd answers, both of which are more remote from educational objectives than the skills required for success in the more traditional examination format.

Examination systems differ substantially in the demands they place on candidates. Differences in content, format, extent of choice, duration, and timing all add up to differences in the burdens candidates must carry. These matters are the subject of the following chapter.

Chapter 7

The Burden of Examinations: Demands Placed on Candidates

The task of filling up the blanks
I'd rather leave to *you.*
—Koko, *The Mikado,* act 1

A nation's educational standards are embodied in its secondary-school-leaving examinations. These tests reflect national assumptions about the knowledge and skills students should acquire during their schooling and about the nature and extent of the burdens candidates can be asked to carry. When those assumptions change, examinations are likely to change, too, though perhaps with some time lag. In the United States, concern over the effects of low levels of school achievement on social conditions and economic performance has led to calls for more demanding examinations. The converse has occurred in France, the Federal Republic of Germany, Sweden, and Japan, where the demands made on students have resulted in attempts to ease the burden of wide-ranging and difficult examinations. Indeed, rarely are examinations considered to be "just right."

Criticisms of examinations for demanding too much of candidates, or too little, imply a judgment in comparative perspective. How do the end-of-secondary-school examination systems of different nations compare with respect to the burdens they place on candidates?

Such a comparative exercise is by no means simple or straightforward. It calls for judgments of what aspects of the examinations can be used to gauge relative difficulty. It requires careful definition of what constitutes greater or lesser difficulty. In addition, nations differ in the organization and use they make of examinations in their respective educational systems, raising a further complex set of problems. All the nations in this study have some form of assessment of student achievement by examination, but some, like Japan, have a single national examination at the end of secondary school; others, for example, the United States, offer several. Some nations distribute examinations over a period of time (Sweden), or give them in two stages (for example, the Soviet Union, Japan, and England/ Wales). In some countries, as in France and Japan, the examination results

Table 1: Examinations by Country

China
  National Unified College Entrance Examinations, Zhejiang Province, 1987,
  1988
England/Wales
  General Certificate of Education, Advanced Level, Oxford and Cambridge
  Schools Examination Board, June 1988; Southern Universities Joint Board,
  1987
Federal Republic of Germany
  Abitur examinations, Nordrhein-Westfalen, Bayern, 1988
France
  Baccalauréat Examinations, 1989
Japan
  Joint First Stage Achievement Test, 1988
Soviet Union
  Examinations for Secondary School Leavers, Russian Republic, 1988–89
Sweden
  National Board of Education, grade twelve tests, 1987, 1990
United States
  Scholastic Aptitude Test, various dates
  American College Test, various dates
  Achievement Tests, various dates
  Advanced Placement Tests, 1989

are critical for a student's future, in others, notably the United States, they
are merely one among a number of factors to be weighed. These differences raise important methodological problems for cross-system comparisons.

In this chapter we address the question by comparing two dimensions
of examinations: the overall requirements of the system and the nature of
the content in two subjects common to all of the national systems, national
language/literature and mathematics. The discussions are based upon the
examination papers listed in table 1.

Comparison of Requirements

Three criteria are used to assess the burden represented by examination
system requirements: the demands imposed on the candidate by the characteristic format of examination papers; the overall load, that is, the number of subjects required; and the duration of the examination(s).

As we have seen in the previous chapter, examination formats in these eight nations cover a considerable range of practices, which impose different demands on candidates. Traditional extended-essay questions, characteristic of the written examinations in China, England/Wales, France, Germany, and the Soviet Union, are more demanding; short-answer questions less so. Multiple-choice, machine-scorable tests, which are the norm in Japan and the United States, are likely to be still less demanding. Although it is possible to devise multiple-choice questions to test fairly complex knowledge and skills, they necessarily provide candidates with prompts and limits to the range of correct answers. Moreover, responses to essay or extended-answer questions require a more self-directed, comprehensive, and sustained effort.

In addition to written papers, and in some cases instead of them, teacher-led orals may form a portion of the examinations. They comprise an important part of the examinations in the Soviet Union, France, and Germany, especially, of course, in foreign languages, as an option in certain subjects for some candidates, or as a requirement for borderline students or in other special circumstances. For most candidates, it appears that oral examinations are less of a burden than written ones. Anxiety and embarrassment may make the occasion more stressful, but the shorter duration usually limits the complexity, depth, and comprehensiveness of the questioning, especially when the one-on-one or panel examination is conducted by the candidate's own teacher.

Practical examinations are a standard part of tests in the sciences, notably in England/Wales, and in history and language/literature it is becoming increasingly common to place original materials before candidates and require them to examine and interpret them. Arguably, such practical tests are more demanding of candidates than written answers, whether long, short, or multiple-choice. The opposite is most likely true where previously prepared work may be submitted for evaluation as part of the examination. Continuous assessment has a growing though variously important part in the final examination results in Sweden, Germany, and England/Wales. This is exemplified by the inclusion of marks for schoolwork and of evaluations of previously prepared work (portfolios) as part of the examination grade.

The effort required of candidates taking the national examination differs substantially from one country to another, in the number of compulsory subjects and in the duration of the individual subject tests and the examination as a whole. Thus, candidates for GCE Advanced-level examinations in England/Wales are free to take no more than one subject at a time, though typically candidates will attempt two or even three. Each test usually lasts three hours. In addition, candidates may choose examinations that include course work done earlier under teacher supervision and/or tests at different levels of difficulty. In some subjects, more than one examination may be required.

Toward the end of secondary school, students in the United States may sit for one or more of four examinations: the SAT, ACT, College Board Achievement Tests, and the Advanced Placement tests. The SAT is a three-hour test, divided into six half-hour sections. All candidates are expected to attempt all six sections—two tests of verbal aptitude, two of mathematical aptitude, one test of standard written English, and a section that provides a further verbal, mathematical, or written English test. The three-hour ACT comprises four tests (English, mathematics, reading, and science reasoning). The College Board Achievement Tests in various subjects each last one hour, and students will often take up to three subject tests at a given sitting, though there is no requirement to do so. Advanced Placement tests run for three hours in each subject, and again there is no requirement to take more than one test at a time.

While examination candidates in England and the United States have large discretion over the number of subjects they offer for examination, Abitur candidates in Germany are required to take four subjects, one of which will be examined orally. Written examinations last three, four, or five hours each. The examination period is intentionally long to allow students to copy their essays in a fair hand before submitting them. In China, France, Japan, and the Soviet Union, six or seven subjects are usually required, though the length of each subject examination varies greatly from country to country. In France, tests may require four hours; in China, they are usually 100 minutes, though 150 minutes are allotted for the Chinese-language paper. Japan's JFSAT examinations are 100 minutes each. In the Soviet Union, the two required written papers (in literature and mathematics) last six and four hours respectively; orals in the remaining subjects last up to about a half hour each. Swedish students are also examined in as many as six or seven subjects, depending on their specialized program, but the examinations vary in duration and are spread over the final year or two of the upper secondary school.

If oral examinations are given instead of written examinations, they rarely go beyond a half hour and are usually set at about twenty minutes. Thus orals demand much less time than a written test in the subject.

Taking into account the minimum number of subjects required and the characteristic duration of the necessary examinations, the minimum burden upon candidates differs substantially among nations: from as much as about twenty hours in the examination room over perhaps a two-week period in France to as little as three hours on one day in the United States.

Figure 2 summarizes data on the overall requirements of the examination systems: the characteristic format of examinations in each country, the minimum number of subjects required, the typical or average duration of an examination in a standard subject, and the amount of time a candidate is usually required to spend, at the very least, in the examination room. Two kinds of information are tabulated here: numbers and judgments. Although it can be assumed that longer and more numerous examination sessions are in themselves more demanding for the candidates, comparisons of the demands on candidates represented by the different formats call for more complex and even subjective judgements. All things considered, open-ended examinations devoted largely to short-answer and essay questions may reasonably be considered more burdensome for candidates than closed examinations containing short-answer questions based largely or entirely on restricted choice.

Figure 3 is a scale of the relative burden placed on candidates based upon the data presented above. The requirements of the examination systems are judged to be most onerous in France, followed closely by those of Germany. China comes next, followed by Japan and the Soviet Union, both quite similar in difficulty and weight of requirements. Then come Sweden and England/Wales, also placed at about the same point on the scale, but for different reasons: the former because of an explicit policy that examinations in different subjects must be spread out over time; the latter because candidates may select a small number of subjects and, within limits, the level of difficulty. All factors considered (format, minimum number of subjects required, examination duration), the United States system presents candidates with the lightest requirements of all.

Comparison of Content

A review of the content and the questions asked comes closer to the heart of the question, "How burdensome are the examinations?"

All examination questions are directed at assessing the candidates' knowledge, understanding, and skills in a particular area. While knowledge-based questions can be confined to the recall of factual material and even to such isolated items of information as names, dates and places, rules, definitions, and formulas, they can be used also to test a candidate's ability to understand and interpret new information, to draw conclusions, or to make inferences. This process requires information recall, but the

Figure 2. The Burden of Examination Requirements

	China	England/Wales	France	Germany	Japan	Sweden	Soviet Union	United States
Format	mixed	open	open	open	closed	mixed	open	closed
Number of Required Subjects	6–7	1[a]	6–7	4[b]	6–7	6–7	6[c]	2[d]
Duration (hours) of a typical written test	1.67[e]	3	up to 4	4–5	1.67	±3	various[c]	0.5[d]
Duration (hours) of total exam in required subjects	11	6[a]	20–24	13–14	10	±15[f]	11.5[c]	3[d]

a. An A-level candidate need take only one subject. There is no compulsory subject. For each subject there are usually at least two papers, hence the total of six given on the bottom line. Candidates normally offer two or three subjects (although there is no requirement to do so, and candidates may offer subjects at intervals of six months, a year, or longer), in which case total examination time will amount to about ten hours.

b. Of the four required subjects, one is taken as an oral, lasting about thirty minutes.

c. Language/literature paper is six hours; mathematics, four hours. There are four oral examinations of about twenty minutes each, for a total of about eleven and a half hours.

d. Figures refer to the Scholastic Aptitude Test, the most widely taken end-of-secondary-school examination. The SAT tests language and mathematical skills (that is, two "subjects") in six sections of thirty minutes each. The ACT is similar in total length. Achievement Tests in subjects (the so-called "College Boards") are one hour long.

e. The language examination lasts for two and a half hours; the examinations in the other subjects last a hundred minutes.

f. Different "lines" of study have different requirements for the number of subjects. There is no "final" examination in Sweden. Instead, the various subject examinations are given over the final two years of senior high school.

Figure 3. The Burden of Examination Requirements: Comparative Scale

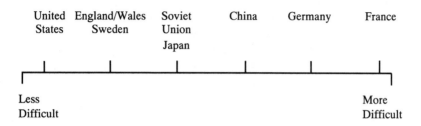

focus here is not merely on isolated facts. Rather it stresses cognitive structures, that is, recognizing the relationships among facts, understanding causes and consequences, and applying knowledge to new facts or groups of facts. Such activities demand a higher order of cognitive skills, and we judge that questions seeking to elicit such skills represent a higher order of difficulty.

We distinguish among three categories of questions that demand such higher-order cognitive skills: those that call, respectively, for comprehension, application, and analysis. The first category involves understanding and interpretation of old and new material, based upon routine operations usually practiced earlier with familiar subject matter. The second and third types of questions, calling for application and analysis, require a longer series of mental steps and treatment of unfamiliar material. Answers involve decision-making and problem-solving tasks. For example, what data and techniques are appropriate to reach valid conclusions in this instance? In particular, application questions require transfer of knowledge or concepts learned earlier to new situations.

Both application and analysis questions are "thinking" questions, requiring higher-order cognitive activity. They call for a considered response based upon judgments of what information, steps of analysis, and techniques must be used and test the respondent's capacity to perform these operations. Thus, in a literature test, matching an author with one of his works, identifying the relationship of characters in a play, or explaining the meaning of a phrase or figure of speech are all examples of relatively undemanding questions that involve no more than recognition and recall. In mathematics, the candidate may be asked only to recall and demonstrate knowledge of textbook material—proving a familiar theorem in geometry, recalling standard trigonometrical identities, or citing the implications of particular coefficients in a quadratic equation for the shape and position of a parabola. As will be shown by examples from examination papers in language/literature and mathematics, questions can rise above this level of performance and target far higher levels of mental activity. We provide examples of what we consider to be more and less demanding questions.

Typical examination questions posed in these two subjects have been categorized using the above criteria: we ask, to what extent do the questions address recall, comprehension, application, and/or analysis? And given that an examination paper will call for more than one or two levels of cognitive skill, we ask, what type of question tends to predominate in a country?

National Language/Literature Examination Papers. Results of the analysis of questions asked in end-of-secondary-school language/literature examinations are presented in figure 4.

All papers require some information recall. Most address cognitive structures, at least in part, and some, to varying degrees, require the candidates to exercise the more complex cognitive skills of decision-making and problem-solving, applied to specific subject matter. To the extent that examinations emphasize the more complex cognitive skills and de-emphasize straightforward information recall, they may be considered more difficult, and hence place greater demands on candidates. Examination papers usually include more than one type of question, and the circles around the check marks in figure 4 indicate our judgments of the predominant emphasis of the language/literature tests in each country.

Questions asked of eighteen-year-olds in England/Wales, France, Sweden, and Germany require significant analysis and synthesis in addition to comprehension and application of principles of language and literary criticism.

A-level candidates in England are, in general, expected to have absorbed and to be able to reproduce basic vocabulary, facts, concepts, and explanatory ideas and techniques in the various texts and topics they have studied. As indicated in chapter 5, the questions require a mixture of broad and detailed knowledge and a general understanding of literary styles and forms, to be demonstrated and applied with reference to some selected works. Candidates are evaluated, too, on their mastery of the written word and especially on their capacity to express themselves in extended, connected prose. A relatively undemanding question in literature will cite a short passage from a Shakespeare set play, asking candidates to render a few lines into plain modern English and to describe its context, the characters involved, or its dramatic/literary style. A more demanding question, based on *King Lear,* may call for an extended discussion of one of the

Figure 4. Difficulty of Examination Content: Language/Literature

	China	England/Wales	France	Germany	Japan	Sweden	Soviet Union	United States
Recall	(✓)	✓	✓	✓	✓	✓	(✓)	✓
Comprehension	✓	✓	✓	✓	(✓)	✓	✓	(✓)
Application	✓	✓	✓	✓	✓	(✓)	✓	✓
Analysis/Synthesis		(✓)	(✓)	(✓)		✓		

following themes: "a play founded on contradictions—fools are wise, the blind can see, and love shows like hate" or "the importance of the mingling of lust with lust for power as a source of dramatic tension."[1]

Candidates in France must apply a series of quite specific language usage techniques—writing a précis, formulating definitions, composing a brief essay, or producing a more extended *commentaire composé* or a literary essay. A relatively simple, minor question from the précis option calls for an explanation, in context, of a phrase from the extract provided. The commentaire composé option presents the candidate with a more difficult task. The question presents a poem or prose extract followed by the words, "Write a commentaire composé." One or two suggested discussion points are given. The candidate must then write an organized critique of the piece, including detailed analysis of the text and the literary techniques employed by the author, the relation of the techniques to the content, an analysis of the theme(s) and sentiments presented, a discussion, where appropriate, of the historical and social setting, and a personal appreciation of the work.

In addition to the written paper, all candidates must take an oral examination. Each submits a list of the works of literature studied in and out of school. The examiner then selects a few lines of prose or poetry from one of the works, and the candidate has some fifteen minutes to prepare a brief *lecture expliqué* explaining the passage and commenting on its linguistic and literary form and qualities. Further questions are asked to extend the scope of discussion to other works, genres, and literary themes. Overall, the language/literature examination assesses a candidate's application of a general, logical system of critical evaluation to a literary work or event and probes the extent to which answers embody a sense of French culture.

Examination questions in Germany resemble those found in France. Typically, an essay question provides, an extract, for example, a poem by Heine and a paragraph on Heine's work from a historical review of German literature, and asks the candidate to analyze the poem and to critically evaluate the methods and theoretical basis of the review.[2] A question from a *Grundkurs* paper is somewhat less demanding, giving a prose extract and asking candidates to analyze the main and subsidiary themes, describe the characters, review the language and literary devices used, and assess the author's purposes and methods of achieving them. Both Germany and France call for critical analysis of literary works according to a more or less pre-

---

1. Oxford and Cambridge Schools Examination Board, General Certificate Examination, Advanced Level. *English Literature Paper I.* June 13, 1988.

2. *Leistungskurs Deutsch, Abitur-Prüfungsaufgaben Gymnasium* NRW (Freising: Stark, 1983).

scribed system of evaluation. Both require attention to form and content, but there is less concern in Germany than in France with the candidate's personal judgments and appreciation of national culture. As in England/Wales, general and particular knowledge is required, and theme, plot, and character are emphasized.

In Sweden, the national examination questions in language/literature do not in themselves indicate levels of difficulty any more than do those in France and Germany. Candidates receive a set of varied materials to study in advance of the examination, all related to a single broad theme, and a number of essay topics with suggestions on how they might be handled. The topics include many possibilities: writing in a particular literary style for a given audience, discussing the use or meaning of factual content, analyzing and arguing for and against particular points of view, evaluating content and style. It is up to the candidates to choose the topic and the approach and in this way to set individual standards of difficulty.

The Swedish national examination in language/literature is both open-ended and comprehensive. It seeks to assess what students have mastered in a syllabus that stresses the various uses of language, its structure and forms, and the candidates' powers of personal expression. Literature is studied as the changing expression of cultural traditions. The essay is evaluated on the basic skills of comprehension and expression; on the candidates' use of the information, opinions, and insights provided and on how well they incorporate these into their own experience; on skills of reasoning, investigation, and persuasion; and on linguistic and stylistic ability. The highest grades are awarded to candidates who meet all the criteria to a high degree and who in addition demonstrate creativity and good literary style.

Examination questions in Japan require mastery of a good deal of factual material, but the candidates are also expected to demonstrate their ability to interpret, apply, and analyze. The multiple-choice format does not allow for the kind of performance required by an open-ended essay, but the questions asked in the Japanese examination paper are varied. For example, substituting one written character for another, matching a poet with a particular poetic style, and choosing the best definition for a term are all relatively straightforward tasks, simply requiring enough knowledge to choose the best of several answers. More difficult questions require candidates to show greater comprehension and finer discrimination by selecting the best critique of a poem or the best explanation of a character's motives.

Although markedly concerned with recall, examinations in China and the Soviet Union also test some comprehension and application. In China questions tend to focus on formal aspects of the subject, with relatively little application to actual situations. Simple questions call for repetition of memorized sentences from texts studied in school and word or phrase definitions, but more difficult questions on a prose extract, for example, test understanding of the author's language usage and writing style or require a brief composition on the extract's theme. In the Soviet Union great emphasis is placed on national language and literature, especially that of Russia. For non-Russian candidates, skill in the Russian language takes precedence over knowledge of Russian literature. Questions in Soviet examinations tend to favor recall of material contained in standard textbooks, rather than the ability to craft individually justified answers, and the ideological content of literary works receives prime attention. A written essay will be complemented by an oral examination in which the candidate picks, sight unseen, one of over twenty cards, each with two questions to be answered. Each card is likely to contain a question selected from eighteenth- and nineteenth-century literature, as well as on the Soviet period. Students are expected to be able to discourse on aspects of the works of Pushkin, Turgenev, Dostoyevski, Tolstoy, or Chekhov and address such topics as Gorky's early revolutionary-romantic works, their artistic uniqueness, and the direction of the ideals expressed; civic motives in contemporary Soviet poetry; the moral cast of mind of the worker-toiler and war in Sholokhov's works; or the problem of historical memory in contemporary Soviet literature. In the non-Russian republics, even before perestroika, curriculum design and the content of examination questions reflected local, national literature, insofar as it was not considered antagonistic to Soviet power and ideals. Once again, as with the Swedish example, it is not possible to discriminate between easy and hard questions when they are briefly stated as essay topics. These topics are by no means open-ended, however, and are intended to be answered using general textbook material.

Finally, the form and content of standardized tests in the United States place a premium on a candidate's ability to choose the right answer rapidly from among a number of possibilities. Candidates in the SAT are asked to recognize information rather than to produce it, since this test deliberately seeks to avoid textbook-based, previously taught material. Although the College Board Achievement Tests do in fact emphasize previously taught material, the questions seek to assess comprehension and the ability to recognize and recall what has been learned, rather than to elicit thoughtful analysis. Common, rather simple, questions in the language examination ask candidates to identify incorrect grammar or usage in a sentence, for example, "He spoke *bluntly* and *angrily* to *we spectators*,"[3] or to rephrase a statement without changing its meaning, by choosing the best of several alternative answers. In place of twenty such questions, candidates may choose an essay question. Candidates are given a topic on which to write (for example, "The more things change, the more they stay the same") and directions on how to approach it, such as, "To what extent do you agree or disagree? . . . Consider how you might apply the saying to a field such as history, literature, art, music . . ." Since no more than twenty minutes are allowed for the essay, candidates have little opportunity for extensive work. The directions acknowledge this with the advice, "How well you write is more important than how much you write, but to cover the topic adequately you may want to write more than one paragraph."[4]

A simple question on the College Board Literature test asks candidates to read a short passage and select which phrase best describes its language: concise syntax, abundance of metaphors, florid diction, coherent organization, regular rhythm. A slightly more difficult question offers two answers in each of five possible choices, asking candidates to exclude the pair that does not apply. The literature test does not elicit critical opinions about a particular work, nor does it require specialized knowledge of authors or periods. Designed to test skill in reading and understanding literary extracts and familiarity with a limited, basic literary terminology, it is limited to comprehension, recall of terms, and application of terms to given extracts.

Mathematics Examination Papers. As with national language/literature examinations, the difficulty of individual mathematics examinations depends upon the kind of competence demanded. Do the questions solely or largely ask for recall and repetition of standard items learned from textbooks and teachers? Or is the emphasis more on questions demanding analysis of the nature of the problem posed, selection of the most appropriate means of solution, and correct application of those means? The latter are clearly more difficult.

In addition, the scope of the questions in mathematics provides another dimension for this comparison of difficulty. We noted in the previous chapter that taking all eight countries together, mathematics syllabi at the upper secondary level cover six broad areas: arithmetic functions, algebra, coor-

3. College Entrance Examination Board, *The College Board Achievement Tests: Fourteen Tests in Thirteen Subjects* (New York: College Entrance Examination Board, 1983).
    4. Ibid., p. 21.

dinate and plane geometry, trigonometry, differential and integral calculus, and probability and statistics, but that not every country requires all of these areas. "Difficulty" then arises in two major respects. First, how many and which of the areas is the candidate expected to know? Second, is the candidate expected to have an elementary, intermediate, or advanced acquaintance with a particular area?

Figure 5 presents an analysis of the eight countries' examination papers in mathematics along these lines. As in figure 4, the predominant emphasis in each nation is indicated by circling a check mark.

Secondary-school-leaving examinations in mathematics in England/Wales and Germany contain very difficult material, though it is important to remember that in these countries the papers are intended for students choosing mathematics as one of their examination subjects. In France, too, a senior secondary school student can opt for a série that will involve a very demanding mathematics paper.

In England/Wales, even though candidates (or their schools) have a wide choice among many different types of examination syllabi and tests, all of the tests present markedly difficult material and span a wide range of topics. In pure mathematics, an example of a compulsory simpler question is:

Determine the range of values of x in each of the following cases:
$x^2 > 3$, and $2 / (x - 2) > 1$.

Perhaps a little more difficult compulsory question is:

Solve the equation $\sin x + 3\cos x = \sqrt{10}$, for $0° < x < 360°$.

At the other end of the difficulty range are questions in a second section of the test, in which the candidate must choose to answer four out of seven questions given. A typical question has the following sections:

O is the origin and A is the point on $y = \tan x$ where $x = \pi/3$.
Calculate the area enclosed by the chord OA and the arc OA of the curve.
Calculate also the volume of the solid formed when this area is rotated through 4 right angles about the x-axis.[5]

The questions on applied mathematics tests are all demanding, but the candidate is usually given a wide choice. In June 1987, the Southern Universities' Joint Board Applied Mathematics Paper 1 offered twenty questions, half in mechanics, half in statistics. Candidates were instructed to

5. Southern Universities' Joint Board, GCE Advanced Level, Pure Mathematics 1, June 10, 1987.

Figure 5. Difficulty of Examination Content: Mathematics

	China	England/Wales	France	Germany	Japan	Sweden	Soviet Union	United States
Recall	⊘	✓	✓	✓	✓	✓	✓	✓
Application	✓	✓	✓	✓	⊘	✓	✓	⊘
Analysis/Synthesis	✓	⊘	⊘	⊘	✓	✓	✓	✓
Number of Areas	4	5	5	2–3	5	2–3	4	2–4

answer not more than seven, of which no more than three could come from statistics. A mechanics questions is:

A particle A of mass m is attached to a particle B of mass $2m$ by a light inextensible string of length a. The particles lie at rest on a frictionless horizontal plane and A is projected toward B with speed u. If the coefficient of restitution between the particles is 3/4, show that the direction of motion of A is reversed after impact with B.

Find:

(i) the speeds of A and B immediately after the string tightens;
(ii) the magnitude of the impulsive tension in the string;
(iii) the time that elapses between the impact and the tightening of the string;
(iv) the total loss of energy due to the impact and tightening of the string.

A question from the statistics section reads:

X_i $(i = 1, 2, \ldots n)$ are n random variables each distributed normally with mean μ and variance o^2. If $Y = X_1 + X_2 + \ldots + X_n$ state precisely the distribution of Y.[6]

As we noted in the previous chapter, candidates may opt to take the S (or Special) paper, which tests mathematical skill and knowledge at a yet higher level.

In France, a minority of candidates take the difficult test; there are less difficult tests for candidates in the nonmathematics and nonscience séries, and these marks are less heavily weighted in the total result. Unlike the test in England/Wales, the baccalauréat tests in mathematics do not normally provide a choice of questions: all are compulsory. Here is one of the simpler questions taken from the 1990 baccalauréat examinations set for candidates in série A1 in the south of France. The question can earn three points out of the maximum possible twenty points for the entire examination:

For the following equations (reals only):

a) $t^3 - 4t = 0$, solve for t.
b) $(\ln x)^3 - 4\ln x = 0$, solve for x.
c) $e^{3x} = 4e^x$, solve for x.

6. Southern Universities' Joint Board GCE Advanced Level, Applied Mathematics 1, June 15, 1987.

The second section of the paper is a question involving techniques of coordinate geometry. An even more difficult third section offers a lengthy, two-part problem carrying twelve of the twenty points. The first part of this section requires the candidate to integrate the function

$F(x) = 1/e^x (x^2 + x)$

and to determine various probabilities of a point falling in particular sections of the area under the curve. The second part presents the superimposed graphs of two curves:

$g(x) = e^{-x}$, and $h(x) = f(x) - g(x)$

and requires the candidate to answer four questions covering the roots, derivative, and range of $h(x)$, as well as the range of

$| f(x) - e^{-x} |$, for $x >= 0.$[7]

We have noted that in Germany mathematics can be offered at the basic (Grund) or advanced (Leistungs) level, but even at the basic level the German mathematics examination contains difficult material. In Bavaria, for example, three questions are to be answered in three hours, one each from calculus, analytic geometry, and probability. In 1988, the calculus question in the Grund examination presented the logarithmic functions:

$h(x) = \ln (x^2/4 + 1)$, and $f(x) = \ln (x^2/4)$

Among other tasks, a series of questions required the candidate to report on the symmetry of the curves about the x- and y-axes; to figure values of extrema; to evaluate the functions for different values of x; to investigate the behavior of the functions as x goes to 0; to sketch the graphs; and to demonstrate that the length of a segment of a line intercepting one of the curves at two points equals a specified quantity. The questions on probability are similarly demanding.[8]

The three-question format of the Leistungkurs paper is similar to that of the Grundkurs, but the questions are significantly more difficult. For example, one of the two calculus questions given in the 1985 examination moves quickly from a section dealing with the determination of intercepts of the function $(1 - x^2) / 2(2 - x)$ to requiring a proof that the function is equal to another (except for $x = 2$). There follow items on the asymptotes

7. Marie-Dominique Danion and Marc Gourion, *Sujets 90 Corrigés: Maths: Terminales A/B* (Paris: Editions Nathan, 1990).

8. *Grundkurs Mathematik: Abitur Prüfungsaufgaben Gymnasium-Bayern,* 11th ed. (Freising: Stark, 1988). pp. 88–1, 88–12.

and absolute values of the function; on confirmation "that the points of the curve with horizontal tangents lie on the bisector of the angle of the first and third quadrants"; on sketching the graph of the function; and on calculating the value of a definite integral.[9]

A student in the oral calculus examination might be asked:

Find $z > 0$, so that

$$\int_1^z \frac{1}{x}\, dx = \int_1^z \ln x\, dx$$

and provide a geometrical meaning for this equality.[10]

Although one can find differences in difficulty of the mathematics papers among England/Wales, France, and Germany, in general their levels are very comparable—and demanding.

Much like France, Japan offers different types (and levels) of mathematics tests to candidates with different specializations. But there is a common core (Mathematics 1). The questions in this core are less difficult than the ones just reviewed, though still demanding. For example, a question gives two quadratic equations:

$$2x^2 - 2ax - a + 1 = 0 \qquad\qquad \ldots \ldots 1$$
$$x^2 - 2(a-1)x - 2a + 1 = 0 \qquad\qquad \ldots \ldots 2$$

and asks the candidate to demonstrate that equation 1 has more than one solution, given that $a = AB \pm \sqrt{C}$. The roots of equation 2 are to be found, and the candidate is then required to identify the roots of equations 1 and 2 combined, given that the values of a and x in the two equations are the same.

Another question defines a triangle with sides of length 5 units and 8 units, and an included angle of 60 degrees. The candidate is asked to calculate the area of the triangle and the cosine of a nonincluded angle. The question then goes on to describe the triangle folded down on a line joining two points, one on each side of the triangle, so that an apex touches a midpoint of the third side. The lengths of three line segments are then to be specified: from the apex to the midpoint; and from each of the endpoints of the fold-down line to the midpoint.

Apart from the common core, each variant of the JFSAT mathematics

9. *Leistungskurs Mathematik: Abitur Prüfungsaufgaben Gymnasium-Bayern,* 11th ed. (Freising: Stark, 1988), pp. 85–86.

10. Kultusminister des Landes Nordrhein-Westfalen. *Gymnasiale Oberstufe: Richtlinien Mathematik,* (Düsseldorf: Kultusminister des Landes Nordrhein-Westfalen, 1981), pp. 144, 149–150.

test has a second section. The questions in this section are at least more specialized, and usually more difficult, than those in the common core. For example, a Mathematics 2 question involving probability in the standard (nonspecialized) mathematics paper cites four teams, A, B, C, and D, playing a tournament. They are paired in three different ways: the winner of A versus B playing the winner of C versus D; the winner of A versus C playing the winner of B versus D; and the winner of A versus D playing the winner of B versus C. It is known that the probability of A winning the final is 1/3 and that the probability of C beating D is 1/2. There are no draws. The candidate is then asked to calculate the probabilities of A, B, or C winning the tournament in the various pairings.

Questions in the common core are all at about the same level of difficulty; similarly the questions in the more specialized sections. In all instances, the level of difficulty is high, but the questions are somewhat less demanding than in England/Wales, France, or Germany. Whatever the Japanese system might lose in establishing a somewhat lower level of difficulty in its mathematics examination for seventeen- and eighteen-year olds, however, it more than gains by ensuring that a higher proportion of the age group studies for and takes mathematics examinations than in England/Wales or Germany.

Written examinations in mathematics for secondary school leavers in the Soviet Union are formulated locally on the basis of syllabus topics distributed by the central education authorities for each Soviet republic. The mathematics examinations to enter institutions of higher education tend to pose significantly more difficult questions than do the school-based leaving examinations.[11]

Overall, in China, the university entrance examination in mathematics is about as difficult as the attestat examinations in the Soviet Union, perhaps a little easier. Short-answer questions cover standard textbook material. For example, from the test given in Zhejiang province in 1987:

Evaluate: $\dfrac{(1+i)^2}{i^3}$

---

11. Specific questions from written examination papers in the Soviet Union are not cited here. Unlike in the case of other countries, our assessment of mathematics examination papers is based on secondary materials from various sources, including examples cited by Nellie Apanasewicz, *Final Examinations in the Russian Ten-Year School* (Washington, D.C.: U.S. Department of Health, Education, and Welfare, 1966); and James Muckle, *A Guide to the Soviet Curriculum: What the Russian Child Is Taught in School* (London: Croom Helm, 1988). We also used questions from oral examinations. Mathematics questions from attestat examinations in Russian schools are reproduced in the Appendix.

and:

> Given two points, A and B, with coordinates $(-1, 2)$ and $(-10, -1)$, respectively, find the length and slope of the line segment AB.

No questions as easy as these appear on the mathematics test in England/Wales, France, or Germany, nor do the papers in these countries' examinations break down the candidate's work into such discrete, small items. The questions become harder however, as the test progresses. For example, two branches of a hyperbola are shown, together with specified points on the curves and the axes. The candidate is required to prove certain relationships among the points and to prove that a given angle is a right angle.

But such complex and difficult questions are not characteristic of the mathematics papers in China. The result is that marks tend to bunch up toward the top end of the scale, weakening the discriminating power of the examination. Indeed, critics charge that the papers must be made more difficult if they are to identify effectively the few really high achievers to whom a place should be awarded from among the mass of candidates who, although capable, cannot be accommodated in higher education.

In Sweden, students completing two- or three-year upper secondary school courses take a combination of locally and centrally provided tests in mathematics, but the range and difficulty level of the papers vary with the particular line, or curriculum, followed. Our discussion focuses on the centrally provided tests. In general, the questions are at a modest level of difficulty. For example, students in the natural sciences/technology lines in 1987 were given a test that opened with the following question:

> A sphere has the same volume as a cube of side 2.58m. Find the radius of the sphere.

A more difficult question involves integration of the expression $y = 6 - (x^2 / 6)$ and its use in calculating the value of a particular intercept on the y-axis, given some data about the volume formed by rotation of a segment about the y-axis.[12] Somewhat curiously, in the test for these students there is a marked absence of practical problems to be solved. Considering the specialization of the candidates, the examination is relatively undemanding.

For those studying the social sciences and economics, the mathematics test contains even less difficult material. There is no coordinate geometry,

12. Centralt Prov Matematik Ak 3 NT 1987-10-22.

no calculus, and no probability/statistics. The level of knowledge required in algebra and trigonometry is elementary. What is stressed instead is what may be called "business mathematics": compound interest, present value, and descriptive statistics. Questions are generally cast in a practical problem mode. No very deep mathematical thinking is required to answer the questions correctly. A simple question, for example, provides the candidate with average scores for three school classes (2.83, 2.69, and 3.38), together with the size of each class (21, 16, and 31, respectively), and asks for the average score overall. A more difficult question states:

X kg. of coffee costing A kroner/kg. were blended with Y kg. of coffee costing B kroner/kg. Give an expression for the cost per kg. of the blend.

Calculus is represented at the following elementary level:

Find the maximum and minimum points on the curve: $y = 3x^2 - x^3 + 1$. Draw the curve.[13]

Thus we place Sweden toward the less difficult end of the continuum represented by the eight countries.

In the United States, students taking the SAT are faced with some exceptionally simple questions often involving a comparison of the size of quantities. For example, one question along these lines gives the two fractions 1,058/23 and 1,058/46. Which is larger? Another gives the two time periods "12 minutes less than 3 hours" and "2 5/6 hours." Which is larger? Only a very few questions could be termed somewhat difficult, for example:

If x, y, and z are three positive whole numbers and $x > y > z$, then, of the following, which is closest to the product xyz?

(A) $(x-1)yz$ (B) $x(y-1)z$ (C) $xy(z-1)$
(D) $x(y+1)z$ (E) $xy(z+1)$.

Placed in a comparative international perspective, the content of the mathematics section of the SAT is elementary.[14]

As with the SAT, the content of the mathematics section of the ACT can hardly be considered demanding for students coming to the end of twelve years of education:

13. Centralt Prov Matematik Ak 3 SE 1988-02-03.
14. Admissions Testing Program of the College Board. 5 SATs (Princeton, N.J.: Educational Testing Service, 1981), pp. 85, 87.

In a certain city, the assessed value of a house is 40% of the house's market value, and the property tax is 3.8% of the assessed value. What is the property tax on a house with a market value of $60,000?
A. $520.00   B $912.00   C. $1,520.00
D. $2,280.00   E. $9,120.00.

Trigonometry does not go beyond presenting a right triangle having two other interior angles of 40 and 50 degrees, with one of the sides adjacent to the right angle being 4 units long. The candidate is asked to find the length of the other side adjacent to the right angle and is given the usual five options from which to choose. Even at its most difficult, coordinate geometry is represented by a question showing a scaled graph of an ellipse centered on the origin and asking the student to choose the correct equation for the ellipse from among the five options given.[15]

Level 1 of the College Board Achievement Test in mathematics is comparable in difficulty to the Swedish test for the social science/economics line; Level 2 compares with the Swedish natural sciences/technology test. For example:

Three vertices of a cube, no two of which lie on the same edge, are joined to form a triangle. If an edge of the cube has length 1, what is the area of the triangle?

(A) $\dfrac{\sqrt{6}}{2}$ (B) $\dfrac{\sqrt{3}}{2}$ (C) $\dfrac{\sqrt{2}}{2}$ (D) $\dfrac{\sqrt{6}}{4}$ (E) $\dfrac{\sqrt{3}}{4}$

and,

The graph of $y = 3 + \cos 2x$ intersects the Y-axis at the point where $y =$
(A) 0   (B) 1   (C) 3   (D) 4   (E) 5.[16]

Because few American students take it, we do not include the Advanced Placement test in mathematics in our considerations. In the previous chapter, we described mathematics for Advanced Placement as quite limited in its scope (mostly calculus, with some trigonometry in one of the options), but within those limits, we judge the questions to be comparable in level of difficulty to those in the JFSAT Mathematics 2 section in Japan. More-

15. American College Testing Program. *Preparing for the ACT Assessment* (Iowa City, Iowa: American College Testing Program, 1989), pp. 17, 19.

16. College Entrance Examination Board. *The College Board Achievement Tests: Fourteen Tests in Thirteen Subjects* (New York: College Entrance Examination Board, 1983), pp. 245–283.

over, unlike the other external mathematics examinations in the United States, the format of the Advanced Placement test is not exclusively short-answer, multiple-choice. Instead, it includes a section of extended-answer, "free-response" questions taking up half the total examination.

An example of a multiple-choice question is:

The normal to the curve represented by the equation $y = x^2 + 6x + 4$ at the point $(-2, -4)$ also intersects the curve at $x =$

(A) -6 (B) $-9/2$ (C) $-7/2$ (D) -3 (E) $-1/2$.

The questions rapidly become more difficult. For example:

For all real b, $\int_0^b |2x|\, dx$ is

(A) $-b|b|$ (B) b^2 (C) $-b^2$ (D) $b|b|$
(E) none of the above.

A free-response question might cite a region enclosed by an axis, a line parallel to the other axis, and a line formed by a logarithmic function. The candidate is asked to determine the area of the region and to find the volume of the solid generated by revolving the region about the x-axis.

Basing our evaluation on the SAT, ACT, and Achievement Tests only, however, we consider that mathematics examinations in the United States are the least demanding of all eight countries.[17]

To summarize these comparative judgments on a scale from most to least difficult, we place national mathematics examinations in the following order: most demanding are those of England/Wales, France, and Germany; next comes Japan, followed by China and the Soviet Union. We consider that overall Sweden offers somewhat easier papers and the United States the least difficult, except for the Advanced Placement examination.

Difficulty of Language/Literature and Mathematics Examinations

Figure 6 summarizes these judgments, combining each nation's language/literature and mathematics examinations on a single scale of relative difficulty.

Although our analysis showed differences from one country to another in the amount of attention given to recall of memorized material, comprehension, and applications of knowledge, the major discriminating factor

17. It is important to remember that the SAT does not claim to be a direct test of school achievement, though the ACT is a little more forthcoming in this respect.

Figure 6. Difficulty of Examination Content in Language/Literature and Math Comparative Scale

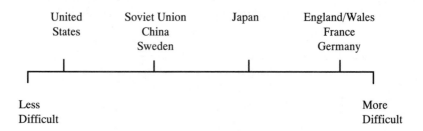

was whether the examination papers include questions testing such higher-order cognitive skills as analysis, synthesis, and evaluation. In mathematics, this means questions that require solutions to complex problems, involving several steps and choices among alternative paths of reasoning. In language and literature, such questions require using appropriate and often creative language, as well as critical appreciation and evaluation of a wide variety of genres and individual works. We found that these more difficult tasks were virtually absent from the examination papers in some countries, whereas they accounted for a large number of the questions in others. Moreover, there is a strong positive relationship between difficulty levels in the two subjects.

Discussion and Conclusions

Examination systems are most demanding when students must bear a heavy load of required subjects and lengthy tests and when the questions call for high-level cognitive skills as well as detailed and broad knowledge. Open-ended essay questions in language/literature papers and "free-response" problem-solving exercises in mathematics are generally more demanding, we consider, than multiple-choice, fill-in the-blanks questions and short answers. Given all these criteria, the examinations in France and Germany stand out among the eight nations as placing the heaviest burdens on candidates. (See figure 7.)

By contrast, candidates in Sweden and the United States face far easier tasks. In Sweden, as a matter of policy, graduation from upper secondary school and entrance into higher education are based only in part on examinations, and pressure on students is deliberately reduced by spreading examinations at intervals over the final two or three years of upper secondary

Figure 7. Overall Difficulty of Examinations: Comparative Scale

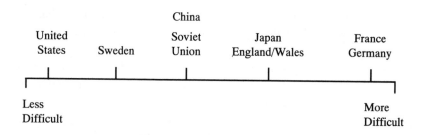

school. Students in the United States, as in Sweden, do not depend only (or, in many instances, largely) on examination results for entrance to college. In comparative perspective, the Achievement Tests, and the commonly taken SAT and ACT, are exceptionally undemanding with respect to content, format, and other requirements. Examination papers in the United States contain difficult content only for the very small proportion of the age group who take Advanced Placement examinations, though, even here, there are no required subjects. In both Sweden and the United States, school-based testing and teacher evaluations complement the results of the nationally recognized examinations when college-admission decisions are made about individual students.

Advanced-level GCE candidates in England/Wales face a set of very demanding examinations, but they have considerable discretion over how hard they wish them to be, depending on the number and type of subjects they select and the level of difficulty they choose. We therefore rate that system as less burdensome for candidates than those of France and Germany, though overall substantially more difficult than the United States and Sweden.

The examination system in Japan, we judge, also lies in an intermediate position. The content and format of examination papers may not be as demanding as those of France, Germany, and England/Wales, but the examination requirements are notably burdensome. Moreover, the exceptionally high degree of attention paid to individual results, and the associated parental, school, and social pressures to perform well, place severe stress on many students.

Students in the Soviet Union and in China also carry a considerable burden of requirements, but have a relatively easy task with respect to content. However, because of external circumstances (social pressure, shortage of places) they too are under great pressure to perform well. We therefore locate these nations also in an intermediate position, but on the less demanding side of Japan and England/Wales.

Several general observations are in order after making these judgments on the burdens that the several examination systems place on candidates. First, it has been noted that an assessment system reflects the goals and expectations of an educational system. Examination syllabi and question papers embody society's understanding not only of what knowledge is of most worth, but also of what burdens can appropriately be placed upon candidates. Second, the examination papers differ in the demands they place on candidates; obviously some questions are harder than others, and certain cognitive demands are "objectively" greater. But the comparative exercise we have performed in this chapter underscores the difficulty of specifying the "objective" difficulty of an examination. The content of question papers is but one element in determining level of difficulty, since the associated regulations governing the number of required subjects, the timing and duration of examination sessions, and the type of format are all part of the challenge to candidates. Conversely, we should remember that the hardest of all questions for the examinee are those requiring knowledge and skills that have *not* been studied! Moreover, even the most challenging and profound open-ended question may trigger no more than an exercise in recall if the student has been well drilled. In France, for example, candidates may have been so extensively rehearsed in the techniques of producing a lecture expliqué, or a formal composition on literary history and criticism, that to deliver such a presentation in the examination, complete with illustrative examples and suitable citations, may require less in the way of high-order cognitive activity than might be supposed at first glance. Thus the simple inquiry "How hard are the examinations?" turns out to be not so simple to answer persuasively.

We conclude with a final, policy-related point. Use of comparative data on the relative difficulty of examination systems can be seriously misleading unless it is informed by an appreciation of the school and social context within which those examination systems operate. Policies designed to make "esay" examinations more demanding, or to reduce the difficulty of "hard" examinations, will inevitably have consequences for the entire educational system of a nation. Sometimes those consequences are quite unexpected. Policymakers who are interested in minimizing such surprises are advised to study carefully the different experiences that other countries have had with their various difficulty levels of examinations.

In later chapters we will consider some of the causes and consequences of efforts to change examination systems, the issues raised, and the policy choices to be confronted. But before proceeding to discussion of these matters, we present another approach to estimating the burden that national systems of secondary-school-completion examinations place on candidates. The next chapter contains a comparison of rates of examination success among the nations, opening the way to discussion of the status of examinations and the value of their associated credentials.

Chapter 8

Academic Success Rates: Causes and Consequences

In serving writs I made such a name
That an articled clerk I soon became;
I wore clean collars and a brand new suit
For the pass examination at the Institute.
   And that pass examination did so well for me,
   That now I am the Ruler of the Queen's Navee!
—The Rt. Hon. Sir Joseph Porter, K.C.B., *H.M.S. Pinafore,* act 1

Success rates are important because they throw light on the relation between the school system and the rest of society, indicating how wide the doors to subsequent opportunity are. This chapter presents a cross-national review of success at the end of secondary school and the characteristics that help explain the differences among countries. As we proceed, we will discuss the reputation, or status, of credentials obtained through those examinations, some of the rewards for success, and the consequences of failure.

Students who finish their secondary school studies with "success" typically pass some examination, receive a diploma, and/or are rewarded for their achievement with a place, scholarship, or fellowship in higher education. The specific token of success, and more particularly the specific token of "high success," varies from country to country. In England/Wales, Japan, the Soviet Union, and the United States, the offer of a place at a prestigious university is the standard signal of high success. In France it is a good aggregate mark (say, seventeen out of a possible twenty) in one of the more difficult séries of the baccalauréat, followed by admission into a *classe préparatoire* for entry into one of the grandes écoles. In Germany high success is associated with gaining a place in medical or dental studies, or elsewhere where numerus clausus limitations are applied, whereas young people in China, given the scarcity of college and university places there relative to the demand for them, view admission to virtually any university as evidence of great success.

While everyone cannot be highly successful, lesser degrees of success may be perfectly satisfactory to those who achieve them. In that sense, success resides in the eye of the beholder. A marginal pass in the examination, when everyone, including perhaps even the candidate, expected a failing grade, may be hailed as a fine achievement. For some individuals, particularly those coming from low-income, low-status families, simply remaining in secondary school through the final year is enough to mark them as academic successes.[1] They will display their completion diploma with justifiable pride, no matter that others might regard its academic content and level as meager.[2] At the other extreme, there are those for whom "only the best will do," giving rise to the phenomenon in the United States and Japan of senior-year students in secondary school equipped with stellar SAT or JFSAT scores viewing themselves as failures because Harvard, Princeton, or Yale, or Todai or Kyoto University, has turned down their application for admission.

For these reasons, to define an objective cross-national and interpersonal standard of success is hardly possible; and if we are to construct measures of success for the purpose of comparison, we are forced to make some fairly subjective decisions as to what we will count as success in each country.

Certainly, in those countries where there is a national, external examination in school subjects taken by most senior-year secondary school students, passing the examination is the standard signal of success. This is so in England/Wales with A levels, in France with the baccalauréat, in Germany with the Abitur, and in the Soviet Union with the examinations confirming the award of the attestat zrelosti. Indeed, it is difficult to overstate the significance of externally regulated examinations taken at or toward the end of secondary school. Although some countries give them a more central place in national life than others, external end-of-secondary-school examinations are never considered merely routine. As economic and social life becomes more formal and bureaucratized, schools are drawn to fit their procedures to the surrounding society. Certificates of completion of a course of study become valuable pieces of property, and examinations are a means to ensure that such certificates reflect degrees of learning rather than merely attendance. Success in the examinations is universally regarded as a validation of and reward for effort and ability, as a door opened to further educational and employment opportunities, and as a predictor of future success. In this way, examination systems function as gatekeepers. Rather

1. Some philanthropists in the United States have offered to pay the college expenses of students who stay on to complete secondary school, thus implicitly defining "success" as not dropping out.

2. There are, of course, those reports of Indian secondary school graduates who are quite happy to announce that their highest credential reads, "Failed London University Matriculation."

than simply evaluate candidates, they control the overall number of individuals who are to receive the reward called success and its inherent opportunities. Moreover, not having the opportunity to take examinations or, perhaps even worse, taking them and failing, can be a very serious matter indeed, likely to deprive a young person of major educational, social, and economic benefits.

In some societies, those in charge of examination systems may decide to exercise very tight control over pass rates, limiting them severely in order to fit the number of "successes" to the number of subsequent opportunities; in other systems, more lenient standards may be applied as part of conscious policy. Cutoff points, pass rates, and success, therefore, should never be regarded as objective standards given to examiners by the state of human knowledge or springing from the natural order of the world. Rather, they are more accurately viewed as deliberate choices, designed to help achieve certain specific, even if unstated, goals.

The ways in which examination results are reported differ from country to country. In England/Wales, France, and Germany, candidates are informed whether they have passed or not, and they receive a grade or score indicating how well they have done. In China a student's aggregate university entrance examination score is either above or below the cutoff point, adjusted each year to produce the number of freshmen desired by the central and provincial authorities. For these four countries, we can cite relatively unambiguous success rates. In the United States and Japan a score is provided, but with no indication whether this represents a passing grade or not; that judgment is left to college admission offices. In the Soviet Union, examinations graded three and above on the five-point scale are deemed to be passing, but both there and in Japan after the first examinations, candidates for higher education usually take a second-stage examination set by each university. Thus, for these three countries and for Sweden, any measure of success must refer principally to college or university entrance, rather than to examination pass rates. This difference should be kept in mind as we describe success rates among the eight countries.

Comparative Academic Success

Whether we are citing examination pass rates or rates of admission to higher education, success rates can be figured in three ways: with respect to the number of candidates, with respect to the number of students enrolled in the relevant grade level, and with respect to the size of the relevant age cohort. The first ratio, the number of passes as a percentage of the number of candidates, is the conventional formulation of the success rate. But this figure indicates only how wide or narrow the road to success is *once an individual is admitted to take the examination*. For this reason, comparisons based solely on the ratio of passes to candidates can be quite deceptive. Retention rates at the upper secondary level and the policies governing who is permitted, or obliged, to take the examinations differ widely among nations. Different proportions of young people remain in school beyond the compulsory years, and even then not all of them become examination candidates. They may be "prescreened" before the end of upper secondary schooling, sometimes for entrance into upper secondary school, sometimes in the final year or two before the examinations.

In Germany the selection process begins as early as age ten, when pupils are sorted into a tripartite secondary school system; in Japan a critical selection point occurs at age fifteen, with examinations to enter upper secondary school; in England/Wales the GCSE examination at age fifteen or sixteen effectively determines who will continue into upper secondary school and have the opportunity to study for the GCE A-level examinations. In the United States and Sweden, however, the doors to the end-of-secondary-school examinations and the associated credentials are wider than in the other countries and remain open for longer in the student's school career. The second and third ratios acknowledge these differences in practices.

Similarly, in the second group of four countries, where candidates are not explicitly informed whether they have passed, the number of those admitted to college can be figured as a percentage of those applying, as a percentage of those enrolled in the relevant age group, and as a percentage of the entire age cohort.

China. Most young Chinese do not complete upper secondary school, so they never have the chance to sit for the examinations to enter higher education. Even for those who do, the supply of places falls far short of the demand.

Figure 8 underscores how difficult it is to achieve examination success in China, where roughly four out of five candidates in the National Unified College Entrance Examinations will fail. Overall, a mere 2 percent of the age cohort can expect to pass. With tight quotas for each institution and for each faculty, the Chinese are operating a college- and university-wide system of numerus clausus. Success for the individual candidate means achieving a final score above a cutoff point in a fiercely competitive examination. Fractions of a point in the final score can make the difference between success and failure. In consequence, Chinese commentators argue for more difficult and, they hope, more discriminating examinations—even though China is by far the least generous of the eight countries in handing

Figure 8. Probabilities of Success

Higher ◄————————————————————————————————► Lower

United States	Sweden	France	Germany	Japan	England/Wales	Soviet Union	China
No pass/fail examination. Approximately 66 percent of high school graduates enter college.	Secondary-school graduation diploma awarded on basis of achievement test results. Approximately 60 percent of high school graduates enter college.	Approximately 66 percent of baccalauréat candidates receive a passing grade.	Most (over 95 percent) of Abitur candidates receive a passing grade.	No pass/fail examination. Approximately 66 percent of high school graduates enter college.	Approximately 70 percent of A-level candidates receive passing grades.	Virtually all who remain in secondary school through the final year receive a "certificate of maturity."	Approximately 22 percent of candidates gain admission to higher education.
Approximately 66 percent of final-grade enrollment enter college.	Approximately 70 percent of final-grade enrollment enter college.	Approximately 64 percent of final-grade enrollment gain a baccalauréat pass.	Approximately 38 percent of final-grade enrollment gain an Abitur.	Approximately 41 percent of final-grade enrollment enter college.	Approximately 32 percent of final-grade enrollment receive A-level passing grades.	As above.	Approximately 23 percent of final-grade enrollment gain admission to higher education.
Approximately 60 percent of the age cohort enter college.	Approximately 67 percent of the age cohort enter college.	Approximately 33 percent of the age cohort pass the baccalauréat.	Approximately 30 percent of the age cohort gain an Abitur.	Approximately 36 percent of the age cohort enter college.	Approximately 16 percent of the age cohort receive A-level passing grades.	Approximately 18 percent of the age cohort enter higher education.	Approximately 2 percent of the age cohort enter higher education.

Notes and Sources

United States. High school graduates are about 85 percent of the age cohort.

Japan. While the JFSAT is not a pass/fail examination, the second-stage individual university admissions examinations are, in the sense that candidates are either offered or refused admission.

England/Wales. Figures are for at least one subject passed at A level.

Soviet Union. About 18 percent of the age cohort enter all types of higher education: full-time, evening, and correspondence. Ten percent of the age cohort enter full-time day higher education.

China. The figure of 23 percent of final-grade enrollment is higher than the figure of 22 percent of candidates, owing to the large number of repeating candidates.

Primary sources used for calculating percentages:

England/Wales: *Annual Abstract of Statistics 1990*; *Social Trends 20*. London: Central Statistical Office.

France: *Annuaire statistique de la France 1989*. Paris: Institut Nationale de la Statistique et des Etudes Economiques. *Repères et Références Statistiques sur les enseignements et la formation 1988*. Paris: Ministère de l'Education Nationale.

Germany: *Statistisches Jahrbuch 1989*. Bonn: Statistisches Bundesamt für die Bundesrepublik Deutschland. *Grund- und Strukturdaten 1987/88*. Bonn: der Bundesminister für Bildung und Wissenschaft.

Japan: *Japan Statistical Yearbook 1989*. Tokyo: Census Bureau.

China: *Statistical Yearbook of China 1987*. Beijing: State Statistical Bureau of the Peoples Republic of China.

Soviet Union: *USSR: Facts and Figures Annual*, vol. 14 (Gulf Breeze, Fla.: Academic International Press, 1990); *Narodnoe Obrazovanie i Kultura v SSSR: Statisticheskii Sbornik* (Moscow: Finansy i statistiki, 1989).

Sweden: *Statistik årsbok 1990*. Stockholm: Statistika Centralbyron.

United States: *The Condition of Education*; *Digest of Education Statistics 1988*; *Statistical Abstract of the United States*. Washington, D.C.: U.S. Government Printing Office.

Also: *Education in OECD Countries 1986–87, 1987–88*. Paris: Organization for Economic Cooperation and Development.

out success. What is certain is that government policies have made success so difficult to achieve that passing is endowed with exceptional significance, powerfully reinforcing an older Chinese tradition of regarding examinations and their results as very serious business.

Sweden and the United States. At the other end of the spectrum, Sweden and the United States are exceptionally generous in providing at least the label of success, if, as in China, success is defined as the chance to enter some form of postsecondary education.

Just over two-thirds of the relevant age group in Sweden make this transition. The country has gone to great lengths to play down the importance attached to test and examination success. The government abolished the system of final secondary school graduation examinations entirely, substituting in its place a set of centrally and locally administered tests given over the entire senior high school career. In addition, a variable proportion of university admissions each year is reserved for applicants who are at least twenty-five years old and who have had at least four years of work experience: the so-called 25/4 policy.

It is commonly accepted in the United States that there is a place in United States higher education for any young person who wishes to attend, regardless even of high school graduation, let alone any particular score on the SAT, ACT, Achievement Tests, or Advanced Placement examinations. As the entry on the third line indicates, not all, of course, do attend, although approximately 60 percent of the relevant age group enter a college or university. Because of the ready availability of postsecondary education in the United States, what counts as success there is not so much graduation from high school, high test scores, or even the opportunity to go on to higher education, as the offer of a place at a prestigious college or university. As a rule, this will be decided only after an admissions committee has weighed a much wider array of the applicant's characteristics than just test scores.

In Sweden, as in the United States, the examination burden on students toward the end of secondary school, as described in chapter 7, is comparatively light. This, combined with the general expectation that a majority of secondary school students will go on to higher education, means that, taken alone, a measure of success in the tests and examinations is an expectation for most and carries relatively little importance.

Germany. Germany relies heavily on the general academic credential, the Abitur, for evidence of school completion and suitability for future academic study. Virtually all who take the Abitur examinations are successful, a tribute to the power of preselection and to the careful preparation of the candidates. However, many who are enrolled in school at age eighteen or nineteen, other than in a Gymnasium, do not attempt the Abitur, so there is a sharp drop from the first to the second ratio cited in figure 8, with a further drop from the second to the third ratio. Less than a third of the age group achieves the success represented by an Abitur certificate.

France. The figures for France show a much lower success rate for candidates than Germany, but a much higher rate in relation to grade-level enrollment and a slightly higher rate with respect to the age group. Hence, although France and Germany run very similar examinations at the end of secondary school, enrollment in the types of schools preparing for these examinations by no means guarantees success in France in the way that it does in Germany. However, a much higher fraction of the age group in France has the opportunity to take the baccalauréat examinations than can take the Abitur in Germany. Against this, it should be noted that German students have a major alternative route to a secondary-school-completion qualification via the dual system of apprenticeship and release-time schooling.

England/Wales. Apart from China, England/Wales has one of the lowest ratios of examination success in relation to the age cohort, though the other two ratios of success are roughly in the middle of the distributions. In particular, the overall pass rate for candidates in the A-level examinations (70 percent) is comparable with baccalauréat pass rates, though markedly lower than in the Abitur. This is so despite relatively strict selection for A-level preparation and candidature and regulations that permit A-level candidates to take just one or two subjects, whereas baccalauréat and Abitur candidates must take many more. Either or both circumstances should result in a higher pass rate for the A level.

Japan. In recent years, about 21 percent of the age group (including repeaters) sat for the JFSAT, which selects those qualified to take a second-stage selection examination set by the higher education institutions. As in the United States, individual scores are recorded and sent to candidates, but there is no indication of "pass" or "not pass." The percentages for Japan in figure 8 are therefore based on entry into higher education.

Many candidates send their scores to specialized private companies for analysis and advice on where they stand the best chance of gaining a place in a higher education institution. Although a higher percentage of the age cohort enters a college or university than in either France or Germany,

many of these students, as in the United States, are attending relatively nonselective institutions. Neither they nor their parents are likely to claim that their JFSAT scores or their second-stage results represent great success. In the Japanese context, as in that of the United States, success comes from admission into a top-level university, here one that is publicly supported with low tuition.

The Soviet Union. Virtually every student who stays in secondary school to the end of the final year is awarded the certificate of maturity, signifying success much as in the United States. But, as in England/Wales, obtaining the certificate affords no right to attend higher education; and, as in Japan, it is usually necessary to pass a second-stage examination administered by the higher institute or university in order to secure a place there. Only a relatively small number (about 10 percent of the age group) are able to continue into full-time higher education. Like the Chinese government, Soviet authorities have been reluctant to expand higher education enrollments fast enough to accommodate larger fractions of the rapidly growing numbers of high school graduates. Hence, in the Soviet Union, success for the graduating high school student is not simply earning the certificate of maturity. At the very minimum, success means going on to the next stage, passing the entrance examination into some higher institute or university; optimally, it is landing a place in one of the more prestigious institutions.

   Reading across from left to right in figure 8, the order of countries reflects our conclusion that based upon all of the evidence, success in these terms (as measured in four of the countries in terms of passing the examination and in the other four in gaining admission to higher education) is easiest to attain in Sweden and the United States, most difficult to achieve in China, relatively available in both Germany and France, and somewhat less so in England/Wales and Japan. In the Soviet Union, success, when defined as gaining admission to higher education, is quite difficult to achieve, though by no means as restricted as in China, where success rates are strikingly low.

A Model of Causes and Consequences

We see from the foregoing that examination success rates differ from country to country. The causes and consequences of these differences are complex and are presented schematically in Figure 9.

   A factor likely to affect success rates is the difficulty of the examination, meaning not only the level of difficulty of the questions, but also other elements of the burden on candidates, like the number of required

Figure 9. Examination Success Rates: Causes and Consequences

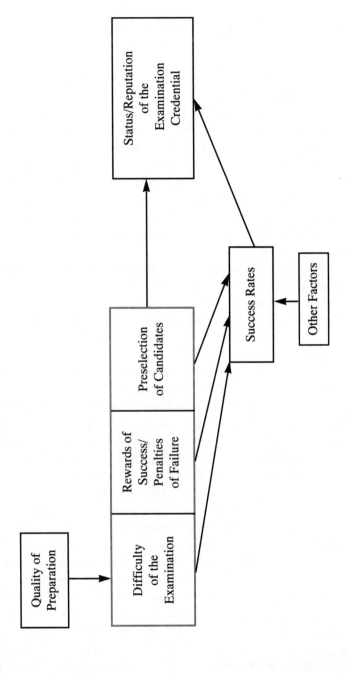

subjects, the format of the examination papers, and their duration. This was analyzed in chapter 7. Thus we might expect to find easier examinations associated with higher pass rates, and we use the conclusions of the previous chapter about the relative level of difficulty of the examinations to explore this possibility.

In addition, pass rates are influenced by the extent to which there is preselection of candidates. Countries emphasizing preselection should show higher pass rates with respect to the number of candidates entered, but perhaps lower rates with respect to the size of the age cohort. On the other hand, countries that favor "open candidacy" are likely to offer relatively easy examinations. The degree of preselection and the level of examination difficulty will probably show some mutual interaction: difficult examinations will promote preselection, and preselection will promote more difficult examinations.

Presumably, incentives persuade students to take their studies seriously, and we sketch in broad outline the "carrots and sticks" associated with examination success in each of the countries. The rewards for passing the end-of-secondary-school examinations and/or gaining the school completion certificate vary substantially among the eight nations, as do the penalties for failure.

We do not claim that these three factors are the only ones likely to influence success rates. Other factors include the level of the cutoff scores separating a pass from a fail; the allotment of school time to each subject and in total; the quantity and quality of textbooks and other pedagogical resources; and the training, skill, and efforts of teachers. We have chosen not to examine these, but instead to limit the analysis to those we consider to be prima facie relevant, though we recognize they do not exhaust the set of plausible factors influencing success rates.

Turning from the causes of success rates to their consequences, we note that the status of the credential is likely to be influenced directly by each of the three factors affecting success rates: the difficulty of the examination, the extent of preselection, and the rewards associated with passing.

We recognize, too, that although it is probably true that the richer the rewards for examination success, the greater the incentive to work hard and do well, high and rising rates of success are likely to erode the level and perceived value of the rewards. Passing "easy" examinations that are open to all is unlikely to radiate an aura of brilliant success. Nor will such examinations be taken very seriously by students and teachers, if only because success in them is not expected to open any well-guarded doors to further study or employment. The opposite will most probably hold for examinations at the difficult end of the spectrum: success in a difficult examination with restricted entry is likely to enjoy high prestige, conveying rewards of high value. In this sense, success in examinations exhibits some of the characteristics of money: perceived value is inversely related to the overall quantity available.

Discussion. In figure 9, three factors influencing the different success rates observed are identified on the upper left-hand side. Figure 9 also illustrates the conjecture that there is a relationship between success rates and the status or reputation of the examination credential.

The first factor listed on the left-hand side of the figure is the level of difficulty of the examination. We concluded in chapter 7 that the United States and Sweden offered the least difficult and least burdensome examinations, followed in increasing order of difficulty by China and the Soviet Union. Then came Japan and England/Wales, and finally France and Germany, with the most difficult examinations (see figure 7).

The relatively easy examinations in the United States and Sweden are clearly associated with high success rates. France, Germany, England/Wales, and Japan run difficult examinations, and their success rates are quite low with respect to the age cohort, although not with respect to the other two bases (candidates and enrollments). In Germany, as well as in England/Wales and in France, preselection of candidates helps keep pass rates high, even in the face of difficult examinations. If China presents an apparent exception to the generalization, it is because government policy has kept the supply of university places well below the level of demand. Overall, we judge that the evidence broadly supports the assertion that cross-nationally, the more difficult the examination, the smaller will be the percentage of the age cohort passing, though not necessarily the percentage of candidates passing.

The identification of a second influence on success rates, the rewards for success and the penalties for failure, also seems to be broadly justified. The underlying theoretical point is simple, even simplistic: Significant, large rewards for passing the examinations should stimulate students' and teachers' efforts and be reflected in higher pass rates. France and Germany certainly offer very significant rewards to successful baccalauréat and Abitur candidates—automatic university admission, if so desired, and at minimum financial cost—and their examination success rates are high. In England/Wales, two or three "good" A-level passes will most probably lead to an offer of a university place, and most students, until recently, also received a substantial study grant from public funds to cover tuition fees and living costs. China seems to be an exception to the "rule," for the high reward of a university place is associated with low measured success rates. These low pass rates, however, are the purely arbitrary reflection of

China's strict quota system for university admissions. The severity of the competition is likely to discourage some secondary school students from even trying to succeed. In addition, there were reports during the second half of the 1980s that low salaries in urban areas, and especially in white-collar occupations, were a disincentive to students to complete upper secondary school and to aspire to higher education. Nevertheless, the high reward of a university place no doubt helps explain the strong demand for upper-secondary-school preparation, even though much of even that demand goes unsatisfied under contemporary Chinese conditions. In the remaining four countries, we explicitly use college entrance rates, rather than examination pass rates, so the link between rewards and success rates cannot be established along the above lines.

Penalties for failure are not necessarily the mirror image of rewards for success. The examination systems we discuss are designed to sort students according to demonstrated academic abilities. Substantial numbers of students fail the examinations (about 30 percent in A levels in England/Wales; one-third of the candidates in France; four-fifths in China). In practice the severity of the penalties is softened by alternative routes to success, as well as by opportunities for the failing candidate to try again. But failure is typically a serious matter, at a minimum imposing additional costs of time, effort, and money to retake the examination, even if it does not permanently damage future prospects for education and training, employment, and social advancement. Such penalties have been especially high in Japan, China, and the Soviet Union. In the United States, although the consequences of low scores on the various aptitude and achievement tests at the end of high school may not be as great as they are in these countries, nevertheless the penalties of "dropping out," that is, of failing to get a high school diploma, are severe. On average, males aged twenty-five to twenty-nine without a high school diploma earn only 60 percent of what those with just a high school diploma and no college study make, and their incidence of unemployment is twice as high.[3]

Similarly, in England/Wales failing A-levels will normally close off the chance for a university education and many opportunities for higher-level public-sector employment, but it will certainly not be as harmful to the individual as similar failure is in, say, China.

In Japan, achieving poor examination grades *is* a serious matter, but repeat candidacies are common. There are multiple opportunities to continue study for a second try, especially in the adult cram courses, called

3. U.S. Department of Education, *The Condition of Education 1990* (Washington, D.C.: U.S. Government Printing Office, 1990), 1. 40–43.

yobiko. These opportunities help mitigate the penalties of initial failure. In Germany, selection at age ten into the tripartite secondary school system means that many citizens have not had the opportunity to study for the Abitur. The doors are not completely closed to those who missed out during their school days, however. There is a *zweiter Bildungsweg* (second educational path) that enables mature individuals to study for the Abitur, take the examinations, receive their certificate of readiness for higher education, and apply for admission to a university. We have already mentioned the Swedish 25/4 provision for older students with work experience to enroll on a preferential basis in the universities. Repeat candidacies are becoming more common in all of the countries.

We identified the preselection of candidates as a major influence on the relatively high success rates of candidates in England/Wales, France, and Germany. In many of the prefectures in Japan, too, entrance examinations are administered to select the most academically able junior high students for enrollment in the top senior high schools. It is expected that candidates from these schools will win a disproportionate share of places in prestigious universities. Thus in four of the eight countries, the initial conjecture, that preselection is associated with higher success rates, is supported. In the other four countries, China, Sweden, the Soviet Union, and the United States, the association between selectivity and success rates is not confirmed. China has a very selective system with low success rates. The other three all run relatively nonselective upper secondary school systems, but Sweden and the United States promote high rates of college entrance as a matter of policy, whereas the Soviet Union limits access to higher education, even while pushing toward complete secondary education for all. About all we can safely conclude is that there is evidence that in some countries preselection is associated with higher success rates, but that wider participation rates in upper secondary education by no means lead automatically to lower success rates.

Our final supposition, that the perceived value or status of the credential is likely to be related inversely to success rates, is also broadly confirmed. In the United States, where over 80 percent of the age group from eighteen to twenty-five has a high school diploma or its equivalent, its mere possession has little status. Good to superior SAT or ACT scores do not guarantee a place at the country's most reputable universities; admission to many universities and colleges is perfectly possible without taking Achievement Tests or Advanced Placement examinations.[4] Colleges look at many other

4. An estimated 80 percent of universities in the United States admit students solely on the basis of SAT scores supplemented by school grades, and without any Achievement Test

characteristics of the applicant. If test scores, together with school grades, are moderately respectable (minimally in, say, the upper quarter), acceptance at a prestigious college is likely to turn on the admissions committee's assessment of such nontest factors as the applicant's leadership qualities, athletic, musical, dramatic, or literary talent, record of community service, race, or alumni connection. The weight given to these factors serves to blunt the ultimate importance of test scores.

Sweden, too, has made success easy to achieve, and at the same time and for that very reason, has made examination and test success much less important.

At the other end of the spectrum lies China, with its startlingly low access to examination success, defined as admission to higher education. High test scores are indispensable for admission, and it is difficult to exaggerate the emphasis and value placed on examination success in China. This remains true in spite of there being some important nonexamination conditions for success: even outstanding scores on the examination need to be supported by attestations of civic-mindedness and political reliability. Such attestations usually take the form of testimonials and recommendations from school principals, teachers, youth organization leaders, or political personnel. The weight accorded to political reliability diminished somewhat in the years before 1989, but after the government's repression of student demonstrations of that year, it once again became important. In addition, some provinces and large cities have introduced high-school-completion examinations on a noncompetitive basis. These are intended to help screen out weak candidates before they add to the already large numbers failing the university entrance examination, as many as two million a year in the late 1980s. This development should not be given too much weight, however. To date, China has done little to diminish the status of examination success, and its importance will likely remain very high.

In France and Germany the examinations and their associated credentials possess exceptional value and status. Success—passing the baccalauréat or the Abitur—is clearly more difficult to achieve, and scarcer, than in the United States or Sweden.

Although the Abitur confers the right to enter a university, it does not give the right to be admitted to all degree programs. Admission quotas were introduced in the more expensive and popular specialities, such as medicine and dentistry, in response to the pressure of numbers and rising demand. This, combined with a national effort to achieve greater compa-

results. R. F. Harnett and R. A. Feldmesser. "College Admission Testing and the Myth of Selectivity," *APHE Bulletin* 32 (1980): 3–6.

rability and equivalence across the regions, means that small differences in Abitur scores can be crucial in determining acceptance to the institution or academic department one chooses. The result is more competition and greater personal and public attention to the examinations, thus raising the status of the credential, even at a time when more candidates than ever are turning toward preparation for careers in business, industry, and technology rather than in the academic and more traditional professions.

Paradoxically, somewhat weakening the value of the Abitur is the continued popularity of the dual system, comprising apprenticeship in a firm combined with continued part-time schooling during release time from the business. This provides a parallel path of upper secondary schooling culminating in alternative examinations and credentials for technical and vocational preparation. These are widely known to employers and valued by them; moreover, they have official status. In addition, the traditional distinction between these two career paths is becoming blurred and so, by the same token, is the function of the Abitur. Increasing numbers of Abitur holders are turning toward apprenticeship or technical training rather than academic careers. Together with the past growth in numbers of students gaining the Abitur, these pressures may in time lessen its traditionally high status.

As in Germany, the relative scarcity of the baccalauréat qualification, plus the similar legal right it carries to attend university free of tuition, maintains the perceived value of the baccalauréat at a high level, though perhaps not quite as high as in Germany. The elevated status of the baccalauréat is perhaps best indicated by its extraordinary public visibility. During the examination season, newspapers often describe the events associated with the baccalauréat. Later, some print the questions and model answers, as well as the national results. This may even make front-page news, accompanied by analyses by leading intellectuals of the cultural implications of the examiners' choice of topics and even the specific wording of questions.

In recent years the status of the baccalauréat has been subject to contradictory pressures. The rise in the number gaining the credential tends to detract somewhat from its status. Reinforcing this downward pressure are the government's announcement that it hopes to have 80 percent of the age group enrolled in the pre-baccalauréat terminale grade by the year 2000 and the associated vigorous development of vocational tracks. All of these plans and changes have the effect of raising doubts whether the modern baccalauréat is as demanding as the traditional one and whether those who earn it should continue to deserve high regard.

This is by no means the whole story. Although the baccalauréat remains a passport, visa, and ticket to higher education, the days when there was basically one class of travel are now gone. Entry into the most prestigious and remunerative lines of study (the classes préparatoires leading to the grandes écoles, and faculties of medicine and dentistry, and certain other sciences) requires more than merely obtaining the credential. High scores in the more difficult séries are virtually indispensable for entry to the "fast track." G. Neave has used the phrase *université à deux vitesses* to describe the situation in which the majority enters higher education immediately with the baccalauréat while a small group enters selective programs and institutions to participate in the concours, the highly competitive examinations that follow usually two years later.[5] Ever-sharper competition to enter the best postsecondary institutions or tracks has so far outweighed potential negative factors, so that the status of the credential shows no signs of serious decline, even though it probably enjoys somewhat less public esteem than the Abitur does in Germany.

In Japan, overall success rates are roughly comparable with those of France, perhaps a little more restrictive. Although a good score on the JFSAT is no guarantee of admission to the better universities, it is indispensable for the opportunity to sit for their entrance examinations. Much of the high prestige and perceived rewards of success in the JFSAT, therefore, come from competition for admission to the top national and provincial universities, although only a fraction of all secondary school graduates can hope to obtain a place there. Curiously, then, the importance, value, and prestige of examination success in Japan is perhaps as high as it is in China, despite the much greater availability of success in Japan.

The competition and tension surrounding the JFSAT and the subsequent university entrance examinations are extraordinarily pronounced. As a result of concern over their impact on Japanese schools and students and over the restrictive effects upon the subsequent careers of graduates, demands for change have been voiced from time to time. For example, the questions of undue pressure on students and alleged inappropriate curricula and instructional methods were considered by former Prime Minister Nakasone's national council on educational reform (1984 to 1987), and they continue to be studied and debated among other groups. But they have been ignored by those who hold the competitive, examination-driven system in the highest regard, because they consider it to be a primary contributor to Japan's past, present, and future achievements. Any reform initia-

5. Guy Neave, "Visions of Mortality: Some Views on Entrances and Exits from Higher Education in Western Europe," *Compare* 16, no. 2 (1986), pp. 167–173.

tives that might impair the status of the examination system in general and the JFSAT in particular currently have small hope of success.

The status of the certificate of maturity has been high in the Soviet Union. Education and credentials were heavily promoted as a proper arena for "socialist competition," and schooling became one of the major avenues of upward social mobility. Moreover, the relative scarcity of places in higher education has reinforced the traditionally high value attached to examination credentials—perhaps not as high as in Japan or China, but still substantial.

In the mid-1980s admissions committees in the Soviet Union became concerned that the academic quality of applicants was declining and that in their anxiety to secure a place—any place— in higher education, many were applying to faculties where they thought they had a good chance of acceptance, irrespective of individual talents and interests. Applicants have been asked to come for interviews, to check on their real aptitudes and career goals. Since the "objective" evidence offered by the entrance examination results is no longer the sole determinant of who will be offered a place, the result may be to devalue the status of examination success a little, but hardly enough to be of great significance.

England/Wales provides some anomaly. Success in the sense of access to higher education, though it has been increasing, remains quite restricted: only 16 percent of the age cohort passes in one or more A-level subjects. Yet this marked scarcity of success does not coexist with high prestige for the qualification. Several reasons may account for this. Unlike the practice in France, Germany, and Japan, the GCE A-level qualification is not an explicitly official, state-issued credential. Moreover, passing in one, two, or even three subjects is no guarantee of admission to any university— much will depend on the "quality" (grade) of the particular passes, the applicant's previous school record, and recommendations, the results of an interview at the university itself, and even the social class of the applicant. Finally, the A level attests more to the holder's depth of specialization than to the breadth of his or her education and culture. These characteristics have probably harmed the prestige and perceived value of the A level credential more than its relative scarcity has helped. England/Wales, however, seems to provide the only exception to the generalization we have ventured.

Conclusion

Success rates in examinations differ quite markedly across nations, but each nation appears to regard its own particular rates as somehow part of the natural order of things. For example, in France from year to year and even from académie to académie, the pass rate on the baccalauréat has moved only a few percentage points above or below two-thirds; and the general belief in France is that it could hardly be otherwise. In England/ Wales, too, roughly the same success rate for candidates obtains. Yet the evidence of the other countries demonstrates that there is no natural law ordaining that two-thirds of the candidates shall pass and the remainder fail. Rather, the observed pass rates in France and England/Wales, as in the other countries, are the result of choices, some deliberate, some less conscious, made within educational, examination, and political institutions. For this reason, success rates are best regarded as artifacts of national policy, deriving sometimes from the overriding need to select a small set of "winners" from among a large number of candidates, as in China, Japan, and the Soviet Union or, as in England/Wales, from a rather small field; or perhaps from the desire and the resources to spread opportunities widely and to be as inclusive as possible, as in Sweden and the United States; or perhaps from a conviction that success in the examination must certify mastery of a demanding curriculum that embraces the most vital elements of the national culture, as in France and Germany.

Difficult examinations appear to reduce the proportion of the age cohort passing, but preselection practices keep success rates with respect to the number of candidates high. Rewards for success are clearly powerful incentives for candidates in France and Germany, and the penalties of failure are substantial in most countries.

Success rates do seem to be inversely related to the status and value of the credential. We should add that abrupt changes in success rates, especially increases, are usually regarded with a certain degree of suspicion, heightened if the rise in the rate is accompanied by an increase in the number of candidates, as occurred in Germany after the 1972 reform of the Abitur. The value of the credential was widely held to have been devalued, and the examination regulations were restored partly to their former rigor. Concern has also been expressed in France that the announced goal for the year 2000 of having 80 percent of the age group at the baccalauréat level will require a lowering of standards and will lead to a fall in its perceived status and value.

Concerns like this are substantial, but they are by no means the only issues centering on examination policies. We now turn to consider the ways in which examination policy can become the focus of dispute and conflict, both within the educational system and in the broader political arena.

Part 3

Analysis

Chapter 9

The Politics of Examinations: Issues and Conflicts

A bias to disclose
Would be indelicate—
—Marco, *The Gondoliers*, act 1

Hitherto, our primary focus has been on the examinations themselves: what part they play in the school and personal lives of secondary school students, how they are managed, and their form and content. In addition, the relative difficulty of national examination systems has been compared in two ways: in terms of the demands placed upon students and with respect to rates of success. We now turn to the broader context to consider an array of conflicts involving examinations.

Examinations become the object of debate and dispute especially when the focus is on what should be taught and how learning should be evaluated. But they can also become footballs in the broader field of national politics, punted hither and yon in the course of ideological clashes. Because they function as instruments of control of the curriculum and teachers' activity, examination systems can become targets for contending parties who seek to maintain or establish a particular vision of what education and society should be. Conflicts are over power as well as over the purported ends of education, over who controls what, in what ways. Not that the boundary between the more narrowly educational and the wider national political scene is always clearly defined: rather, the educational and political issues involving examinations are inevitably intertwined, and play upon each other.

Disputes readily become highly contentious, in part because they reflect the views and claims of different interest groups and in part because the debates over examinations are often debates over fundamentally different philosophies of education and different views of what is good for society. Do the schools exist primarily to serve the interests of their students, or the broader interests of society? To be more specific, should the schools seek above all to develop individual talent, or should they give most attention to equipping young people with the knowledge and skills that government or the labor market are currently demanding? How much of the curriculum should be devoted to optional subjects designed to meet individual aspirations and talents, and how much to conveying a core of knowledge common for all children? Should access to further study and jobs be determined strictly according to academic merit? If not, what other characteristics—for example, ethnicity, sex, social class, record of community service, athletic talent—are to be considered, what weights should be given them, and what limits set? Views on these questions will most likely color preferences expressed about the content and structure of the examination system.

At one extreme, critics raise doubts about whether examinations are a legitimate way to determine individual merit; at the other, defenders of examinations insist that they are in practice the *only* defensible way to allocate opportunities. Ranged against those who argue that examinations should be abolished entirely are those who want greater reliance on even more demanding examinations. In between are the many who see opportunities for "improving" the examination system, in ways calculated to change schools or society in directions they consider desirable. In particular, changes in examinations are often advocated and implemented in the hope that they will affect the way teachers go about their business in the classroom.

This chapter is directed at two questions: What are the issues involved in debates over examinations? Under what conditions do examinations become the focus of serious debate and struggles? We attempt to answer these questions using two approaches. First we examine the educational and political issues arising in debate and conflict over examinations, indicating the countries in which these issues have had major importance. Then we proceed country by country to describe the nature and current status of such debates and conflicts. In conclusion, we discuss the political nature of those common elements that make the subject of examinations prone to conflict.

Issues, Educational and Political

Some questions are located primarily within the realm of professional educational debates, but spill over into disputes over examination policy. For example: who should control the curriculum *content* of the upper secondary schools—a question that continues in the forefront of debate in England/Wales and the United States; to what extent should the curriculum be *differentiated* to take care of the different aspirations, talents, and ability levels of different students—an issue that has been raised most notably in France, Germany, and Sweden, but also in England/Wales and the United States; and is it desirable and efficacious to use examinations to help control *teachers'* efforts? This question is of particular salience in Japan, but has been prominent too in the debates over examinations in England/Wales and the United States and has been echoed in Sweden.

Another issue, with even more direct impact on examination policy, has been the desirability of introducing alternatives or complements to traditional examinations. A frequently mentioned alternative is the assembly, submission, and evaluation of student schoolwork in place of the "one-shot," traditional, closed-book examination. Typically, "progressive" teachers and researchers hold this view, whereas it is resisted by more cautious teachers and administrators who fear loss of comparability among candidates and loss of objectivity among graders.

In the United States, Vermont has led the way in introducing assessment on the basis of portfolios;[1] and in England/Wales a movement to promote these alternatives has been influencing the structure and procedures of the GCSE. Another proposal is for the provision of profiles of students' achievements, competences, and characteristics recorded over fairly long periods of time, in place of the usual bare numerical or alphabetical grades. In Sweden proposals made in the late 1980s to introduce a so-called holistic assessment of each student would have gone far beyond reporting measures of academic achievement to include sports activity and performance levels, health status, psychological, especially motivational, characteristics, family background and conditions, and so forth. This ambitious goal has run into opposition on both political-ideological and financial grounds.

Controversy also surrounds the question of the kind of examinations to be given, specifically their format, length, and comprehensiveness. These are all under discussion in the United States and were extensively debated in England/Wales in the 1980s. In the Soviet Union, France, and Germany, there has been much questioning of the limited degrees of choice in examination subjects; whereas in England/Wales questions are being raised from the other direction, in the form of expressions of concern over an excessively broad range of examination subject choices available to the schools and their candidates.

Last among the primarily "within-education" disputes over examinations, we should note the opposition of teachers and their professional organizations in England/Wales, the United States, and Japan to the growing use of examination results to evaluate schools and even individual teachers in the name of public accountability.

---

1. Portfolios are organized collections of the student's work in the various school subjects. They will usually include teachers' evaluations, and sometimes even the student's own reflections on items in the portfolio.

Issues generating conflicts in the broader political arena may have re-percussions on the schools and on end-of-school examinations. These is-sues are often couched in ideological terms: for or against holding schools accountable for achieving national political, economic, and social goals; for or against providing greater autonomy to regional administrations, teaching staffs, or parents in matters of school governance and curriculum decision-making; for or against sorting and "labeling" individuals by reg-ular, comprehensive evaluation of students' performance; and for or against employing an "input-output" model of schooling and using examination results as indicators of output.

The debate over examinations has extended even as far as questioning whether to have examinations at all. Calls for their abolition have been heard from time to time in Western Europe and the United States. From the 1920s through the 1960s, the suppression of in-course and completion examinations was a major element in the credo of the New Education Fel-lowship, an international movement for the reform of schooling. After vig-orous debate, Sweden abolished the traditional end-of-secondary-school examination in 1972, hoping that in-course tests would provide more reli-able indicators of each student's academic achievement, would rid the schools of the hothouse cramming and tension that accompanied the end-of-school examinations, and would lead to wider extension of postsecondary educa-tion to hitherto underrepresented groups.

In the Soviet Union and China, when completion and selection exami-nations were abandoned, the motivation was more narrowly ideological: to "level the playing field" by removing the greater opportunity for advance-ment that the children of the middle and upper classes had over peasants' and workers' children. But in both countries, the "reforms" did not last more than a decade, and new leaders, Joseph Stalin in the Soviet Union and Deng Xiaoping in China, ordained their reversal.

A corollary to the spread of examinations to larger proportions of the secondary school population has been a trend toward proliferation of cre-dentials for employment in even low-skill jobs. Criticism is voiced in such terms as "the diploma disease," "the overeducated American," and "cre-dential creep," language expressing the concern of those who believe that curricula, examinations, and diplomas have lost much of their relevance for the job tasks high school graduates must perform.[2] This judgment is

2. See Ronald Dore, *The Diploma Disease: Education, Qualification, and Development* (Berkeley: University of California Press, 1976); Ivar Berg, *Education and Jobs: The Great Training Robbery* (New York: Praeger, 1970); and Richard Freeman, *The Over-Educated American* (New York: Academic Press, 1976).

contested strongly by other observers who stress the role of examinations as a prime means of maintaining or raising national achievement levels. They call for more and revised testing and examinations, and more attention paid by employers to diplomas, as ways of focusing the attention of students, parents, and teachers on the importance of study, effort, and credentials.[3]

Above all, examinations have been accused of being systematically unfair and biased against females and minorities, charges that have been leveled in the United States, France, England/Wales, and even in Japan, China, and the Soviet Union. Accusations of gender, ethnic, and regional bias are not only common, but politically explosive. Critics argue that examinations have been exceptionally effective instruments for allocating life chances and that the biases built into them are perpetuated over the lifetimes of candidates who have been unfairly discouraged or eliminated by flawed examinations. The critical importance for life chances of end-of-secondary-school certificates and test scores means that more attention than ever before is focused on the tests' validity, reliability, and fairness.

As the following instances will show, the issues involved in debates over examinations and in changing policies combine educational and broader social considerations. Even questions that arise in technical, psychometric form are likely to carry implications beyond the immediate problem to be solved. Debates and disputes involving examinations, like those over educational arrangements in general, only too often end up in the political arena.

National Debates over Examinations

A country-by-country review of experience during the past two decades shows that examination policies and arrangements have been the subject of active dispute in some countries, but not in others. Test and examination policy has been caught up in vigorous political debate and struggle in the United States, England/Wales, Germany, Japan, and China, whereas in France, Sweden, and the Soviet Union controversy over examinations has been much less in evidence.

The United States. In the United States until the late 1960s most criticism of the schools came from the "progressive" viewpoint, though there were

---

3. John H. Bishop, "Why High School Students Learn So Little and What Can Be Done About It" (Cornell University Working Paper no. 88-01, Center for Advanced Human Resource Studies, School of Industrial and Labor Relations, mimeographed). 1988.

those like Arthur Bestor and Admiral Hyman Rickover who even during the 1950s and 1960s called for a "return to basics" and tougher standards. But as evidence of low average achievement levels accumulated from National Assessment of Educational Progress (NAEP) reports, IEA studies, and declining SAT and similar test scores, the direction of criticism reversed itself. The slogan "school reform" now meant the imposition of stricter requirements, fewer options, higher standards, a curriculum focused on a basic, common canon of knowledge, and more assessment of student progress by achievement tests. Taxpayers and employers were to be reassured that students were receiving a "quality education" in return for money spent. The publication in 1983 of *A Nation at Risk,* a report commissioned by the U.S. Secretary of Education, signaled the opening of a reform campaign, which continues to show signs of strength almost a decade later.

The absence of a federal role in regulating secondary school examinations has severely limited the power of national authorities to influence, let alone control, what goes on in the school systems and schools of the fifty states. The situation is comparable to that in England/Wales before the legislation of the late 1980s took effect. On occasion the federal government has been able to exercise influence by offering funds for specific educational programs, for example, to change curricula in mathematics, the sciences, and foreign languages and to encourage the provision of vocational education. But budget constraints have always worked with administrative precedents to prevent federal authorities from acquiring long-term, consistent power over the schools and their curricula. Power that may be unavailable in Washington, D.C., is very much present in state governments, however. There the introduction of new curricular requirements has been reinforced by the growth or establishment of regular testing programs during the course of schooling and the introduction of final examinations to try to ensure some minimum level of competence before the award of the high school diploma. By 1990 most states were requiring regular assessments of students' academic achievement and were mandating explicitly defined minimum course requirements and levels of achievement for the award of a high school diploma. The NAEP has received an infusion of federal funds and a mandate to report its findings so that state-by-state comparisons of school achievement are possible. A few states have even begun to publish such data at the school district level.

Although the education scene in the United States may appear at first sight to be hopelessly chaotic and uncoordinated—and compared to many more tightly organized national systems of education, it is—the contemporary school reform movement has been one of those occasions when a national consensus on a program of change has emerged and when broadly similar measures have been put in place from one end of the country to the other. Consensus on the need to pay more attention to what the schools are doing, to raise standards, and to introduce more frequent and more difficult tests of achievement cuts across political party lines. Democrats and Republicans alike support school reform, backed up by testing. For example, the president's Education Policy Advisory Committee has stated that national tests are indispensable for monitoring progress toward reaching the president's six National Education Goals for the Year 2000. Similarly, the National Education Goals Panel, which includes state governors, congressional representatives, and members of the administration, is actively promoting the concept of national tests.

Criticism of multiple-choice testing has not been lacking.[4] The tests have come under increasing attack for their alleged undesirable effects on what and how teachers teach and on student learning, thinking, and ability to write acceptable prose, and for the message they convey to students about the nature of academic skills and knowledge. The criticisms appear to be having some effect. The American College Test now advertises itself as more than an aptitude test; and the Educational Testing Service is reported to be revamping the SAT. Finally, a movement to establish some national achievement criteria for high school graduation and to assess individual students by examination has been gaining momentum.

Proposals to reform the work of the schools have by no means been confined to public authorities. Early in the 1980s, three years of nationwide consultation and consensus-building led by the College Board resulted in the publication in May 1983 of *Academic Preparation for College: What Students Need to Know and Be Able to Do,* the so-called Green Book. This was followed by a set of suggestions on how to achieve the competencies and knowledge specified in each of six basic school subjects. More recently, the pace of recommendation and examination construction has quickened. The National Commission on the Skills of the American Workforce recommends, "A new educational performance standard should be set for all students to meet by age 16. This standard should be established nationally and benchmarked to the highest in the world."[5] The National Center on Education and the Economy, which nurtured the commission, is collaborating with Lauren Resnick and others at the University of

4. For example, Lauren B. and Daniel P. Resnick, "Standards, Curriculum, and Performance: A Historical and Comparative Perspective," *The Educational Researcher* 14, no. 4 (April 1985): 5–20.

5. National Commission on the Skills of the American Workforce, *America's Choice: High Skills or Low Wages?* (Rochester, N.Y.: National Center on Education and the Economy, 1990), p. 5.

Pittsburgh's Learning Research and Development Center to develop a new model for a nationwide high school examination system. Yet another new, private, not-for-profit organization, Educate America, headquartered in New Jersey, is also preparing tests for all high school seniors.[6]

The earlier recommendations did not assume that tests and examinations were to be among the major levers of change, as these later initiatives do. The intent of the College Board in its Green Book was "to suggest curricular change (and then to modify the tests to reflect such changes as did occur) and not to force curricular change by first changing the tests."[7] While the board has given priority to reforming its testing instruments, it specifically abjures use of college admission tests as a means of changing the secondary school curriculum.

Criticism of reform via more tests comes from individual teachers and administrators, researchers, parent-teacher associations, and the like. They raise a variety of objections, arguing that the policies represent an overreliance on a single instrument to motivate students and teachers, while ignoring other, less mechanistic approaches; that emphasizing testing attacks the symptoms, not the causes, of poor school performance; that what the schools really need is more money, not only for the schools themselves, but to finance a comprehensive national policy for the support of families and children, reduce malnutrition, improve child health care, and deal more effectively with the effects of broken homes; and that more and harder tests will serve only to increase the number of failing students, especially among those groups already experiencing high failure rates. The harshest criticism accuses the tests of systematic bias against blacks, Hispanics, females, and rural residents and argues that the last thing America needs is more of the same.

The strongest challenge to tests and examinations in the United States comes from specifically established public interest groups, such as Fair-Test, in Cambridge, Mass., which oppose testing in general, rather than seeking to improve current tests.[8] But even so, compared to the strength and authority of the voices raised in support of current school reform policies, these critics are not making enough noise, nor are they making it loudly enough, to shake the broad consensus described. State or national action to impose examination requirements along the lines of western European countries is nowhere in sight.

6. Educate America, *An Idea Whose Time Has Come: A National Achievement Test for High School Seniors!* (Morristown, N.J.: Educate America, 1991).

7. John A. Valentine, *The College Board and the School Curriculum* (New York: College Entrance Examination Board, 1987), p. 164.

8. See chapter 4.

England/Wales. In the late 1980s a revolution of sorts occurred in England/ Wales with respect to educational policy in general and to government participation in particular. Traditionally, the central government had refrained from close control of the curriculum of the schools and the structure and content of external end-of-secondary-school examinations. By 1990 this long-standing, hands-off stance had been abandoned and the Education Act of 1988 had taken effect, giving the central government direct control of the schools' curricula and the examination system, together with an entirely new program of national testing of pupils' school achievement at four age levels.

The legislation, which amounted to a virtual revolution in educational policy in England/Wales, was to a large extent a reaction to changes made in the two decades after 1960. As in the United States, through most of this period criticism of the schools was characterized by charges that schools were too oppressive, too demanding, and too inclined to evaluate and label students. Examinations and tests were regarded as part of the problems of education, certainly not as part of the solution. Opposition focused on the selection examination for entering secondary schools (the eleven-plus examination). Critics charged that the age of eleven was far too early to decide a child's educational fate; that too much depended on which educational authority was responsible, for some had made much more provision for academic secondary education than others; and that the tests favored children from upper- or middle-class families. The Labour party in opposition campaigned vigorously for the abolition of the eleven-plus examination, and local education authorities began to abandon it, even before 1965 when the Labour government announced its intention to introduce comprehensive secondary schools in place of the existing tripartite system of grammar, technical, and modern schools. At the same time a new examination for sixteen-year-olds (the Certificate of Secondary Education), giving teachers a larger role in setting syllabi and grading, was established as a less academic alternative to the GCE O level.

But as early as the late 1960s, the tenor of criticism began to change. The new direction was signaled by the publication of a series of so-called Black Papers, beginning in 1969 and culminating with Rhodes Boyson's *Crisis in Education*. The critics charged school and university curricula with being unstructured and watered-down: domination of school policy by education professionals had substituted faddish, "easy" subject matter in place of solid knowledge that had proved its worth over time. As a result, it was alleged, Britain was sinking into mediocrity, unable to produce the quantity and quality of graduates required by a first-rate nation. It was absurd, the Black Paper critics asserted, to try to organize the educational system along lines that produced no clear winners and losers. The message of an effective education system should be that there *are* winners and losers, and examinations exist to allocate the prizes.

A degree of support from more official quarters was not long in coming. In 1976 a parliamentary committee concluded that too many options were available far too early in secondary education and recommended consideration of a core curriculum, to be determined under the leadership of the Department of Education and Science (DES) and Her Majesty's Inspectors of Schools. In the same year, concern for acquiring data to use in judging the efficiency—or inefficiency, as the government suspected—of education's use of public resources led to the establishment of the Assessment of Performance Unit, charged with the task of testing student achievement as measures of the condition of the schools. In 1977 the DES itself expressed the need to prune drastically an overgrown curriculum, to concentrate on essentials rather than continually to expand options, to reduce the wide range of differences between schools, and to introduce a core curriculum within a national framework.

Although these calls for change were initiated under a Labour government, the policy direction continued and the rhetoric hardened with the shift to Conservative government. Indeed, a direct line leads from these preliminaries to the passage of the Education Act of 1988. The act provides for revolutionary changes in education. Among them are the establishment of a national core curriculum (to cover at least 40 percent of total school time) and a national system of periodic assessment of students' achievement (at seven, ten, fourteen, and sixteen years of age). Together with the new examinations for the General Certificate of Secondary Education, the innovations are intended to change principals' and teachers' behavior in ways that will support the national curriculum and elevate standards of achievement.

Successive Conservative governments under Margaret Thatcher's leadership were profoundly critical of the way many local government authorities, especially those in the hands of the Labour party, were managing local services in general. In Britain, educational services have been a major responsibility of local government, so the government's disapproval of local authorities' performance also took the form of disapproval of their educational performance. The strongest thread running through the changes embodied in the Education Act of 1988 is the central government's desire to curtail the educational prerogatives of the local authorities: to reduce their curricular discretion; to put them at risk of losing control of their schools to the minister in Whitehall should a majority of parents so vote; to limit their financial powers; to divest them of their sixth-form colleges and their tertiary-level institutions; and above all to force upon them greater accountability by subjecting their pupils to regular testing and by publication of school-by-school results.[9]

To help achieve these goals, and to give the central government more control over the external secondary school examinations, the number of GCSE examination boards has been sharply reduced (to five regional groups, each comprising former GCE and CSE boards) and their work subjected to close oversight by the newly created School Examination and Assessment Council (SEAC), the members of which are appointed by and report to the minister. All external examinations at the secondary level are now required to receive the SEAC's imprimatur.[10] These changes represent a decisive expression of faith in the power of examinations to shift the locus of control of education away from the periphery—individual school principals and local education authorities—toward the central authorities, reversing what has been a fundamental tenet of educational administration in England/Wales since the beginning of public education over one hundred years ago.

The government's campaign against the local educational authorities, the establishment of a national curriculum, and the preparations for centrally organized, periodic assessment of pupils' achievement have all attracted substantial criticism and organized opposition from teachers. Meanwhile, the Labour party, again in opposition, is on record as opposing the Conservative government's program of regular assessment of school

9. For details of the removal of the sixth-form colleges from local authority jurisdiction, see the February, March, and April 1991 issues of the *Times Educational Supplement*. Debate has been provoked over assessing the performance of head teachers by using, among other indicators, levels of student success in public examinations. The *Sunday Times* published the results of a first-ever survey, listing the top 250 schools across the country, ranked by the quality of their A-level results (September 8, 1991): 9. The publication of this list provoked protest and criticism from some head teachers and their association: "Independent schools have been thrown into turmoil by the publication of league tables of their A level examination results in national newspapers. Heads .. .. . were anxious to distance themselves from tables of raw results, echoing state school heads, who claim they tell little about a school's performance in improving academic progress." *Guardian Weekly* (Sept. 29, 1991): 5.

10. In December 1990 the government announced a further revolutionary implementation of testing in British education: local authorities are to test their teachers on a regular basis in order to ascertain their continued competence. The government's program of radical educational change continues unabated under Thatcher's successor. Cries of alarm were heard immediately from the opposition. The response by teacher unions was mixed: they had earlier agreed to support such a scheme so long as it was not linked to pay or to dismissals. But Education Secretary Kenneth Clarke's announcement did not appear to satisfy earlier understandings: that teacher assessment would not be compulsory, that it would not interfere with regular teaching, and that it would be sufficiently funded. *Times Educational Supplement* (Dec. 14, 1990), 6.

achievement and is likely to abolish or severely curtail it if it is returned to office.

The examination system that developed to satisfy the university entrance requirements has led secondary school students into exceptionally early and intense subject specialization. The British are divided about this feature of their upper secondary schooling. Probably a majority still judges the high level of specialization in sixth form (grades twelve and thirteen) to be a most positive feature, and equate the A-level examination with a "gold standard" that ensures high quality and value. Others deplore the fact that English youngsters can and typically do abandon the sciences and mathematics, the humanities, or the social sciences by age sixteen to concentrate on their sixth-form studies. This is an examination system that makes little or no effort at the upper secondary level to ensure some equivalent of the French *culture générale,* or the German *allgemeine Bildung,* let alone the Soviet polytechnical ideal.

The Conservative government has strongly supported the present structure of the GCE Advanced level, arguing that it admirably defends traditions of sixth-form subject specialization and depth of study against fashionable but shallow innovations aimed at "rounded," "general" education.[11] The Higginson Committee, an official review of the structure and content of the A-level examinations, reported in favor of substantially broadening studies and examinations.[12] The government saw fit to reject the recommendations in toto on the day of their publication. In May 1991 the government's White Papers on further and higher education announced a continued official commitment to the present A-level arrangements.[13]

But criticism of the sixth-form curriculum and A-level specialization is rising to such a pitch and covers such a wide spectrum of interest groups and opinion that some more flexible response by the government would seem to be inevitable.[14] In the autumn of 1990, a British Broadcasting

11. "There seems to be a group of people whose central aim in life is to get rid of A-Levels, which have proved a highly effective route into the university." Kenneth Clarke as quoted in David Tyler, "A-Levels under a Cloud," *Times* (December 2, 1991): 27.

12. *Advancing A Levels. Report of a Committee Appointed by the Secretary of State for Education and Science and the Secretary of State for Wales* (London: Her Majesty's Stationery Office, 1988). This is known as the Higginson Report.

13. *Education and Training for the 21st Century,* 2 vols. (London: Her Majesty's Stationery Office, 1991).

14. The response appears to be taking the form of an attempt to establish greater parity of esteem between A-levels and revamped vocational training qualifications. Support for the established A-level structure appears to remain as strong as ever within the cabinet. But John Major's Conservative government has intensified support for the National Council for Vocational Qualifications (NCVQ), which began work in 1987 to bring some order and greater

Corporation survey of school heads showed that 97 percent of state secondary school heads wanted reform of the A level, although a majority of
the heads of the famous public schools wish to retain the present content
and structure. The Committee of Vice-Chancellors (of universities) has announced, "The Vice-Chancellors are committed to the total reform of A
Levels. We want to see a much broader examination, more like the French
baccalauréat." The Confederation of British Industry, an influential employers' association, concurs: "The system of A-Level examinations has
served us well in the past but it needs to be changed." On this matter even
the Trades Union Congress agrees with the employers: "A major obstacle
to widening access to higher education continues to be the government's
reluctance to broaden the narrow traditional A-Level route."[15] The Labour
party has weighed in with a pledge to abolish A-level examinations entirely, basing its criticisms partly on the Higginson report and partly on
proposals by the Institute of Public Policy Research and the Secondary
Heads Association.[16] Thus, the immediate prospect in England/Wales is
for another stormy political dispute over examination policy and practices,
this time centered on the A levels.

Germany. Unlike the United States, where disagreements about school organization and examinations often cut across party political lines, quite the
opposite characterizes the politics of education in Germany, where Social
Democratic party (SPD) and Christian Democratic party (CDU) policies are
sharply defined and systematically in conflict. Although the politics of education in general and of the Abitur in particular are primarily conditioned
by the sovereignty of the eleven Länder in educational matters and the
differences among them in party political allegiance, changes in the bal-

status to the tangle of vocational training courses and qualifications. Newly designed National
Vocational Qualifications are to be available for four-fifths of the work force by the end of
1992. On January 23, 1992, Major "announced details of a new qualification for those 16 or
over. The Advanced Diploma will be awarded for satisfactory performance in A-levels, or in
level 3 NVQs, or in a mixture of the two. The aim is to create parity of prestige between
vocational and academic education and increase participation in further education. Sixteen-
year-olds will no longer have to choose between narrow A-levels and equally narrow vocational qualifications." *Economist* (January 25, 1992): 35.

   15. All these observations were cited in *The Economist* (April 27 and May 3, 1991): pp.
13, 64.

   16. "Labour to Abolish A-levels," *Times Educational Supplement* (May 3, 1991): 2. A
more recent report suggests that Labour party policy has softened somewhat and that "a
Labour government would introduce five 'leaner, broader' A-levels as the best way to widen
sixth-form education." David Tyler, "A-Levels under a Cloud," *Times* (December 2, 1991):
27.

ance of party power in the federal government have signaled changes in policies affecting the Abitur. Six Länder (the city-states of Hamburg and Bremen, plus Hesse, Nordrhein-Westfalen, Saar, and Schleswig-Holstein) have remained staunchly or mostly Social Democratic, whereas five (Bavaria, Baden-Württemberg, Rheinland-Pfalz, Lower Saxony, and West Berlin)[17] are solidly or mostly in the CDU or allied camps. The Christian Democrats have been conservative in their education policies, in particular opposing any tampering with the division of secondary education among the three types of schools, Gymnasium, Realschule, and Hauptschule, and resisting changes to curricula and the examinations at the end of schooling. The Social Democrats initially pushed hard to sweep away the tripartite structure in favor of installing comprehensive secondary education (*Gesamtschulen*). They have achieved only very limited success in this direction, but they have been much more successful in their policies directed to widening access to the Gymnasium, diversifying curricula in the direction of adding more directly vocational subjects, and providing more options in the Abitur.

The arrival in federal power of the Social Democratic Party in 1969 was followed in 1972 by changes to the Abitur. Regulations were relaxed to permit a much wider choice of subjects and levels of difficulty. In 1982 the political pendulum swung back to the Christian Democrats and five years later the changes of 1972 were partially rolled back, withdrawing some of the options previously made available—the so-called reform of the reforms. As has been described in chapter 4, debate, conflict, and ultimate resolution of inter-Land differences in these matters takes place within the Kultus Minister Konferenz. After the 1972 reform of the Abitur, ministers from some Länder threatened to withdraw their recognition of Abitur certificates from other (Social Democratic) Länder, calling those certificates "discount Abiturs."[18] A particular point of dispute was the new Abitur certificates introduced in Nordrhein-Westfalen, where alternatives to the traditional Gymnasium had been established in the form of twenty-four so-called *Kollegeschulen*. These new schools sought to provide a "dual" Abitur with substantial vocational elements, providing access to a skilled trade as well as to the universities, and hence abandoning

17. We should note that the Christian Democrats lost Lower Saxony to the Social Democrats in May 1990, Hesse in January 1991, and Rheinland-Pfalz in the Land elections of April 1991—this last a wholly unexpected outcome after forty-five unbroken years of CDU rule. The 1991 losses are the fallout from what was widely perceived to be Chancellor Helmut Kohl's broken promise not to raise taxes to pay for the unification of the two Germanys.

18. Gerold Becker, "Gymnasiale Oberstufe: Das Ende einer Illusion?" *Pädagogik Heute* 5 (May 1987): 7–11.

the exclusive concentration on studies for *allgemeine Bildung* (broad, humanistic education) that has been a traditional hallmark of German secondary education.[19]

Criticism of the movement to include vocational elements in the curriculum came, as expected, from the West German [University] Rectors' Conference and from the association of Gymnasium teachers, the Philologenverband. Both organizations charged that freshmen would be inadequately prepared for their university studies if they were permitted to substitute specialized vocational subjects in place of German and foreign languages and mathematics. The Gewerkschaft Erziehung und Wissenschaft, a trade union organization especially concerned with education, policies, was equally vocal in its view that the traditional humanistic, academic curriculum had outlived its usefulness and should be radically restructured to meet Germany's current situation and needs as an advanced industrial and postindustrial power.

This conflict, partly political, partly professional, over the innovative Abitur courses was eventually settled in a compromise toward the end of 1987 by the "reform of the reforms." This set minimum requirements for the Abitur while recognizing the right of the individual Länder to establish variations on the traditional upper secondary school course.[20] For the time being, at least, the Abitur question in the "original" eleven Länder offers relatively small points of controversy, compared with the vigor of the disputes of the past two decades. Concern has moved on to more pressing matters: the restructuring of secondary education and the Abitur in the five Länder incorporated into the Federal Republic as a result of the dissolution of the German Democratic Republic (GDR), and the problems likely to be raised for Germany's secondary education by the approaching integration of the labor markets of the European Community countries. These questions have in turn sparked a discussion of the advisability of reducing the course of study leading to the Abitur from thirteen years to twelve. The desirability of such a move has been in part raised by the fact that students in the former GDR needed, and still need, only twelve years to graduate. In part, also, there is concern that German students already take too long to graduate and that they will be at a growing disadvantage vis-à-vis students from other European Community countries as labor mobility across the Common Market increases.

19. Paul Bendelow, "Undecided over Ultimate *Abitur*," *Times Educational Supplement*, (March 13, 1987): 15.

20. *Frankfurter Allgemeine Zeitung* (January 21, 1987, February 11, 1987).

Japan. In recent years, Japan has become the model to be admired if not emulated by some other nations. Motivated for over a century by the desire to catch up to and overtake the more industrialized world, Japan has so successfully adapted foreign educational practices that today many of the features of its educational system are the envy of others. During the United States occupation of Japan at the end of World War II, aptitude tests replaced achievement tests for the purpose of selecting high school graduates for college admission. Abandonment of achievement tests represented a rejection of a fundamental Japanese value: the principle that individual effort to master the curriculum is the key to success, rather than the mere possession of talent or special gifts. As soon as the occupation forces were withdrawn and Japanese sovereignty over its own education system restored, aptitude tests were abandoned in favor of achievement tests. Although the Japanese have experimented with different formats and agencies of control for these tests, in all their forms they have been heavily weighted with factual material, requiring students to memorize large numbers of often isolated facts. It is this feature that has primarily aroused the opposition of the generally left-wing secondary school teachers in Japan. They and the Ministry of Education are frequently on opposite sides of the struggle for control of schools, curriculum, and examinations. Teachers tend to deplore the extreme burdens the JFSAT loads on to secondary school students, the constraints the examination imposes on their pedagogical freedom, and the determining power of the JFSAT over the curriculum. For a brief period in the mid-1980s there was a degree of official support for these views, as Prime Minister Nakasone established a committee to review the Japanese educational system and to recommend changes. But other parts of the government, business interests, and most parents did not agree with the prime minister that large changes were needed in the way the schools operate. Rather, the Japanese typically voice their approval of the work of the school system, accepting their country's position at the top of the international "league tables" of student achievement with a large measure of pride, and regard continued Ministry of Education control of the JFSAT, more or less on current lines, as an essential guarantee of high standards. Even before Nakasone ceased to be prime minister, the early reformist momentum had significantly slowed. With his resignation in 1989 what remained vanished. The conflict between those who desire to continue the traditional emphasis on promoting individual effort and those who want to relax the pressures on students—either because they believe current practice is inhumane or because they believe the continued progress of Japan requires a greater degree of creativity and independent thought among the graduates—has once again been resolved decisively in favor of the former. Their victory is supported by the widely shared conviction that only a difficult examination based upon an equally tough curriculum can guarantee fairness in allocating college and university places.

China. China's experience with respect to examinations and control of the schools has been the most volatile of the eight countries studied, swings of policy having occurred at roughly 10-year intervals since the establishment of the People's Republic in 1949. Changes in educational policies have followed closely upon changes in the political climate. Examination policy has played a role in the political debate and has been a focus for the different views held on educational policy in general. On one side are those who support a strenuously competitive national college entrance examination, arguing that this will provide a powerful incentive to students and their teachers to work hard and to master the knowledge required for building a socialist society. The proponents of the examination system also point to it as the only defensible way to allocate scarce university places. Opposed are those who see in highly competitive university entrance examinations a tool for the reproduction of privilege, leading to the distortion of pedagogy and projecting damage far down into the earliest grade levels. As the official policy pendulum has swung back and forth, the first view, then the second, then the first again have gained ascendancy.

From 1949 to 1959, Soviet influence was strong and policy was directed to building China along the lines of a Marxist-Leninist-Stalinist model. Educational policy emphasized the importance of knowledge and skills: to be "expert" was as important as to be "red." Control of the schools and the transfer of students was centralized in Beijing's hands. A national system of college entrance examinations was introduced in 1952, reinforcing the central authorities' control over the schools and focusing much of Chinese schooling on preparation for the college entrance examinations. Enrollments in secondary education were still small, however, and for some years there were barely enough secondary school graduates to fill the available freshman places in the universities.

A second period of Chinese policy opened in the late 1950s. In July 1960 Soviet assistance all but ended with the precipitate departure of all Soviet advisers. Nevertheless, the college entrance examinations remained in full force, along with the influence they exerted on the schools. It was not until 1966 that this changed.

Mao called on young people to mount a Great Proletarian Cultural Revolution, to mobilize and destroy the power of bureaucrats, not only in

Beijing, but also in the provinces and localities. Administrators in education and teachers were especially targeted, accused of conveying false, especially Confucian, doctrines, encouraging the reestablishing of elites, and placing obstacles in the path of youngsters from peasant and worker families. Many colleges and universities were closed and in the remainder ideological campaigning and political activism took the place of formal teaching, study, and research. The most brutal abuse of educational personnel occurred in the two or three years following 1966, but imprisonments, forced labor, and exile to the countryside continued throughout the ten years following.

In the course of this Mao-inspired "second revolution" against the governmental bureaucracy in general, and the educational establishment in particular, examinations were abolished. Students were no longer expected to prepare themselves for academic tests; transfer at the end of secondary school depended on evidence of appropriate social class origin, record of political and social service, and demonstrated enthusiasm for the new radically populist policies. Meanwhile, following a policy of opening education much more broadly to sectors of the population previously excluded, a great expansion of enrollments in secondary education took place, from about 14.5 million in 1965 to over 58 million in 1977, although the quality of the education provided left much to be desired. "Expertness" took a backseat, "redness" became the paramount virtue.

The fourth turn of the wheel came in 1976, with the overthrow of the government controlled by Mao's widow. The ouster of the so-called Gang of Four brought a restoration of central control over education and a marked shift of emphasis back to "expertness." In 1977 the highly selective, nationwide end-of-upper-secondary-school examinations were reinstated. In the struggle between those who had agitated for a populist egalitarianism and those who preferred a hierarchically organized society based on a mixture of party allegiance, educational credentials, and work position, the latter had decisively won, with predictable results for the role of examinations in the educational system and in the wider society. Although examinations again became critical for admission to higher education, and also for entrance to the key-point schools, the results also served as an important barometer of success for the schools themselves. Poor examination results could threaten a key-point school's priority status in obtaining scarce resources and admitting superior students.

During the 1980s substantial administrative authority over the examinations devolved to the provinces and to a few of the larger cities, Beijing and Shanghai in particular. General directions were issued by the State

Education Commission, but implementation was in the hands of the provinces. In like manner, secondary-school-graduation examinations began to be instituted by provincial authorities, beginning with Shanghai and Beijing, and were increasingly used as first-stage examinations, screening candidates for the National Unified College Entrance Examinations. Other local and private initiatives were also introduced in the mid-1980s, including pilot projects whereby a university might admit students at its own discretion, ignoring examination scores. Such measures were viewed with suspicion and hostility by many: decentralization, local variations, and encouragement of choices all represented challenges to more orthodox Marxist thinking and party control over higher education.[21]

In the second half of the 1980s, yet another swing of policy back toward greater central control of the examinations became evident: devolution and decentralization of the examination system was allegedly becoming too costly. Construction and validation of examinations by each of the provinces was said to impose undue financial burdens on the educational system. In order to reduce costs and improve comparability and objectivity, the State Education Commission encouraged the introduction of new formats, such as short-answer questions and multiple-choice, machine-scored tests.[22]

One of the enduring aspects of education in China has been the tiny fraction (2 percent) of the age group admitted to higher education. Thus far the Chinese people have been willing to accept the legitimacy of severe "selecting-out" by the examination system. Chinese university students represent an intellectual elite, guaranteed access to privileged jobs, financial security, and social status. The economic reforms initiated after 1979 have reduced these expectations of automatic privilege, at the same time that economic liberalization has not been accompanied by any substantial political reform. Student protests against lack of democratic freedoms were not unknown before May 1989, but the demonstrations, sit-ins, and hunger strikes in Beijing's Tiananmen Square, Shanghai, and other large towns

21. See Wolfgang Mitter, "Chinas Hochschulen im gesellschaftliche Wandel: Tatsachen und Probleme gegenwärtiger Entwicklung," *Bildung in sozioökonomischer Sicht* (Cologne: Böhlau Verlag, 1989), pp. 361–384. (*Festschrift für Hasso von Recum*).

22. See *Third Symposium on the Reform of Examinations and Recruitment of Students by Ordinary Higher Education Institutions* (Beijing: Higher Education Press, 1989). This collection of papers by Chinese educators and researchers includes discussion of all of the points mentioned and criticizes current examination practices. Authors press for greater "objectivity" in the examinations and support more autonomy for the higher education institutions in selecting students for admission.

were on a scale and of an intensity to give the government and party pause. The leadership is caught in the predictable dilemma of governments that wish to develop economically and materially without sharing political power more widely. It desires the technical, economic, and military benefits to be had from a highly educated set of cadres; it does not, however, wish to provide substantial political freedoms to those individuals or to the population at large. After Tiananmen Square, the Chinese government has once again rethought the policy of relying primarily on examination results to allocate university places. Admission scores remain important, but graduation examination results are generally a prerequisite to taking the entrance examination. In addition, school references on the health, "moral qualities," and other "special characteristics" of applicants are now given more attention than previously.[23]

At the time of its abolition in 1905, the imperial examination system that had survived for centuries was viewed as a worthless, even damaging, relic of an outmoded system of education, an obstacle to westernization. Subsequently, Western-type examinations were regarded as an ideal means to modernize the education system. This positive view of examinations lasted until the decade of the Cultural Revolution, when once again they were seen as instruments of the status quo—this time as obstacles to building a progressive, egalitarian socialist society. For a decade after the Cultural Revolution had spent its force, examinations were regarded once again in a positive light, as valuable instruments of educational change. Now China is once again changing its mind about the merit of relying primarily on the results of competitive examinations to stimulate effort and to allocate educational opportunities. In few other countries have there been such violent struggles for the control of education; and in few other countries have extreme alternating swings of ideology and party policy so buffeted examination policies.

The Soviet Union, France, and Sweden. In sharp contrast to these instances, the Soviet Union, France, and Sweden have witnessed much less overt conflict over examination policies than the five discussed above. In the last half-century in the Soviet Union, although debates on the structure and content of education have been virtually continuous, and even at times vigorous, little or no debate about examinations has been reported. Even under the surge toward *glasnost* in 1988, the only effect upon the secondary graduation examinations was to suspend the history examination pend-

23. From a news item in *Shanghai World Report* (February–March 1991), describing the most recent changes in the college entrance examinations.

ing the announcement of new topics for study and the publication of new textbooks. But this order was a matter of curriculum change, not of examination policy itself. In consequence, policies governing the secondary-school-completion examination and university and higher-institute entrance examinations have changed hardly at all.

In France, paradoxically, although political disputes over educational policies, broadly defined, have often boiled over into vehement protests and demonstrations, the radical changes made in the baccalauréat over the past thirty years have taken effect with relatively little controversy surrounding them. The diversification of the baccalauréat has been a powerful instrument for widening the curriculum of French secondary schools and for weakening the privileged position of the academic lycées, which formerly enjoyed a monopoly in preparation for the baccalauréat. The exception has been when the government has proposed measures that could be interpreted as weakening the baccalauréat's status or the entitlements it has traditionally provided. In late 1986 the French government announced a few changes of arrangements in university education, all of them commonly established in other countries. Among other things, it was proposed to give each university greater discretion over what levels of baccalauréat score would be acceptable for admission and to have the degree certificate include the name of the university attended. The untutored observer might regard these as fairly insignificant changes, but university students saw in them an attack on both the national currency of the baccalauréat and the principle of equal status for all universities. Their opposition was manifested in a series of demonstrations, joining university and lycée students and political parties all over the country and culminating in a large-scale sit-down outside the Assemblée nationale in Paris. In short order the minister responsible resigned and the government's proposals were withdrawn.

Although criticism of the baccalauréat is common, it is marked by contradiction. On the one hand are heard complaints that the examination overstuffs the curriculum and overloads students; on the other are dire warnings about the "watering down" of standards due to increasing numbers of candidates and rising pass rates. In particular, lycée teachers (and their students) have expressed concern that the rapid expansion of enrollments has not been accompanied by appropriate expansion of facilities and finance, resulting in inadequate staff, poor physical conditions in the schools, and ultimately a loss of educational quality. These complaints, too, led to massive street demonstrations (in November 1990, most notably), which extracted government promises of more funds and staff for the schools. But for all their vehemence and the support they drew, none of these protests targeted specifically the baccalauréat or the system of examinations in general. Indeed, among the signs held up during the 1990 demonstrations was one that expressed with elegant simplicity the spirit of the protests: "Give us the money, so that we can get our *bacs*."

Sweden presents the paradox of a country that has made the greatest change of all in examination policy—doing away with the classic end-of-secondary-school external examination—without producing political uproar. Although there are criticisms of poor student standards, attributed in part to examinations that have become less demanding, conflict over the replacement of the traditional examination by the current system of periodic tests is virtually absent.

Comparative Discussion

Conflicts over examinations are rooted in differences in political-ideological stance, contrasting views of what education is all about, and struggles over who shall determine the shape and functions of the instrument of control, potentially or actually powerful, represented by examination policies and practices. The struggles for power over the examinations are sharpened by the expectation that they can be used either to promote or to prevent educational change.

Differences in educational views, the interests of various sectors and groups in society, and national politics are so inextricably intertwined that it is hardly possible to isolate the issues from one another. What does seem clear is that a number of common features are involved. Everywhere, examination policy is the stage on which more traditional, uniform, subject- and content-based views of the curriculum confront the alternatives of project-based, individualized, and differentiated curricula.

Furthermore, differences of opinion about examinations, even within a single body of men and women, set the scene for a political struggle between those who view examination syllabi and regulations as valuable tools in a campaign to energize educational activity and those who view them as dead weights reinforcing the inertia of schools.

Britain's Conservative government has wholeheartedly embraced a policy of tests and examinations for all, hoping that this will help build a better sense of the purpose of education for all children and their teachers. The Labour party, in opposition, has mounted a constant attack on the government's proposals, arguing that they are a poor substitute for the necessary investment of money in the education and training systems of the country.

The British government's arguments have been reflected in many U.S. states. Recently, governors and legislatures have joined forces to install new programs of tests, also in the hope that this will help stimulate and focus student and teacher effort. State officials are frequently quite candid in saying that they expect poor test results to lead more frequently than in the past to students having to repeat courses and even be the ground for withholding high school diplomas. None of this goes down well with some groups and their spokespersons, who argue that the tougher standards now being introduced will simply impose a higher probability of failure on children who already have had too much experience of it. More tests and examinations, they argue, are no substitute for more resources to support disadvantaged families, poor and hungry children, and their schools. Examination for assessment distracts from other, more important educational purposes.

Examinations become embroiled in politics because they are inherently contentious. They are criticized by some for the very characteristics others praise, for example, their function of sorting and labeling students in the interest of promoting efficiency. While opening the doors of further opportunity for those who are successful, they slam them shut in the face of those who fail. Although examinations are supported as being effective ways of reducing nepotism, influence, and outright corruption, the contemporary importance of credentials based on examination success means that examinations are constantly under scrutiny for evidence of deficiencies, like bias in favor of some groups or against others, weaknesses in administration, outmoded syllabi, poor question construction, or unreliable grading. Finally, although examinations are valued for the stimulus they can provide to teaching and learning, they are at the same time blamed for undermining teachers' initiative and constraining and overloading the curriculum. Teachers and their professional unions are especially prone to be critical officially of the baneful effects of examinations on the processes of schooling, all the while recognizing that their work is often most valued by pupils and families and their own status in society elevated precisely when they are engaged in preparing their pupils for examinations. Examinations not only can become political footballs between groups holding differing views about their desirability, they are even regarded ambiguously within such specific groups as teachers, members of a political party, or employers. Because examinations present two faces to the world, they are always liable to become embroiled in political struggle.

Distinctly different views of the functions of examinations are at the root of much of the conflict. Teachers and school administrators tend to regard examinations differently from others involved with their results, being primarily concerned with their instructional uses and with student assessments of several kinds. Others, within and outside the educational system, regard examination results as means to assess and rate schools and local school systems. This function has grown in importance with the growth of concerns about standards of education and about gaining value for public money expended on it. Examinations are seen as useful tools for both financial and political accountability.

Employers and postsecondary admission officers are likely to regard examinations in yet a different light: as selection instruments. Common to all nations is the conflict between those groups, in schools and outside, who discern different uses and, consequently, different attributes, both positive and negative, of the examination system depending on their particular interests.

This is not to say that those in a given interest group speak with a single voice. Not all employers' organizations, for example, are in accord about the wisdom of promoting more vocational elements in curricula and examinations. The most one can say is that small-scale employers tend to be somewhat more enthusiastic about vocationalizing school curricula and examinations than their large-scale competitors, no doubt out of self-interest. Small-scale employers probably feel less able to bear the costs of training, preferring this be done at public expense. Also, if their employees switch jobs, employers do not lose as much of their investment as they would if they had borne a large fraction of the training costs. Large-scale employers are likely to feel more secure on both counts.

A common element across countries is the frequent association of examination issues with national and party politics. Supporters of the political center and right wing are likely to accept, and even applaud, the sorting and selection function of examinations. They view examinations as highly legitimate devices, rewarding effort and talent. They are valued as providing appropriate incentives for hard work and regarded as assurances of maintaining the status quo. Left-wing supporters are more likely to criticize examinations as instruments for the reproduction of inherited privilege, providing a veneer of justification for the exclusion of minority-group children and the poor from full opportunity.

These ideological differences in attitudes toward examinations can be seen as much in Communist China as in capitalist America, and as much in France as in Britain and Germany. Indeed, in all of these countries, writers on the left have used such terms as *oppressive, hegemonic,* and *imperialist* in their discussions of examination systems, at the same time that those in the center and on the right look forward to the extension of even more rigorous examinations to even more youngsters.

Views about other particulars of the curriculum and the associated examinations also show a consistent relation to political leaning. In England,

France, Germany, and Japan, opposition to the substitution of broader world history, or general social studies, in place of national history has come strongly from those on the political right, especially those with nationalist leanings. Also in England, France, and Germany, the abandonment of traditional language and literature studies in favor of the development of more general, functional syllabi entitled "communication skills," "applied language arts," "practical English[French/German]," and the like has been the target of severe criticism, generally from the political right. Similarly, the relatively small movements toward the revival of minority languages and the extension of permission to write examinations in these languages (for example, in Breton and German in France), and the movement in the United States to place Spanish on a more equal footing with English, are more often opposed by right-wing than left-wing politicians. It is difficult indeed for politicians to avoid taking a stand on these issues, not only because examinations are important social institutions in their own right, but because decisions about examinations have a way of reverberating through the entire educational system. Thus, political issues having to do with national unity and identity may lie at the root of some of the controversies over curriculum and examinations.

Demographic conditions, specifically the growth of enrollment in upper secondary and postsecondary education, have contributed to conflict over examinations in the public domain. When secondary schooling and its associated examinations were restricted to a small minority of the young population—until 1960 in Germany, only 5 to 6 percent of the age group achieved the Abitur—the potential for political struggle over the associated educational issues was much smaller than it is today, when *Abiturienten* form 30 percent of the age group. Already in France, 60 percent of the age group is enrolled in lycées, and the government talks seriously about raising this figure to 80 percent by the year 2000. Such numbers make it virtually impossible to insulate questions surrounding the secondary school examinations from the political arena. Not only are the numbers affected by secondary school examinations large and increasing, but successful completion of secondary school has become critical for the life chances of young people. Many jobs formerly open to primary school leavers are available now only to those with evidence of at least secondary education. Most of the eight countries of the study have formal, legal, or quasi-legal regulations governing the minimum credentials and education requirements for different types of jobs. Germany is outstanding in this respect, with an exceptionally tight, legally enforced set of education and credential requirements for each occupation. But even in more relaxed systems, for example, in the United States, employers nowadays will routinely expect an applicant to possess a high school diploma for quite low-skill jobs, like supermarket clerk or cashier.

As we have noted, examination policy has been a matter of contention in some countries, and much less so, or even absent, in others. Why have three countries, France, Sweden, and the Soviet Union, not been affected by serious conflict over examination policies? One reason is that they have not had to use examinations to mold school curricula. Rather, by issuing directives and regulations, their governments could exercise direct control of the curricula. In England/Wales and the United States, government power is much weaker in this respect, and the use of examination policy to compensate has led to the involvement of examinations in conflicts over curricula and levels of achievement. Similarly, in Germany, the political party divisions among the Länder, together with Land prerogatives in education, have set the stage for frequent political confrontations over school policy, including the Abitur.

Nevertheless, political conflict over examination policy can also occur in systems in which central governments enjoy considerable power over school curricula—witness China and Japan. China's experience can perhaps be explained by the extreme politicization of education, mirroring closely the politicization of so many other aspects of Chinese society, and Japan's by reference to the exceptional emphasis given to examinations in Japanese society.

Conclusion

If examinations provoke debate and conflict, it is because they are not merely technical devices to evaluate students. The policies and practices they embody carry ideological and political freight. Educational, ideological, and political issues become intertwined, especially over questions of control: who shall control the examinations, and what shall the examinations control?

Neither of these questions finds permanent solutions in any country. Instead, current examination policies and arrangements are best regarded as the outcome of a series of compromises among competing values, interests, and points of view, or as we phrase it in the next chapter, as a set of trade-offs between competing values.

Chapter 10

Findings, Options, Trade-offs, and Dilemmas

Why should we, in vain endeavour,
  Guess and guess and guess again?
—Quintet, *The Gondoliers,* act 1

Even though external, written examinations are a relatively recent phenomenon, they are now regarded as part of the natural order of things. Governments, the press, the churches, political parties, employers and their associations, trade unions, schoolteachers, students, parents, and the public at large—all largely accept examinations and examination results at their face value, as appropriate exercises designed to inform interested parties of an individual's level of knowledge and degree of skill or talent. Extreme attacks calling for the abolition of examinations are rare, even if criticisms of current examination arrangements and proposals for change are common. Examinations possess a high degree of legitimacy in modern society.

Nevertheless, a national examination system is a highly artificial construction. There is nothing natural about the idea of arranging for a sizable fraction of the country's teenage youth to complete their secondary schooling by producing externally graded written answers to a series of externally set questions. The esteem enjoyed by such an examination system derives primarily from the public's estimate of its legitimacy. This in turn depends on the general sense that the examinations are honest, fair, and relevant, that is, administered in secure fashion, discriminating impartially among the candidates, and testing knowledge that is regarded as important. Should any one of these criteria be seen as absent, the legitimacy of the examination system may be questioned.

Acceptance of extant national examination systems is so high that nations appear routinely to operate tests that elsewhere most likely would be termed unacceptably flawed. For example, the SAT and ACT of the United States find little favor in Europe. The emphasis on oral examination in the Soviet Union is usually dismissed as too subjective and too costly for the United States and elsewhere. The many choices of subjects and level of difficulty available in the French baccalauréat do not sit well with the Japanese, who place a very high value on comparability of results among candidates. In turn, the Japanese examinations, with their extraordinarily heavy load of learning imposed on students, would be quite unacceptable even in France and certainly in the United States. Legitimacy is in the eye of the beholder over a very wide range of examination characteristics.

Having said this, it is also true that the rituals and formalities to do with security of the questions before the examination date, the monitoring of the examination halls to exclude the possibility of cheating, the arrangements to ensure the expertise and incorruptibility of the graders, and the reputation and authority of the issuers of certificates and diplomas are all important guarantees of the status and sense of legitimacy enjoyed by the examination. The media attention given to even occasional lapses reflects the importance of security for the public's overall assessment of examination legitimacy. Certainly, when an examination authority fails to maintain the security of its system of constructing, printing, and distributing the examination papers, grave damage is done to the legitimacy of its credentials.

Findings

Examinations at the end of secondary schooling both shape and reflect the characteristics of the schools. Because examinations fulfill so many vital functions, countries find it very difficult to do without them, and those that have tried to abolish them have eventually had to restore them. Of central importance is this study's demonstration of the ways in which examinations operate as powerful instruments of control within education, albeit that different countries are shown to use examinations for this purpose in different ways.

Our study shows that in a number of respects, national examination systems are converging toward common forms and practices. Examination systems that have traditionally been decentralized give strong indications of greater centralization, and those that have been centralized in their control appear to be becoming less so. In every country the secondary school examination system has expanded to embrace a far greater proportion of the population of senior secondary school students. Expansion has been part consequence, but also part cause, of the ongoing differentiation of examinations that traditionally have been quite limited in their range of subjects. The changes have provided candidates with an increased range of choices among subjects and levels of difficulty. Often this has taken the form of including a greatly increased number of employment-related options. Convergence is evident, too, in trends among systems that have relied exclusively on open-ended, extended-answer formats to introduce multiple-choice, machine-scorable items and among those that have emphasized objective tests to introduce more elements of extended answers.

Last, the study highlights the two faces of examination systems. Examinations play a dual role in broader educational change. They can serve both as levers and obstacles to educational change, even within a given country. Although governments are prone to seize upon examination systems as handy instruments for pushing schools and teachers in desired directions, equally common is the resistance mounted to such initiatives by school administrators, teachers, employers, and even parents, using the examination systems to defend the status quo.

Impact and Reach of Examinations. In none of the countries studied does every student coming to the end of secondary education sit for an external examination. Large groups are often unaffected. Some have been selected out of the examination-preparatory tracks. Others attend a school that is simply not engaged in the business of preparing students for the examination. Nevertheless, the influence of an examination system permeates a nation's education system. It affects performance expectations, curriculum content, and definitions of scholastic success and failure. Especially for those who prepare for the examination, the impact on school and personal life is likely to be profound, as in Japan, France, Germany and England/ Wales, where successive years of upper secondary schooling are characterized by a crescendo of concentration and effort. But even in other countries, students' lives in and out of school focus upon examinations. There are exceptions, however. Sweden makes a deliberate attempt to minimize the impact of the tests, and in the United States preparing for and taking the SAT and the ACT is far from the defining experience of the typical student's high school career.

Controlling the Examinations. We have observed many variations in the distribution of authority and responsibilities for national examinations. No nation has a single, centrally determined examination for all possible purposes. Control and ownership of the examinations can be in the hands of the central government, or shared among subnational units, or in a "quango," or even, as in the United States, in a private not-for-profit corporation. In France, China, Japan, and Sweden, the end-of-secondary-school examination systems are controlled mainly from the center by a special agency of each country's ministry of education. But even in these formally centralized arrangements, there are strong elements of devolution to regional or local authorities. Conversely, even when the system is formally decentralized, usually some oversight is entrusted to a central authority. Thus, in the Soviet Union each republic has formal authority over the attestat zrelosti, but took its cue from Moscow. In England/Wales, several largely autonomous regional examining boards are in control, but they collaborate on administrative matters and examination content, and they are increasingly subject to supervision by the central government's Department of Education and Science through the School Examination and Assessment Council. In Germany, though the Länder retain formal sovereign powers over their Abitur examination systems, they enter into voluntary agreements that in practice limit their discretion. In all these countries, control and ownership of the examinations are in the hands of public bodies, either a government department or semi-independent public agency.

The situation is quite different in the United States. Here, although a few states arrange for end-of-secondary-school achievement examinations, none has national currency, nor does the federal government provide a national examination system for the schools. The United States is exceptional in its reliance on private organizations like the Educational Testing Service and the American College Testing Program to provide end-of-secondary-school external tests and examinations, free of federal direction or control.[1]

Apart from who "owns" the examinations, there is the question of the role of teachers—mainly, though not exclusively, secondary school teachers—in performing such specific tasks as constructing test papers, proctoring the examination sessions, evaluating responses, and monitoring the whole process. The latter function can influence teacher-student relationships profoundly. When, as in Japan, China, England/Wales, the United States, and France, all grading of external examination answers is done anonymously, without teacher participation in grading their own students' answer papers, students and teachers can become allies in the business of outsmarting examiners. This is more difficult in Germany and the Soviet Union, where a student's own teachers play a large, overt role in evaluating his or her examination work. In addition, the German and Soviet practice indicates the presence of considerable trust, whether justified or not, in the skill and judgment of teachers, a positive reflection on their professional status. Swedish practice contains elements of all of the above.

The Examinations. Examination systems strongly influence the school curriculum, to the extent that in England/Wales, France, China, and Japan the

---

1. Some states do limit the otherwise unfettered discretion of the testing organizations. For example, New York State requires ETS to provide each SAT candidate with an item-by-item printout of the grading of his or her responses.

subjects examined and the syllabi for the examinations virtually determine the school curriculum and the objectives of teaching. The format and content of examinations reflect what an educational system considers to be the knowledge and skills of most worth. They also reflect and stimulate curriculum changes. New curriculum elements tend gradually to find their way into examination papers, usually at the expense of traditional ones.

Tests incorporating significant practical work, such as laboratory exercises or artistic work—so-called performance examinations—are common in some places, rare or absent elsewhere. Multiple-choice formats are becoming more common, but still remain the exception rather than the rule in the eight nations of this study. Although all examinations test recall and comprehension, more advanced intellectual activities like problem-solving, critical analysis, and creative expression may also be assessed. New forms of evaluation are emerging that involve more than a timed paper-and-pen test. Rather, the new forms take into account an accumulated corpus of the candidate's work in the subject. Some advocate reporting results in more detailed ways, beyond traditional letter or number grades, to reflect fuller "profiles" of achievement.

The Demands Examinations Place on Candidates, Compared. Examination systems define a nation's expectations of students and its standards for educational success. Although all systems impose requirements upon candidates, these vary considerably. Some, like France and Germany, call for many subjects, an extensive syllabus, and long examination papers; others are less burdensome, for example, the United States. All systems offer certain options to candidates in choice of subjects and in level of difficulty, some of them very limited, others more numerous. In France scores for a subject examination are weighted differently in the final overall grade according to the candidate's specialization. In Germany and recently in England/Wales, candidates may take a subject as a major or a minor, with different examination papers based on different syllabi.

Comparing the relative difficulty of examination systems involves evaluating their general requirements, the content and the format of examination papers, timing and time limits, and the available options. Although such an exercise includes some objective data, like the number of examination hours, much rests on subjective judgments. We confined our analysis to the two most frequently tested subjects, national language/literature and mathematics. We conclude that end-of-secondary-school examinations are very burdensome in Germany and France, especially when they are compared with the relatively undemanding tests in Sweden and the United

States. The content of the tests in Germany and France places high cognitive demands on candidates, extended answers are always required, and the time allotment is prolonged. In all respects, the examinations in Sweden and the United States are much less burdensome. Examinations in England/Wales and Japan lie between these extremes, but toward the more difficult end of the scale; China and the Soviet Union toward the less difficult end. Our conclusions refer only to the national external examinations and not to the university entrance examinations given as a second stage in Japan and the Soviet Union.

Success Rates Compared. Some examination systems, like Japan's JFSAT and the United States' SAT and ACT, provide results simply in the form of a numerical score, with no indication whether the score means pass or fail. Other systems, for example, France, England/Wales, and the Soviet Union, provide certification of passing or failing as well as a numerical or letter score. In those countries where the examination serves primarily as a selection instrument for postsecondary education, success is defined in practice as gaining entrance to higher education. In China the score is made known to the candidate, but it is meaningful only as it relates to the cutoff point for admission to college. Therefore, comparative and international study of success rates presents some difficulty.

Differences of organization and practice in secondary school systems, in admission standards to higher education, and in the announcement of results must be taken into account, and complicate comparison even more. Our broad conclusion is not just that success is defined differently but that success rates differ quite markedly across nations and that each nation appears to regard its own rates as somehow part of the natural order of things. Difficult examinations help reduce the percentage of the age group passing, but preselection tends to ensure that success rates with respect to the number of candidates are kept high. The gap between success rates in the United States and Sweden at one end of the scale and China at the other might better be termed a gulf. In the United States and Sweden the doors to postsecondary education are wide open. A high school diploma is not difficult to achieve and there are ways of getting admitted to some college, somewhere, without even completing the standard high school course of studies. This stands in stark contrast to China, where the percentage of the age group entering universities is very small—our estimate is as low as 2 percent of the age group. We conclude that success rates reflect both national resource levels and the willingness to make them available for secondary and postsecondary education. In this way, success rates can be regarded as artifacts of national policies, for they go far beyond the narrow business of determining how much candidates know and how well they can demonstrate knowledge.

The Politics of Examinations. Because we know them to be powerful instruments of control, examination systems can become a focus of attention, even of political debate and struggle. This has been particularly evident in China, England/Wales, and Germany, and the political temperature surrounding examinations is rising sharply in the United States. On the other hand, even though the Swedes have made the greatest change of all by abandoning the traditional end-of-secondary-school examination and moving to a system of periodic local and national assessments, they have engaged in little dispute over examinations. In the Soviet Union, too, although many educational topics have been vigorously discussed, the examination system has generated little if any attention.

Possibly the most important cause of political engagement with examinations in recent years has been the very large increase in the number of students completing secondary education. Examinations that once involved only a tiny fraction of the population now interest a much wider public. Disputes over structure, format, and content of examinations often reflect differences in basic educational philosophy, even standard political ideology. As the number of stakeholders is growing, so are the voices of groups focusing attention on their particular interests and points of view. One important result is an increasing demand for examining bodies to be accountable for decisions and to follow full-disclosure principles as part of normal practice. They are only too frequently caught in a crossfire of charge and countercharge. In the United States the examination authorities, ETS in particular, are criticized for constructing ''unfair'' tests that are systematically biased against ethnic minorities and women. In some instances, the examiners are accused of overemphasizing the traditional aspects of the examined subjects; in others, the charge is that the examinations have thrown out too much of the traditional canon in favor of faddish approaches and material. In history and language and literature, particularly, the ''modernization'' of curricula and examination syllabi has been accompanied in the United States, France, and England/Wales by expressions of concern that national identity, national pride, and knowledge of the national heritage have been undermined by the introduction of world history, multicultural history, non-Western literature, language for communication, and the like.

The Persistence of Examinations. In spite of the conflicts surrounding them, examinations appear to have great survival capacity. Indeed, they have done more than persist, they have positively flourished. Why? First, they fulfill a number of essential functions for the school system and for society at large, namely (a) assessing student achievement, (b) controlling curriculum and instruction, (c) allocating rewards in education and employment, (d) motivating students and teachers, and (e) validating/legitimating knowledge and educational activity.

In addition, social changes have forced the bureaucratization of relationships that once could be satisfactorily maintained on a personal basis. When only a small proportion of the population stayed in school long enough to become candidates for the end-of-secondary-school examinations, everyone knew everyone else, and attendance at a particular school or the recommendation of a teacher could be relied upon to communicate to university professors or prospective employers a comprehensible and reliable evaluation of a student's preparation and performance. In contemporary society, schooling has become a mega-enterprise, public and complex, touching virtually every citizen and, most important of all, widely regarded as critical for individual and national prosperity. Examinations are expected to provide objective, reliable measures of accomplishment on which rational and efficient decisions about the future of individuals can be based, along with national benchmarks that enable citizens to assess the contribution made by the schools to the total national economic effort.

Finally, examination systems have demonstrated great adaptability in the face of changing circumstances. As the content of work has demanded more specifically technical knowledge and skills, so school curricula and examinations have moved to incorporate more applied and vocational elements into subject matter that was once almost exclusively academic and abstract. To meet accusations of subjectivity and unfairness in grading, examination systems have developed tests that lay claim to objectivity. And, reinforcing the trend from norm-referenced to criterion-referenced assessment, there are now signs of movement away from reliance on one-shot, time-limited tests toward the incorporation of such nonexamination criteria as portfolios, profiles, and school records in the final evaluation of candidates. Sweden is furthest along this road, using both continuous assessment (a mix of centrally and locally set examinations, required and optional) and grades from course work done during regular school activities.

The Uses of Comparison

"Instead of each country trying out its own experiments, they should be studying each other's for ideas and pitfalls." So writes the *Economist* in a comparison of health care provisions in several nations.[2] The same might well be said of examination practices. Indifference to international practice is a mistake. This is not because any country has solved "the problem" or because one system is more effective and that therefore another country should adopt it in place of its own. It is rather that there are lessons to be learned from looking at different ways of doing things and the costs and benefits of each. While each set of practices is a product of a particular nation's history and circumstances, together they can provide informative exemplars of alternative arrangements.

In fact, nations quite commonly emulate foreign practices, though they rarely do so as part of a conscious, deliberate policy. British, French, and American models of education have been copied or imposed widely in Africa and parts of Asia. The United States borrowed British models of college education and German models of graduate education. Japan after the Meiji Restoration of 1868 is the best known example of a deliberate search for foreign educational models to adopt and adapt. In this century, the American occupation of Japan after World War II has left a long-lasting imprint on the structure of its education, as the four decades of Soviet influence have done in Eastern Europe.

Although similar examples could be detailed by the score, it remains evident that it is not only difficult to borrow wholesale from foreign examples, but it is even difficult to make practical use of observation of foreign practices. In particular, attempts to learn from other nations' examination arrangements run up against at least two sets of problems.

First, the uses, forms, and effects of an examination system can only be understood in context. Examinations are part of a larger system, educational and national/cultural; they are not like replacement parts, separable and transportable. A country's examination system represents a blend of arrangements, some unique to the country and some shared with others. The bias toward stressing the unique and particular elements in this blend is typically strong, especially when political and ideological aspects of the examination system are thought to be threatened by foreign "lessons." This is so even when the lesson may seem simple: for example, to move to objective, multiple-choice tests—they save money and are less open to accusations of grader bias; or to incorporate the grades for school-based course work alongside the examination scores when reporting the candidate's final examination result; or to require that all candidates take certain core subjects, like national language and literature, mathematics, and world

2. "A Survey of Health Care: Surgery Needed," *Economist* (July 6, 1991): 4.

history. But appearances can be deceptive: these seemingly clear-cut proposals can have subtle and complicated ramifications, going far beyond the immediate issue to implicate major elements of the educational system and social structure.

Second, there are important vested interests in maintaining the status quo: today's decision-makers are products of yesterday's and the day before yesterday's system. They are not necessarily well endowed with the ability to transcend the system that molded them. In addition, examining and testing has grown into a substantial industry, with important jobs and revenues liable to be placed at risk by proposed changes whether or not they originate in foreign models.

In spite of these obstacles, observation of foreign practice can yield benefits at both theoretical and practical levels: it can clarify the problems and issues, draw attention to the possible, and suggest options for consideration. For example, the German dual system of apprenticeship and continuing in-school education has attracted widespread interest, particularly in England/Wales and the United States. The development of achievement profiles and performance examinations in England/Wales has provoked much attention in the United States; and the use of multiple-choice examinations in the United States has been embraced wholeheartedly in Japan and is changing the face of examinations in China.

Options and Trade-offs

Comparative and international observation can go beyond the obvious "good points versus bad points" approach. A series of "What if?" possibilities can be phrased in terms of the trade-offs implicit in specific examination arrangements in particular countries. This should appeal particularly to policymakers and administrators, who are required to negotiate an acceptable path between opposing, even contradictory, goals as they try to achieve one set of objectives without paying too high a price in terms of other desirable outcomes. As in other aspects of a country's social life, examination policies and practices reflect compromises among such competing values and goals. While seeking to increase perceived benefits in one direction, a nation almost inevitably gives up some benefit or exacerbates some problem in another direction. It is in that sense, therefore, that we can view extant examination systems as configurations of trade-offs. Here, for example, are three such sets of trade-offs evident in many countries:

• Administering a uniform examination to all, rather than allowing candidates to choose which examinations and subjects to take, and at what level of difficulty, facilitates comparability of scores, but shortchanges individual, regional, ethnic, cultural, and other differences.

• Machine-scorable formats are economical, but their use risks neglecting the development of those skills that are difficult to test using these formats.

• Moving away from one-shot, time-bound examinations to assessments based on the results of work done over extended periods of time is likely to provide more authentic evidence of a student's capacities, but raises problems of grading standards, fairness, and comparability that are very difficult to solve.

Uniformity versus optionality represents one of the most critical sets of trade-offs in the realm of examinations. Some nations, for example, Japan, China, the Soviet Union, and the United States, in the SAT and ACT, offer limited options in what is essentially the same examination for all candidates, whereas other countries, particularly England/Wales, France, Germany, and Sweden, offer candidates a large measure of choice among subjects, syllabi, kinds or degrees of specialization, and levels of difficulty.

Uniform national examinations facilitate comparability and evenhandedness of treatment for different groups. But uniformity exacts its price: opportunities to adjust the examination to recognize the different needs of regions or groups at different stages of school development are inevitably reduced; regional and local interests may feel slighted; and the center's purposes are likely to be served at the expense of the periphery's. These are the educational and social costs of a single examination, of special concern in countries covering a varied territory or comprising a large and heterogeneous population. By the same token, a large measure of optionality brings the clear benefit of adapting the examination to the subject preferences and aptitudes of individual candidates. Examinations can in this way also be tailored to different educational and occupational prospects and to the broad requirements of society and the economy.

But optionality inevitably weakens the prospects for a national curriculum and the sense of a national culture. It raises problems of comparability and may even provoke concerns about equity. A credential based on a familiar standard set of compulsory subjects is easy for employers and admissions officers to interpret; they can be puzzled indeed by the complex regulations and weighting schemes used to equate the essentially non-equatable assortments of examination subjects offered by candidates.

The retreat from uniformity to diversity is well illustrated by changes in examination policy in France and Germany. The changes made in the baccalauréat represent bold and on the whole successful moves, but they have been achieved at some price. The most obvious has been a loss of comparability of candidates, who take widely different assortments of subjects and different tests in nominally the same subject, with different weights given to the results, depending on the particular option. Only in name, certainly not in practice, is there a single national end-of-secondary-school examination administered to all candidates in France. Instead, a strongly demarcated hierarchy of prestige has emerged, with the mathematical options at the head and the vocational options at the tail. Furthermore, devolution of some limited responsibilities for selecting examination questions and awarding marks has led to the view that standards are not the same across all académies. An examination system that began with a strong commitment to strict uniformity and comparability across the entire country, including even overseas departments and dependencies, has yielded to the need to accommodate a wider spectrum of the student population and broadened definitions of what should be learned at school and assessed.

In addition, despite the persistence of a common core of subjects, the differentiation of the baccalauréat has provoked fear that France is dissipating its intellectual *patrimoine*. Whether this is a benefit or a loss is, we suppose, a matter of taste, but taken simply as a matter of fact rather than of values, French culture générale has become a little less générale.

As with the baccalauréat, the Abitur has been significantly altered to cope with the increased numbers and heterogeneity of candidates. It has changed less radically than the baccalauréat, however, perhaps because the need in Germany to secure some measure of agreement among eleven quite differently oriented Länder sets limits on the possibilities of change. In addition, whereas the baccalauréat is marked by a generally high degree of central direction, a determining characteristic of the Abitur is its school-based control. Especially in Germany, the combination of local control and written and oral examinations raises questions about the extent to which grading standards are kept consistent even within a given Land, let alone across the eleven Länder. Because Germany makes less effort compared even with France to ensure such standardization, an important element of chance and arbitrariness has developed.

Even more than in most centralized countries, the basic stance of the examination systems in both Japan and China is one of strict central control and uniformity of content, characteristics that build upon traditional state practices. Few options are extended to Japanese candidates. They may choose mathematics tests of different levels of difficulty, additional tests in social studies, and a particular foreign language. In China, although the detailed administration of the examinations and the final selection process are delegated to the provincial authorities, they are required to operate within narrowly drawn guidelines. The intent is to ensure a strictly meritocratic selection of candidates for entry into higher education. Although criteria other than examination scores are taken into account, especially evidence of political reliability, work experience, and good health, performance on the National Unified College Entrance Examination remains the major criterion for selection. Considering that the number of candidates is exceptionally large—in 1988, 2.7 million prepared for the national college admission tests, of whom only a fifth were accepted for study—the Chinese system has produced a truly impressive degree of comparability among candidates. But this insistence on a uniform examination has severely limited the range of studies in the secondary schools, as well as the freedom of Chinese teachers to experiment with new materials and methods. To that extent, educational development has been held back in China.

The Soviet Union provides a sharp contrast to China in practice, though not in formal terms. On paper, the center, Moscow, is dominant and only token variations from standard uniform syllabi and examinations are permitted; in practice the republics and the localities enjoy considerable latitude. Each of the fifteen republics has responsibility for setting the content and standards of the examinations for the attestat zrelosti. Schools work within the republic guidelines, but in turn enjoy a good deal of local discretion. The teachers who prepare the students dominate the process of setting the questions and evaluating the responses. Even though many teachers are members of the Communist party, this degree of autonomy presents a curious disjuncture with the tight control the party and the central government exert over school curricula and textbooks. Paradoxically, in a society and a school system that are in most respects characterized by substantial central direction, the school-completion examination is not. Thus, the Soviet Union has settled for a curious compromise between the rhetoric of centralized planning and the practice of local discretion.

Once again, the trade-off for such local discretion is a substantial loss of comparability of marks, and this led the universities and higher technical institutes (the vuzy) to insist on applicants sitting for special, institutionally set and graded entrance examinations, a second stage very much along Japanese lines. In the final years of Soviet power, the universities have received formal encouragement to establish their own entrance criteria and examinations.[3] Diversity and optionality achieved in this manner

3. *Bulletin of the State Committee of the USSR on Public Education.* Professional education series. 1/1991; Poisk 6/91.

entail significant costs and aberrations. The location of the examinations can impose substantial travel costs on students. There is virtually no coordination among the VUZY concerning the dates on which they will hold their examinations; examination syllabi are idiosyncratic; and grading formulas, cutoff points, and so forth are confidential. Admission into higher education has consequently become something of an exercise in game theory, requiring candidates to exercise decision-making skills in conditions of imperfect knowledge and uncertainty. The system appears to be lacking important elements of overall fairness and objectivity, to say nothing of the persistent reports of discrimination against particular ethnic and religious groups, influence-peddling, and corruption.

In Sweden the changes in the examination system since the mid-1970s have gone hand-in-hand with changes in the upper secondary school curriculum. These offered students a much wider choice of courses and devolved administrative authority over the schools from the center to the municipalities. Sweden discarded a fairly uniform national end-of-secondary-school examination, replacing it with a combination of marks gained during regular classroom and home work and in nationally set tests administered at intervals during the upper secondary school career. The goals were to reduce the strain on pupils, produce more valid and reliable predictors of university success, and correct socioeducational inequities in assessment. These were judged to be as important as insisting on a high degree of comparability via a uniform examination.

The new system by no means abandons attempts at comparability across candidates. Teachers keep detailed records of their students' achievements, and much time is given to moderating grading standards, so that variations are minimized within both schools and regions. All of this makes important demands on educational resources, but so far the Swedes have been willing and able to incur the necessary costs in order to try to reconcile the respective demands of individual diversity and national comparability.

There is some evidence that the system may not be working to provide a wholly satisfactory degree of comparability. Beginning in September 1991, high school seniors could choose to take the Swedish Scholastic Aptitude Test (SSAT), a daylong assessment of verbal, quantitative, analytic and problem-solving abilities, and offer their scores in place of the usual high school records when applying for admission to higher education.[4] Previously this route had been open to mature-age students only.

---

4. Kenny Bränberg et al., "The Influence of Sex, Education and Age on Test Scores on the Swedish Scholastic Aptitude Test," *Scandinavian Journal of Educational Research* 34, no. 3 (1990): 189.

If the trend in Sweden has been to devolve authority from the center to the local government units, events in England/Wales since 1987 represent an abrupt acceleration of what had been a slow transfer of authority over the schools from local to central government. In the interest of establishing uniform national curricular standards, voluntarism and localism have been forced to give way.

Since the demise of the General School Certificate and its associated London University Matriculation regulations, it has not been necessary for a given student to take any particular subject or to follow any particular syllabus within that subject, except insofar as he or she wanted to take an examination or the school demanded it. The former GCE O level and CSE offered, and the present GCSE and A level examinations all continue to offer, a truly startling array of options. The government decided that this laissez-faire policy had produced such incoherence in school curricula and such indefiniteness in expectations of what the schools should be doing that it had to go. Hence the quite revolutionary decision to introduce regular national assessment of each student's knowledge and skills, which together with the new GCSE examinations is intended to help implement a national core curriculum.

So far, the government has declined to interfere with the GCE A-level examination system, which continues to offer a rich variety of subjects and examination syllabi to schools and candidates. However, problems occasioned by lack of comparability have been reduced by cooperation among the examining boards to identify core topics in syllabi in such basic subjects as mathematics and literature. In addition, a much greater effort has been made in England/Wales than in either France or Germany, for example, to ensure standardization of grading criteria, both within and between examining boards. For this reason, some of the more serious doubts about the fairness and comparability of marking that are voiced in the latter countries have been restrained in England/Wales, though by no means absent.

In the United States the benefits of local control and optionality have been secured, but only at the price of absence of widely recognized achievement standards. State and local control of the schools in the United States has produced a bewildering array of instructional practices, far exceeding even the variety formerly available in England/Wales. In addition, very few of the fifty states offer an external secondary-school-leaving examination or university selection/entrance examination. A high school graduate's academic achievement is thus reported on the basis of school-based, teacher-awarded course grades, with little or no effort made, as in

Sweden, to ensure comparability of grading standards among schools or even in many instances within a school.

To compensate for the resulting extreme lack of comparability, the "national" examinations of the Educational Testing Service and the American College Testing Program have deliberately provided few options to the individual candidate. In this way a limited amount of comparable information about college applicants is provided. On the other hand, employers hiring the non-college-bound usually have only the applicant's high school diploma as evidence of academic achievement. Sometimes, but by no means commonly, an employer will have a copy of the applicant's high school transcript, but even then may be hard-pressed to divine what a particular grade means with respect to academic ability. Most employers have responded to this uncertainty by ignoring transcripts altogether. So far, the United States has steered away from instituting an officially sanctioned, uniform system of examinations, though recently, as a result of rising concern about achievement standards, the possibility of some form of national school-leaving examination has come under consideration.[5]

Economy versus Pedagogy. The end-of-secondary-school examination typically arrives toward the end of twelve years of schooling. In some countries the final examination occurs after eleven years, and in others, thirteen. The resources devoted to a student's education during those years are considerable. In the United States, for example, twelve years of public school education ending in 1989 would, on average, have cost taxpayers approximately $50,000 per student in constant 1989 dollars.[6] In relation to this sum, how much should be spent on the process of certifying the graduating student's level of knowledge and achievement? What if an inexpensive examination system, chosen for its economy, turns out to have undesirable pedagogical implications?

5. See, e.g., the work of the New Standards Project, developed jointly by the National Center on Education and the Economy, Washington D.C., and the University of Pittsburgh's Learning Research and Development Center. In addition, the National Council on Education Standards and Testing, created by the U.S. Congress in early 1991, is likely to have a major impact on the debate over standards of achievement and modes of assessment in the United States. The preferred solution seems at the moment to be the establishment of a set of nationally recognized standards, identifying a core of subjects and their content, which state educational authorities could adopt, while adding whatever they wish to the state's own examination to meet local preferences. See chapter 9 and note 14 below for further details.

6. Calculated on the basis of data in National Center for Education Statistics, *The Condition of Education 1990* (Washington, D.C.: U.S. Government Printing Office, 1990) pp. 1.82–83. The figure given in the text does not include any interest on the annually invested sums cumulated to year twelve.

Cost and format are intimately linked. Multiple-choice testing lends itself admirably to machine-scoring. It thus has the significant benefit of costing very little per additional candidate, once the often substantial initial expenses of equipment, programming, test construction, and pretesting have been met. Of the eight countries in our study, Japan and the United States are the only two to have adopted an almost exclusively multiple-choice machine-scorable format for their examinations. The Japanese appear to have been persuaded, along with the Americans, that such tests are more objective, provide higher levels of comparability across candidates, and are generally more efficient to administer by examiners who are facing hundreds of thousands, if not millions, of candidates. Perhaps more than in the United States, the Japanese have paid a heavy price for these benefits, producing tests that require candidates to memorize vast quantities of facts and downplaying originality and flexibility of thought.

The United States' embrace of machine-scorable examinations, usually in the form of collections of multiple-choice items, has derived largely from its commitment to widening the clientele served by examinations, resulting in a very large number of candidates. This in turn made it economical to invest considerable resources in formulating, pretesting, and revising banks of items from which question papers could be constructed. The option of retaining the traditional extended-answer type of examination was rejected, mostly because the costs and complexity of organizing a grading system that would be regarded as equitable were thought to be unacceptable. In addition, it was argued that the summative and predictive validity of a multiple-choice test could be made as high as, if not higher than, that of a traditional examination.

Yet even in the United States, many believe that these benefits come at too high a price, encouraging styles of teaching and learning that they would prefer to downplay, if not to avoid entirely. The development of written language skills among the student population has not been a high priority; practice in the careful construction of an extended answer has given way to practice in test-taking tricks and the tactics of guessing. Short-item questions tend to emphasize recall-type learning rather than analysis and problem-solving. These drawbacks are widely conceded, but the price has been paid and the trade-off has been made in order to secure the important political value of a more accessible and objective examination system, as well as the ability to deal reasonably inexpensively with the flood of candidates.

Japan until a few years ago operated a very economical system of selection for higher education on the basis of a single, nationwide, standardized, multiple-choice examination. In view of the extreme importance of the decisions being made on the basis of this single examination, the volume of resources spent on its provision was remarkably low. But in order to improve control over the makeup of their entering classes, the colleges and universities instituted a second level of examinations, set by each institution, thus effectively making the national examination a preliminary qualifying test. This device has enabled Japanese institutions of higher education to retain some measure of control over their student recruitment, but the trade-off has been the significantly higher resource costs now absorbed by selection for postsecondary education. A large share of these resource costs is borne by candidates and their families, who invest time and funds in one-on-one tutoring, after-school coaching in the famous juku, commercial tests and analysis for college advisement, and the expenses of travel to distant cities to sit for the second-level examinations.

Following United States and Japanese examples, the Chinese authorities have introduced substantial elements of multiple-choice and short-answer questions into what had previously been a traditional extended-answer national examination. They have not yet adopted a totally machine-scorable format, but with ever-larger numbers of candidates, the low marginal costs of such formats means an ever-stronger incentive to move further in that direction. At least one authority on examination policy in the World Bank has predicted that the time is not far off when the pressure of numbers on the Chinese examiners will become irresistible and a vast school population of multiple-choice, machine-scored examinees will be added to those of the United States and Japan.[7] If so, there is the distinct danger that the changed format will reinforce the already strong emphasis in Chinese schools on rote learning and the recall of facts.

Although Sweden may have abandoned its final secondary school examinations, there has been no abandonment of tests and examinations in general. Indeed, one might well argue that there is now more evaluating and examining than ever before. But Sweden has chosen a distinctly different path from most other countries, being rich enough and willing to devote the necessary resources to an extensive program of regular assessments. The system requires exceptionally detailed record-keeping, formative and summative, covering personal development and schoolwork, as well as time-consuming consultation and collaboration among teachers in each upper secondary school and among schools in a region. The process of consultation and collaboration means that teachers talk to each other more than in most other countries about essential pedagogical matters: the

7. Stephen P. Heyneman and Ingemar Fägerlind. *"University Examinations and Standardized Testing.,"* (Washington, D.C.: World Bank, 1988).

content of the curriculum, the way that content is being taught, and the results of their teaching. Although we can cite no firm evidence, we surmise that this type of activity is very beneficial for the professional development of Swedish teachers, especially for encouraging a sense of personal responsibility for the outcomes of their teaching.

In many countries, oral examinations used to provide a major alternative format. They were once quite common at the end of secondary school because they offered an opportunity for assessment based on interaction between the examiners and the candidate and permitted examiners to shape standard questions to individual candidates. Nowadays oral examinations are rare, retaining a significant place only in the Soviet Union and Germany, and to a lesser extent in France. Whatever the benefits of oral examinations, they are undoubtedly open to accusations of bias, unreliability, and high cost. The first two charges are very difficult to counter, but high cost can be avoided. Oral examinations have survived where teachers serve as examiners as part of their regular duties and costs can be reduced not only for oral, but also for extended-answer written examinations. Thus, a choice between low cost and satisfactory pedagogy is not inevitable. In addition, as we have noted is possibly true in Sweden, a major benefit of involving teachers in the construction and moderation of examinations lies in stimulating their professional awareness, knowledge, and responsibility. If teachers are to perform these tasks well, however, they must have training and the opportunity to accumulate experience and enjoy a sufficient degree of public and professional trust to lend legitimacy to their decisions.

Authenticity versus Objectivity and Comparability. In England/Wales and the United States in particular, criticism has been directed at both machine-scorable and traditional extended-answer examinations on the ground that they do not provide a valid—the currently favored term is "authentic"—picture of a candidate's achievements and abilities. Instead, it is proposed that examination authorities place more emphasis on evaluating samples of the candidate's work produced over a period of time, perhaps during the course of regular schoolwork, but also partly in response to assignments set by the examining authorities. The assembled work would be presented in portfolios for each subject, tracing the progress made by the candidate over a period of perhaps a year or two and combined with comments, suggestions, and evaluations by the teacher(s) and even the candidate.[8]

8. Patricia Broadfoot, "Toward Profiles of Achievement: Developments in Europe," in Max A. Eckstein and Harold J. Noah, eds., *Examinations: Comparative and International Studies* (Oxford: Pergamon Press, 1992), pp. 61–78.

There is little doubt that at least in combination with the standard time-limited examination, proceeding along these lines would provide a more complete and perhaps more valid assessment of the candidate. But difficult problems of grading standards, fairness, and comparability will remain to be solved. In particular, there may be a cost in terms of lost confidence in the fairness and objectivity of the results.

These problems have already surfaced in England/Wales, where a number of GCSE subjects and options permit or require the submission of work done outside the examination room. They also concern those in the United States who are working on the reform of the SAT and other standardized tests.[9] Some reformers there seek a uniform examination containing a substantial component of essays and extended answers alongside the introduction of portfolios and profiles of achievement.[10]

In addition to these three broad options, other difficult choices face examination authorities.

Should the *scope of the examination* be broad, covering many subjects, or should it be narrower, focusing more tightly on and probing more deeply into fewer, perhaps more specialized, subjects? The examination systems we have considered tend toward breadth and comprehensiveness, understandably, since they are aimed at a large proportion, if not the majority, of the secondary school population. Germany and England/Wales offer a more specialized examination, in the Abitur for Leistungskursen and at the GCE A level respectively, though, as we have shown in earlier chapters, degrees of specialization, depth, or difficulty of the subject matter are not easy to compare. The other nations, with the exception of the United States, opt for breadth as indicated by the number of subjects required, at various levels of generality. There is a price to pay for a high degree of specialization: as former practice in many countries indicates, it is a deterrent to participation in the examination, setting a limit on student access to higher education as well as to upper secondary education. On the other hand, a highly specialized examination, such as the A level in England/Wales, makes possible a relatively short period of undergraduate study, usually three years, leading to the first degree.

Should the examination system focus on *selecting candidates in, or selecting them out?* Selecting-in emphasizes certifying that candidates have reached levels of performance qualifying them for the next stage in their lives, either further education or employment. Selecting-out emphasizes

9. See Joan Knapp, "Commentary," in Eckstein and Noah, *Examinations*, pp. 88–91.

10. Learning Research and Development Center, University of Pittsburgh. *The New Standards Project: An Overview*. No date.

the winnowing of a large number of candidates in order to fill a limited number of college places or jobs. Japan's university entrance examinations offer the prime example of selecting-out. They function as a very effective, socially acceptable device for controlling access to the most prestigious institutions of higher education and thereby to the most valuable career opportunities. Allocation of opportunity according to examination success is supported because it forces candidates to study hard, thereby promoting efficient use of the public resources spent on providing secondary and university education. Not all of the consequences of the system are positive, however. Apart from the tangible resource costs of such a system, important intangible costs arise from the intense competition for places in the best universities and the resulting academic and psychological pressure on candidates. Indeed, the competition is so intense and the pressures are so great during the secondary school period that the universities commonly complain that students arrive burned-out, determined to make up for their lost youth, and unwilling to continue to study with the intensity that characterized their secondary school careers.

Selecting-out is also the goal of the examinations in China, where resource limitations severely constrain entrance to higher education and higher-level training in the secondary technical schools. Overall, only about 2 percent of first graders can go on to higher education. Intense competition to succeed leads to pressures on students that are every bit as severe as in Japan. Ideological faith and socialist good works counted for little in the decade or so after the Cultural Revolution; nor was peasant origin any longer so helpful. Examination success was the all-important criterion. "Expertness" was valued more highly than "redness." Since the student demonstrations in Tiananmen Square in 1989, political orthodoxy and a good record of social contributions have again become important. But admission still depends heavily on success in the examinations at the end of senior secondary school, reflecting the determination to select on a strictly equitable basis the best and the brightest of Chinese youth for university education.[11]

All this is in sharp contrast to the United States, where the tendency is to use examinations more for selecting-in than selecting-out. The examinations typically offer a large number of relatively easy questions, with only a few questions toward the end of the paper that might reveal outstanding ability. Most students expect to qualify at some acceptable level. One consequence is that United States high schools are accused of failing

11. This is not to deny that favoritism, connections, and even outright bribery do not also on occasion play some role in securing a college place.

to challenge their students sufficiently, so that first-year college students are liable to suffer shock as they confront for the first time major demands upon their time and intellect.

Sweden's system of in-school examinations too is characterized by selecting-in. In the 1960s and after, Social Democratic political policy strongly favored opening up what had been a restrictive, traditional system of higher education. The abandonment of Abitur-type examinations was intended to facilitate expansion of postsecondary enrollments, especially for the children of those social groups that had previously been poorly represented in such education. In addition, the "25/4" regulations and tests, which allocated a percentage of places for use by those who were at least twenty-five years of age and who had at least four years of work experience, were also designed to promote the selecting-in of mature students.

In England/Wales, the GCSE is intended to provide a credential for the majority of students completing compulsory schooling. For this reason, it too has a significant selecting-in character, more so than the GCE Ordinary level and CSE examinations that it replaced. Similarly, in the Soviet Union, the attestat zrelosti certifies satisfactory completion of upper secondary studies, something that is expected of the majority of students there.

In an attempt to obtain the benefits of both selecting-in and selecting-out, five of the eight countries studied operate a two-stage examination system at the end of secondary school. In Japan and the Soviet Union, the two stages are quite explicit. The Japanese JFSAT and the examinations for the attestat zrelosti are essentially certifying and qualifying examinations for the next stage, which is in the hands of the individual institutions of higher education. China is moving toward a similar two-stage pattern, with its new provincial graduation examinations and the subsequent national examination for university selection. In England/Wales and France the two stages are not so explicit, but nevertheless are strongly present. In England/Wales the GCSE qualifies and certifies, and the GCE A-level examinations select; in France the baccalauréat qualifies and certifies, and the concours selects.

Lessons for the United States

The United States is unique among the countries we have studied in having no coordinated, public, national system for assessing student achievement at the end of secondary school. It lacks any systematic and general way of certifying completion of a specified course of secondary school study and, unlike other countries, has no consistent national criteria or means for selection beyond that stage, whether for employment or for particular types of postsecondary education and training. In addition to certification and selection, other countries use their end-of-secondary-school examinations for a variety of other functions: for example, to define what knowledge and skills are of most worth, to set performance expectations of students, teachers, and schools, and to provide yardsticks against which individual schools and the school system as a whole can be assessed. Although none of these functions is fulfilled by a national examination system alone, it does serve to support them. In the United States the gap has had to be partially filled by resort to ad hoc alternatives, such as school subject curricula issued by national associations of teachers of the several school subjects and, on a more official level, by the National Assessment of Educational Progress.

For the last decade or so, the schools have been subject to severe criticism. This is not exactly a novel situation for educators. In the 1960s and 1970s they were accused of running inhumane, uncaring, and bureaucratized schools and failing to meet the needs of significant minorities, especially blacks and Hispanics.[12] The contemporary accusation is that incompetent teachers are making pitifully inadequate demands on their students, while textbooks have been "dumbed down" to accommodate the students' low academic standards. As a result, it is charged, the schools are turning out high school graduates who know little and can do less. Scores on international surveys of students' achievement levels are cited in support of the claim that if America is losing ground in the struggle for economic competitiveness, much of the blame can be laid at the schoolhouse door.[13]

To make matters worse, public confidence is so eroded that even those most central to the schools—teachers, administrators, and academics—are not trusted or empowered to devise the appropriate remedies, let alone implement them. Hence the growing support for the establishment of national scholastic standards, supported by a national examination system at the end of secondary school. In January 1992, the National Council on

12. See, e.g., Edgar Z. Friedenberg, *Coming of Age in America* (New York: Random House, 1965); Nat Hentoff, *Our Children Are Dying* (New York: Viking Press, 1966); Jonathan Kozol, *Death at an Early Age: The Destruction of the Hearts and Minds of Negro Children in the Boston Public Schools* (Boston: Houghton Mifflin, 1967).

13. "If an unfriendly foreign power had attempted to impose on America the mediocre educational performance that exists today, we might well have viewed it as an act of war. As it stands, we have allowed this to happen to ourselves .. .. . We have, in effect, been committing an act of unthinking, unilateral educational disarmament." *A Nation at Risk: The Imperative for Educational Reform* (Washington, D.C.: National Commission on Excellence in Education, 1983), p. 5.

Education Standards and Testing, established by the U.S. Congress, issued a report entitled, "Raising Standards for American Education." The council called for just such national standards, "to serve as a basic core of important understandings that all students need to acquire, but certainly not everything that a student should learn." [14] The Council went on to recommend that the national samples by the NAEP be supplemented by a nationally approved and certified assessment of each student.

Recommendations in this vein run into immediate opposition. At the same time the council's report was released, some fifty prominent figures in education cautioned against a headlong rush toward national standards and examinations, though they agreed that dramatically higher educational standards are needed for American schools. Their statement questioned whether a national examination was necessary to achieve that goal. Even more contentious is another of the council's recommendations, that the results of individual assessments be used to monitor the work of each school and each school system.

The vigor of the debate over national standards and national assessment raises the question of how participants in the current debates can benefit from the findings of a comparative study of examinations, despite the distinctive character of the United States. What lessons are there for the United States? [15]

Probably the single most important lesson is that although the United States is definitely odd-man-out in not operating an official national examination system, there is no single best system to serve all purposes. National systems vary considerably in the ways they fulfill their various functions within their respective educational and social systems. Some contexts have called for, and produced, totally centralized examinations, others have fostered a large measure of decentralization, even down to the school level; some systems set a uniform examination, others incorporate large elements of choice of subjects and difficulty; some systems use the results of the examination to monitor school and system performance, others do not. With all these variations, however, the benefits of some form of national assessment system are so widely acknowledged that it is only

14. "Council Calls for a New System of Standards, Tests," *Education Week* (Jan. 29, 1992): 30.

15. Note the recent publication of *Testing in American Schools—Asking the Right Questions*. Washington, D.C.: Office of Technology Assessment, 1992). The OTA was asked by Congress to report on educational testing, with emphasis on new approaches. It devoted considerable attention to studying foreign practices and in the complete report, which is due to appear shortly, will respond in part to this question. It points to the advantages and drawbacks of various practices and approaches and to federal policy options.

too likely that the United States is forgoing considerable advantages by its unwillingness and/or inability so far to install one.

There are other, more specific pointers provided by the evidence from abroad, particularly with respect to the major trade-offs discussed earlier in this chapter. First, because the United States is a federally organized polity, it has to lean heavily in the direction of decentralization and optionality. Like Germany, the United States has located ultimate jurisdiction over the schools at the level of the states. This together with the heterogeneity of its student population, its regional diversity, and its traditions of localism and individualism all speak strongly against any large degree of examination uniformity. Students and school systems must have choices among subjects, syllabi, levels of difficulty, and forms of examinations. But the example and achievements of other countries support the notion that this diversity should be built upon a common core of knowledge in basic subjects. Moreover, other countries have found it expedient to set explicit standards of performance to define minimally acceptable, average, and superior achievement in those studies. In addition, as the example of Germany also shows, a strongly held sense of state-level prerogatives in schooling need not prevent formal, sustained consultation, collaboration, and agreement among the states. Federal encouragement of interstate cooperation, rather than federal legislation, can be a more appropriate way to raise standards throughout the system.

The second major trade-off touched on the claims of pedagogy versus those of financial economy in choosing among alternative examination formats. In comparative perspective, the United States and Japan have overemphasized machine-scorable formats, partly in search of a greater degree of "objectivity" than extended-answer formats are expected to provide, but partly in search of economy. In the United States as well, competition among the testing services has focused attention on keeping costs per candidate low. The paradoxical result is that school systems routinely spend tens of thousands of dollars bringing a student to the point of graduation from high school and are then content to settle for a cheap machine-scored assessment (costing about thirty dollars) of what that student knows and can do.

Other nations, not necessarily richer than the United States, have quite properly feared the side effects of heavy reliance on multiple-choice formats—and they have been willing to bear the extra costs that choice involves. Although there is a definite role for limited-choice, machine-scorable assessment, the wholesale abandonment of extended-answer alternatives has had unfortunate, albeit somewhat different, effects on schooling in both Japan and the United States. The United States has practiced a false economy that other countries have been wise to avoid.

None of this is an argument for simply turning the clock back to the old-style exclusive reliance on one-shot, essay-type examinations. This brings us to the third trade-off discussed above, between authenticity and objectivity. Other countries are experimenting with performance-based assessments that go beyond the traditional one-, two-, or three-hour examination session and beyond essay-writing. In the United States, Vermont has introduced an assessment system based upon the submission of a portfolio of student work. These nascent efforts at so-called authentic assessment presage a major change in procedures, even though they bring with them severe problems of grading integrity, fairness, and comparability. Here the lesson to be drawn from the experience of other countries to date is that it is important not to let the goal of completely reliable, statistically impeccable tests override other equally, if not more, pressing needs at this juncture in the United States: to institute modes of assessment that encourage, rather than frustrate, the desire and ability to learn; that foster teachers' creative involvement with their students' efforts; and that give all parties concerned—students, teachers, parents, school administrators, admissions and hiring personnel, politicians, and voters—confidence that what is being measured and reported represents a broader rather than narrower picture of students' past achievement, present capacity, and potential for the future.

The international, comparative scene offers strong support for the American practice of leaning more toward the selecting-in than the selecting-out function of examinations and of providing multiple opportunities for demonstrating talent, actual and potential. Although the approach taken in United States and Sweden reduces incentives to achieve academically by relieving some of the competitive pressures on students, it gains by increasing the chance that those with talent are not eliminated from subsequent educational opportunity. On the other hand, China, the Soviet Union, and England/Wales have operated examination systems largely devoted to selecting-out. The approach in these countries has been based on the assumption that success in formal written and oral examinations is the best way to identify those innately talented and/or hard-working students who most deserve to benefit from state-subsidized postsecondary education. But examination success is also a result of the quantity of resources that parents devote to their children's upbringing, so that in these countries, as in others, there is a bias in favor of selecting candidates coming from the more privileged sectors of society. Apart, therefore, from the loss of the primary rationale for using examination results as a strict selecting-out mechanism, these three countries have most probably failed to uncover a reservoir of talent that existed but was not being discovered by the examination system. The Japanese have been able to reduce such losses by instituting the widely accepted device of the yobiko, giving those who have not reached their desired goal on their first attempt an opportunity to try again. In any reform of United States assessment patterns and procedures, it will be important to keep such evidence from other countries in mind, taking especial care to avoid selecting-out procedures as much as possible and recognizing that continued reliance on selecting-out has not served China, the Soviet Union, or England/Wales well.

The Persistent Dilemmas of Examination Policy

While the example offered by other countries gives strong support to the notion that a national, external, end-of-secondary-school examination is useful, and even necessary, its introduction into the United States should not be regarded as a panacea for the country's educational ills. In addition, although there are clear advantages accruing to Germany from its Abitur, to France from its baccalauréat, and to Japan from its JFSAT, the critical policy question when trying to adapt foreign institutions to domestic purposes is: How can the United States secure these advantages, while avoiding, or at least minimizing, the disadvantages that may accompany them?

Entirely satisfactory solutions for such policy problems are rare indeed. Moreover, as the circumstances of an examination system change, so a new set of compromises among the competing goals is likely to be required. For these reasons, the choices that must be made are best regarded as persistent dilemmas that examination authorities have to learn to live with, leaning sometimes to one side, sometimes to the other. Among such dilemmas are the following:

Dilemma 1. How to retain the function of the examination as a stabilizing element in the educational and social systems, while:

(a) providing flexibility and opportunities for change in content and format of the examination;

(b) introducing new, nonexamination criteria of assessment, for example, course work and portfolios;

(c) expanding the number of candidates.

Dilemma 2. How to promote examination results that are comparable and understandable, while:

(a) introducing new, more sophisticated ways of reporting results;

(b) introducing nonexamination criteria of assessment;

(c) introducing new subjects and differentiated levels of subjects.

Dilemma 3. How to maintain the value of the credential earned by examination success, while:

(a) increasing the number of successful candidates;

(b) introducing nonexamination criteria of assessment;

(c) reducing the burdens and pressure on students;

(d) controlling examination costs.

Dilemma 4. How to ensure a sufficient degree of regional authority and school or individual autonomy, while:

(a) implementing national standards of content and quality;

(b) recognizing the claims of internationalism;

(c) using examination results to monitor school system performance.

Dilemma 5. How to use the examination to select for subsequent education, training, and jobs, while:

(a) also certifying satisfactory completion of secondary education;

(b) not discouraging too many candidates, that is, picking winners without creating too many losers;

(c) providing flexibility of examination content, in particular, access to new subjects.

Dilemma 6. How to incorporate the new information technologies in the examination system and secure the promised benefits of greater efficiency and cost savings, while safeguarding teaching and learning from undesirable side effects.

Dilemma 7. How to maintain and increase the professional autonomy of teachers, while:

(a) using examination results to monitor school system performance;

(b) strengthening national curricula and national standards.

Dilemma 8. How to raise standards of performance, while:

(a) increasing the number of successful candidates;

(b) using nonexamination criteria of assessment;

(c) reducing the burden and pressure on students;

(d) reducing examination costs;

(e) not discouraging too many candidates.

Each of these dilemmas represents a potential problem associated with use of the examination system to control either individual destinies or what occurs in schools. In consequence, as the United States quite properly considers reform of the testing and examination system as a way to lever education to a higher level of performance, policymakers need to be constantly mindful of the likelihood of unintended, undesirable consequences of their decisions. Other countries have often "been there before," and the consequences of going in this or that direction are available for inspection.[16] If for no other reason, the record of other countries' examination experience repays attention.

16. Albert Shanker, president of the American Federation of Teachers, calls attention to the experience of other countries, as follows: "People who predict disaster [if the United States were to adopt national standards and assessments] should look at how these systems work in other industrialized countries. Some of these systems are better than others, but none is a disaster, and there's no reason to believe we'd have one here. In fact, there's every reason to believe we could make such a system work." "National Standards and Exams," *New York Times* (March 1, 1992): 4.7.

Appendix

Selected Examination Papers and Questions: National Language/Literature and Mathematics

This appendix presents English-language translations of either part or the whole of selected end-of-secondary-school examination papers in language/literature and mathematics in each of the eight countries of this study. It should be noted that for some countries, the authors had to choose among several alternative papers; in most instances, only portions of the papers could be presented, either because of their length or, in the national language papers, because of the difficulties of finding English equivalents. The material offered will provide the reader with an indication of the types of questions set and the extent of the knowledge, skills, and understanding expected of candidates taking specific examinations in the several countries.

Where necessary, the authors have added explanatory notes. These are enclosed in brackets.

China: Language and Literature

Shanghai Citywide Senior High School Examination, Chinese Language/Literature, 1987

[The test lasts 150 minutes.]

I. *Basic Knowledge* (10 points). The first nine questions have only one correct answer each. Put answers in parentheses.

[The ten questions cover punctuation, word usage, grammar, comprehension, and recognition of authors and their works. All except the last one are multiple-choice. Three examples are given here.]

1. The sentence with the correct punctuation is . . .

A. What do you mean, only you can see us again without being ashamed?
B. What does Dong Kun look like. Does he look like Uncle Shang in our hometown?
C. If you have anything to say? You should let me know?
D. Are you applying to liberal arts school? Or science school?

4. The authors of *On the Landscape, Hunter, Random Memories,* and *Visit of Ancient Sites in Inner Mongolia* are . . .

A. Mau Dun, Wu Boxiao, Ye Shentao, Jian Bozhian

B. Wu Boxiao, Mao Dun, Tang Tao, Jian Bozhian
C. Mau Dun, Wu Boxiao, Tang Tao, Jian Bozhian
D. Wu Boxiao, Mao Dun, Jian Bozhian, Tang Tao

9. The sentence without a figure of speech is. . .

A. The sweet fragrance of the breeze reminds people of the drifting melody from those distant tall buildings.
B. Most of the time, dark clouds gathered from all directions, like those layers of mountains in Chinese landscape paintings.
C. Mountains without streams, just like a person without eyes, seem to lack the expressive intelligence.
D. There are some pink lichees such as "March Red" and "Cassia Green" from Guangdong Province.

II. *Modern Chinese Language* (30 points)

[Two brief and two longer prose extracts are provided, each followed by several questions testing comprehension and literary knowledge, analysis, and judgment. One such example is given here.]

4. Read the story "Coin Dumpling" and answer the questions (10 points).

[The narrator tells of his involvement in the Cultural Revolution, his punishment, and his worries that his family, in particular his grandmother, would suffer from his errors. As he celebrates his release with his family at a New Year's dinner, each member secretly transmits the good luck symbol to the next until it ends in the grandmother's bowl. Several sentences in the text are underlined.]

1. The sentence, "I was worried that my mother would leave me for another world," means . . .

A. Mother felt that I failed to be a good person and planned to leave me.
B. Mother was very weak and needed to go to the hospital.
C. The suffering was so much for Mother that she could not make it.
D. Mother might leave home to avoid witnessing her son's humiliation.

2. In the second underlined sentence, why did the author use the word "surprisingly"?

3. The third underlined part describes Mother's responses at three different levels. What psychological changes do these descriptions seek to suggest?
First:
Second:
Third:

4. The fourth underlined sentence is necessary for the further development of the story. Without it, the story would be:

5. As the last underlined sentence describes it, "Mother started to laugh and laugh until tears covered her wrinkled cheeks." Why?

IV. *Composition* (40 points)

Today's students have various views on their extracurricular reading, including whether to read, what to read, and how to read. For example, some say, "Reading can nurture one's thinking and increase one's knowledge"; others feel that the curriculum has been sufficiently demanding to cover all necessary aspects; some students feel that reading provides them with things they can share with their peers. Please write a short essay to express your opinions.

Directions: focus on one point; write about 700 words.

Source: Examination paper, 1987.

England/Wales: Language and Literature

General Certificate of Education, Advanced Level, Examination Papers, English Literature, June 1987

[Candidates take three tests in the subject, for a total of eight hours.]

ENGLISH LITERATURE 1 (3 hours)

[The test is divided into four sections: Poetry, Drama, Prose, and General. Candidates answer four questions from at least three of the sections. Candidates have with them a copy of the poetry text(s) they have studied in section A. They will have studied the works of one or two of the authors in each section. Each question is given with an alternative.]

Section A—POETRY

[Sixteen questions are given on the works of eight poets (Donne, Milton, Keats, Blake, Shakespeare, Hardy, Yeats, and Eliot).]

Milton: Comus and Lycidas

2. EITHER: (a) "Both *Comus* and *Lycidas* are too artificial to be enjoyed today. The conventions of masque, elegy and pastoral poetry are not ours and we cannot respond sympathetically." Discuss both works in the light of this comment.

OR: (b) "Comus is a more attractive figure than any of his virtuous adversaries." Do you find this so? If so, why? If not, why not?

Section B—DRAMA

[Ten questions are given on the works of five authors (Marlowe, Jonson, Webster, Miller, and Stoppard).]

Miller: Death of a Salesman

12. EITHER: (a) What have you found of particular interest in Miller's use of language and his stagecraft in *Death of a Salesman?*

OR: (b) Contrast the responses of Biff and Happy Loman to the demands made on them by their family and background.

Section C—PROSE

[Ten questions are given on the works of five authors (Austen, Dickens, Hardy, Joyce, and White).]

Joyce: Dubliners

17. EITHER: (A) Show some of the ways in which Joyce introduces significant detail to illuminate character and mood in *Dubliners*.

OR: (b) Show how "The Dead" is an impressive short story in itself *and* represents a culmination of some of the ideas and themes in the book.

Section D—GENERAL QUESTIONS

[Eight questions are given; candidates will select one, or at most two, to answer. Questions are to be answered by reference to literature related to the texts prescribed in sections A, B, or C, or to the texts themselves, where appropriate. Candidates will not receive credit for material already used in answer to questions in other sections.]

19. Explore the use of rhyme by a poet set for this paper and by another not among those set this year.

26. How "political" can literature become without ceasing to be literature? Show how two works, one of them in the syllabus and the other outside it, illustrate the difference between propaganda and literature.

ENGLISH LITERATURE 2 (3 hours)

[Candidates are instructed to answer four questions: nos. 1, 2, and 3 and either 4 or 5.]

1. Choose ONE of the following extracts and (a) write a critical commentary on the extract; (b) discuss the importance of the extract, relating it to the whole work from which it is taken; (c) paraphrase the underlined passage(s) clarifying any expressions that would not be readily understood today.

[Five extracts are given, of about twenty-five lines each, from *King Lear, As You Like It, The Tempest, Canterbury Tales,* and *The Prelude.* Here is part of the extract given from *The Tempest:*]

Ferdinand: Admir'd Miranda!
                    Indeed the top of admiration, worth
                    What's dearest to the world! Full many a lady
                    I have eyed with best regard, *and many a time,*
                    Th' harmony of their tongues hath into bondage

Brought my too diligent ear: for several virtues
Have I liked several women—never any
With so full soul, but some defect in her
Did quarrel with the noblest grace she owed,
And put it to the foil . . . But you, O you,
So perfect, and so peerless, are created
Of every creature's best.

2. EITHER: (a) Discuss some of the ways in which the scenes on the heath, in the hovel and in the farmhouse in the central section of the play reflect Lear's crisis and his response to it.

OR: (b) "*King Lear* is marred by an excess of needless cruelty, both physical and moral." Do you agree?

3. (a) "Touchstone, Jaques, and Rosalind all display, in different ways, a healthy scepticism about life." Show the various forms taken by their scepticism, and its dramatic purpose.

OR: (b) . . .

OR: (c) Discuss some of the ways in which *The Tempest* explores the conflict between ideal and cynical responses to life.

OR: (d) What various aspects of the theme of lawful authority and usurpation are explored in *The Tempest?*

4. EITHER: (a) "Although many of his pilgrims are nothing if not worldly, Chaucer himself attaches great importance to the Canterbury pilgrimage as a religious experience." Discuss this view, making sure that you consider an appropriate range of characters, and also the opening of the poem.

OR: (b) How far would you agree that Chaucer celebrates the vitality and love-life of the young in *The Miller's Tale?*

ENGLISH LITERATURE 3 (2 hours)

[Both questions must be answered. The poem (thirty-nine lines long) is "A Holiday from Strict Reality" by Christopher Reid; the prose passage (about eight hundred words) is from J. B. Priestley's *Angel Pavement.*]

1. Write an appreciation of the poem.

2. Write an appreciation of the prose passage, making any points of comparison or contrast with the poem that seem interesting or relevant to you.

Source: Southern Universities' Joint Board for School Examinations, *Examination for the General Certificate of Education, 1987,* Advanced Level and Special Papers. Bristol, England, papers Nos. 9005/1, 9005/2, 9005/3. (Courtesy University of Cambridge Local Examinations Syndicate, Cambridge, England.)

France: Language and Literature

Baccalauréat Examination Paper, French, June 1991

[The candidate must select one of the three subjects. The examination lasts four hours.]

Subject No. 1

The City as an Architectural Object

[This is a prose passage of approximately seven hundred words from a work by Ricardo Bofill, *Espaces d'une vie* (1989).]
Questions:

1. *Resume* (8 points)

Write a précis of the text in 175 words. A margin of plus or minus 10% is acceptable. At the end, give the exact number of words used.

2. *Vocabulary* (2 points)

Explain the meaning in the text of the two underlined phrases: "continuity in urban design" and "introduce a rhythm."

3. *Discussion* (10 points)

Do you agree with the architect Ricardo Bofill that the city "has ceased to be a meeting place and has become simply a network of paths of communication"?

Subject No. 2

My first book of lessons was a great winter, when I went to school between two walls of snow taller than I was. What have they done with those great winters of yesteryear, white, solid, lasting, beautified by the snow, tales of fantasy, pine trees, and wolves? As real as my childhood, are they now as lost as it is? As lost as old Miss Fanny, shadowy ghost of my elementary school teacher, who lived on romantic novels and hardships? Now and then, Miss Fanny would emerge from her romantic dream and make a neighing sound that announced the class lesson . . . That year, we were learning to read in the New Testament.[1] Why the New Testament? Because it was there, I think. And the ghostly old schoolmarm beat out the rhythm of the sacred syllables with her ruler on the desk as we chanted[2] in chorus: "In those days, Jesus said to his disciples, . . ." Sometimes an infant pupil, sitting on her heater[3] for warmth, would utter a sharp cry because she had just burned her little behind. Or a column of smoke would rise from the heater, giving off the smell of a chestnut, a potato, or a winter pear that one of us was trying to roast in the heater. All around us, it was winter, silence broken by the crows, by the mewing wind, by the scrape of wooden shoes, winter and the woods surrounding the village . . . Nothing else. Nothing more. A simple country picture.

1. New Testament: one of the two major parts of the Bible, devoted to the life of Christ.

2. chanted: recited together in a monotone.

3. heater: a metal box with holes in the lid, in which you put embers, to warm your feet.

Write an essay on this text showing, for example, how Colette manages, not without humor, to convey to the reader at the same time her nostalgia, as well as her love of nature and life.

Subject No. 3

Isn't the function of comedy merely to amuse?

Base your thinking on analysis of specific examples; do not limit yourself only to the field of literature.

Source: Examination papers, June 1991.

Germany: Language and Literature

Abitur Examination Paper, German—Grundkurs/Basic Course, Province of Nordrhein-Westfalen

[The test lasts five hours.]

ANALYSIS OF A NONFICTION TEXT

Analyze the following text; above all, bring out Walser's conception of "the reader."

Text: Martin Walser: "Why, in General, Do We Read?"

Our grandmothers no longer tell us stories; either they are dead, or they have finally established themselves in front of the television set. Why don't I, too, at last arrange myself in front of the television? Because it's tiring for me to remain passive for a long time. Is it only a myth that a passive existence, doing nothing, is exacting work, or is there something to it? If consciousness, or the soul, or the spirit—it does not matter what we call our inner disquiet—if this imaginary milk of our being is prevented from boiling up for a long time, it turns sour. Our consciousness-soul-spirit itself wants to be a movie, a movie that runs continuously; it comes to an end if it is subjected to merely the bombardment or pleasure of ready-made films from outside. Does the soul or our consciousness become more active during reading than during watching a film? Yes, because what is written is incomplete and has to be brought to life and thus completed by each reader: not a whit different from the notes written down by the composer that are brought to life by the singer, the pianist, and so forth. The reader is rather to be compared with someone who makes music, than with someone who hears it.

[The text, about 900 words in all, develops the theme of reading as a participatory activity in which the reader experiences an actual encounter with the writer's words.]

ANALYSIS OF A FICTION TEXT

Analyze the following text.

[The text presented is Arthur Schnitzler's short story "The Green Tie," a piece of approximately 530 words.]

Source: *Grundkurs Deutsch: Abitur Prüfungsaufgaben Gymnasium Nordrhein-Westfalen* (Freising: Stark, 1986), pp. 1–2, 29.

Japan: Language and Literature

Joint First Stage Achievement Test, Japanese Language, 1988

[This is a one hundred-minute, multiple-choice test containing four literary excerpts: a poem of about three thousand characters, an excerpt from a modern novel, and portions of a Japanese and a Chinese classic. Each is followed by eight questions (some with subquestions) referring to marked parts of the text and dealing with content, form, language, and character motivation. Here follow examples of the questions asked on the second excerpt, four pages describing an incident on a train journey—a near-accident involving a child.]

Directions: read the text and answer the questions.

1. Select the sentence that best explains reasons for the author's feelings [at the beginning of the story]:

A. the shaking of the train, boredom of travel, and the flutter of the butterfly;
B. he could no longer think clearly because of the shaking of the train and the unbearable heat;
C. he was looking at the passengers who were irritated by the hot day;
D. he was looking at the expressions of the passengers exhausted by the heat;
E. he was oppressed by the stuffy air of the humid train, crowded with passengers.

3. Choose the answer that best expresses the kind of "joy" described in the text:

A. A selfish joy. He was glad because nothing had happened to him.
B. Happy as an observer. Though in the audience, he was glad that the child was saved anyway.
C. Self-centered joy. He was glad he was safe. He does not care about the child at all.
D. A sense of relief, after a breathtaking, frightening moment.
E. Personal happiness, unrelated to anyone else.

4. Choose the best explanation for the meaning of the words marked in the text: [three phrases, each with five alternative answers]

6. Choose the best explanation of the mother's feeling for her child in [the marked portions of] the text:

A. She expresses her affection toward her child by scolding. In this sense, there is no difference between (f) and (g), though there is anger at the child's carelessness in (f), and her regret has developed in (g).

B. In both (f) and (g) she was surprised at the crowd and then scolded her child, worrying about what others might think . . . In (f) she is mainly worried about what the conductor and driver think of her. In (g) she is concerned about the crowd.

C. Upset about the accident, she suddenly hit her child. Both extracts show that she is trying to shift responsibility for the accident to the child's carelessness.

D. In both extracts, she scolded just because she loved the child so much. In (f) she was still upset about the accident, but in (g) she was glad her child was again safe.

E. When she saw the crowd, she became upset and scolded her child because of anger and shame that he had caused an accident. In (f) she is trying to apologize, and in (g) she is scolding his carelessness again.

7. Choose the answer that best describes the different reactions of the young man and the petty official to the accident:

A. The young man spoke and behaved roughly, but cared about the child and acted rapidly. He played a leading role. The official played a supporting role, excited about the child's miraculous escape rather than happy that the child was saved.

B. The young man played a leading role in this story. He picked up the child, worried whether the child was injured, protested to the conductor. The official took care of the child tenderly, and attended to the details.

C. The young man played a leading role, feeling anger at the impassive driver, never speaking to him but speaking to the conductor and the child's mother. The official took a supporting role, helping the young man and, with his greater experience, talking to the driver (he was impressed at the driver's skill).

D. The youth took a leading role, talking to the mother and taking pride in what he had done. The official took a supporting role, taking care of the child, providing some humor . . .

E. The young man was troubled about treating the child, but still took a leading role . . . as he saved the child. The official played a supporting role, comforting the child by his tender actions such as washing the dirt from the child's face.

Source: Examination paper, 1988.

Soviet Union: Language and Literature

Cards for the Oral Graduation Examination, Literature, 1989

[Candidates choose a card from among a number arrayed facedown on the examiners' table. Each card contains two questions based on the topics listed. See chapter 5 for a description of the oral examination procedure.]

Card 1

1. Modern Soviet literature as a reflection of Communist party policy.
2. The philosophical poetry of A. S. Pushkin.

Card 2

1. The article by V. I. Lenin, "Party Organization and Party Literature."
2. The author's personality in A. S. Pushkin's novel *Eugene Onegin*.

Card 3

1. M. Gorky as a person and as a writer.
2. The theme of "the people" in A. S. Pushkin's literary works.

Card 5

1. Lenin's image in Soviet drama.
2. Satire in modern Soviet prose.

Card 6

1. Lenin's image in Soviet literature, 1950 to the 1980s.
2. Ideas and characters in modern Soviet poetry.

Card 20

1. The moral image of a man as a worker and as a warrior in the works of M. A. Sholokhov.
2. The problem of historical memory in modern Soviet literature.

Card 21

1. Heroic deeds of the Soviet people in the Great Patriotic War (citing one or two works of modern Soviet literature as examples).
2. Man and nature in Soviet literature.

Card 22

1. Past and present of the Soviet country in A. T. Tvardovsky's poem, "Beyond the Horizon."
2. Moral problems in Soviet literature.

Source: Ministerstvo narodnogo obrazovaniia RSFSR, Glavnoe upravlenie soderzhaniia obrazovaniia, metodov obucheniia i vospitaniia, *Bilety dlia vypusknykh ekzamenov za kurs srednei shkoly na 1988/89 uchebnyi god* [Cards for graduation examinations for secondary school courses, 1988–89 academic year] (Moscow: Prosveshchenie, 1989), pp. 6–8.

Sweden: Language and Literature

National School Board Examination, Swedish, 1990

[As indicated in chapter 5, materials for the examination were distributed a week before the examination date, consisting of varied pieces for study on a given general theme. In 1990, the subject was "Travel" and the sixteen-page pamphlet contained the following materials:

Eight lines from Homer's *Odyssey,* in Swedish translation;

Frans G. Bengtsson, "Happy Journey," a 1,500-word essay by a well-known Swedish author (1938);

Karen Boye, "In Motion," a ten-line poem (1927);

Ake Andersson and Ulf Stromquist, "The Great Liberation," a 650-word extract from a book on the growth of travel (1988) with two charts giving related statistics;

Karen Soderberg, "Fighting the Clock and Hurrying to See the Sights," a brief newspaper extract on planning a trip, describing alternative tourist possibilities;

Per Ewald, "Worlds within Reach," a 1,000-word account of a sixteen-year-old girl traveling by train in Europe;

three poems and eight additional prose extracts all related to some aspect of travel.

Candidates are directed to read all the extracts carefully and be prepared to write for up to five hours on a chosen theme, making specific use of pieces relevant to the topic selected.]

Assignment. Write an essay on one of the following:

1. "The Swedes and Their Travel Habits."

2. "Great-grandmother and Her Great-grandchildren."

3. "Happy Journey!"

4. "Tourism for Good and Ill."

5. " 'On the Road' by Rail."

6. "The Trials and Tribulations of Traveling."

7. "Armchair Travel."

8. "The Art of Telling Travel Tales."

9. "Local Travel."

Source: Examination booklet published by the National School Board.

United States: Language and Literature

College Board Achievement Test, Literature, December 1982

[This is a one-hour, sixty-question, multiple-choice test. The following questions were selected from an actual test administered in December 1982 and reproduced in a College Board publication intended to enable candidates to familiarize themselves with the actual tests. The full test contains seven extracts from different literary works (poetry and prose, older and modern works) followed by questions on their content, form, and style. Two extracts and the questions on each are reproduced here.

Directions: This test consists of selections from literary works and questions on their content, form, and style. After reading each passage or poem, choose the best answer to each question and blacken the corresponding space on the answer sheet.

Note: Pay particular attention to the requirement of questions that contain the words NOT, LEAST, or EXCEPT.

Questions 1–6. Read the following fable carefully before you choose your answers.

> A weaver watched in wide-eyed wonder a
> silkworm spinning its cocoon in a white
> mulberry tree.
> "Where do you get that stuff?" asked the
> (5) admiring weaver.
> "Do you want to make something out of it?"
> inquired the silkworm, eagerly.
> Then the weaver and the silkworm went their
> separate ways, for each thought the other had
> (10) insulted him. We live, man and worm, in a time
> when almost everything can mean almost
> anything, for this is the age of gobbledygook,
> doubletalk, and gudda.
> MORAL: A word to the wise is not sufficient if
> it doesn't make any sense.
>
> From *Further Fables for Our Time,*
> published by Simon & Schuster.
> © 1956 James Thurber. Originally
> printed in *The New Yorker.*

1. The central idea of the fable is the

   (A) frequent failure of language as a means of communication
   (B) unstable nature of casual relationships
   (C) richness of language, even in everyday situations
   (D) unwillingness of people to listen to each other

(E) possibility of misunderstanding in any relationship

2. The silkworm intended "make" (line 6) as a synonym for

(A) imply
(B) arrange
(C) start
(D) draw
(E) weave

3. The characters were insulted because the words "stuff" (line 4) and "make something out of it" (line 6) were misinterpreted as

(A) "nonsense" and "cause a disturbance"
(B) "material" and "weave a garment from it"
(C) "junk" and "use it as a reason for a quarrel"
(D) "garbage" and "make a mountain out of a molehill"
(E) "rubbish" and "take it for your own use"

4. The effect of the phrase "man and worm" (line 10) is to

(A) suggest that the narrator is hostile toward the two characters
(B) demonstrate that human language is appropriate for a wide variety of situations
(C) emphasize the close relationship among all living creatures
(D) indicate the narrator's concern for sophisticated and unsophisticated creatures
(E) suggest the gently satiric attitude of the narrator

5. The primary reason that the misunderstanding between the two is ironic is that

(A) weavers and silkworms seldom talk to each other in such a way
(B) neither the weaver nor the silkworm means to be hostile
(C) the silkworm is a creature that is useful to people
(D) the weaver and the silkworm are not wise
(E) the weaver and the silkworm are using language incorrectly

6. The misunderstanding between the two characters might have been prevented if they had paid more attention to

(A) grammar
(B) sentence structure
(C) imagery
(D) tone
(E) alliteration

Source: College Entrance Examination Board, *The College Board Achievement Tests: Fourteen Tests in Thirteen Subjects* (New York: College Entrance Examination Board, 1983), pp. 54–57. Reprinted by permission of Educational Testing Service, Princeton, N.J., the copyright owner.

China: Mathematics

Zhejiang Province High School Graduation Mathematics Examination
(for Science Candidates), 1987

[The test runs one hundred minutes.]

I. Fill in the blanks (3 points each, 30 points total)

1. If A is an odd number set, B is an even number set, and Q is a rational number set, then $A \cap Q = $ ____, $B \cup Q = $ ____, $A \cap B = $ ____.

2. The field of definition of function $y = x^{-3/2}$ is _____ (to be expressed in set).

3. If $tg\alpha = 2$ and $tg\beta = 3$, then $tg(\alpha + \beta) = $ _____.

9. Fill real numbers in the blanks: If complex number $Z = 1 + 5i$ and $W = 3i$, then $Z + W = $ __ $+ 8i$, $ZW = -12 + $ __ i.

10. If parametric equation $\begin{cases} x = \alpha + \cos\theta \ (\theta \text{ is the parameter}), \\ y = \alpha\sin\theta \end{cases}$

then the conic equation is _____; the equation in polar coordinates $\rho = 2\alpha\cos\theta$ (α is a constant) can be expressed by an equation in rectangular coordinates _____.

II. Multiple choice (4 points each, total 24 points)

Each question has four answers, but only ONE is correct. Put the letter of the correct one in the parentheses.

1. If a line $(Ax + By + C = 0)$ is the line $x = 0$, then coefficients must be ( ).

(A) $B, C = 0$.
(B) $A \neq 0$.
(C) $B, C = 0$ and $A \neq 0$.
(D) $A \neq 0$ and $B = C = 0$.

2. If the logarithmic function $y = \log_a x$ and $y = \log_b x$ are graphed in the figure, then the relation and the range of a and b must be ( ).

(A) $a > b > 1$.
(B) $b > a > 1$.
(C) $1 > a > b > 0$.
(D) $1 > b > a > 0$.

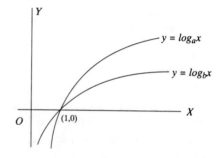

6. The correct proposition is (   ).

(A) The origin of a complex plane is not on an imaginary axis.
(B) Two lines without common point are lines on different planes.
(C) The focus of a parabola $y = x^2 - 2x + 2$ is on the y-axis.
(D) The circumference ratio of function $y = \sin x/2$ is π.

III. Give brief answers (5 points each, total 20 points)

1. If $\cos \beta = \sqrt{3}$, find the value of $\sin (2\alpha + \beta) - 2 \sin \alpha \cos (\alpha + \beta)$.

4. If $(x - 1)/(x - 2) = \cos \theta$, and $\pi/2 < \theta < \pi$, $x = ?$

IV. (Up to 8 points)

Use mathematic inductive method to prove:
$C_n^0 + C_n^1 + C_n^2 + \ldots + C_n^n = 2^n \ (n \in N)$.

VI. (Up to 9 points)

If a is the side length of the cube $ABCD-A'B'C'D'$, E and F are the midpoints of $B'B'$ and $C'D'$ respectively, find:

(1) The ratio of two volumes intercepted by the cross-section $BEFD$;
(2) The angle formed between the cross-section $BEFD$ and $BCC'B'$ (give the one less than 90°).

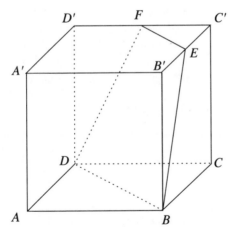

EXTRA (10 points each, 20 points total)

1. Find the derivative of $y = \ln \arcsin (1 - x^2)/(1 + x^2)$. $(0 < x < 1.)$

2. The function $f(x) = \ln x$ satisfies $f(b) - f(a) = f'(\zeta)$ at $(1/2, 2)$, find ζ value at $(b - a)$.

Source: Examination paper, 1987.

England/Wales: Mathematics

General Certificate of Education, Advanced Level, Examination Paper, Pure Mathematics 1/Mathematics 1, June 1987

[In addition to this three-hour test, candidates may take additional tests in pure mathematics and in applied mathematics.]

Attempt ALL the questions in Section A and FOUR questions from Section B. Credit will be given for the methods used. They should be clearly set out. Calculators and slide rules may be used. Marks: Section A: 44; Section B: 56

SECTION A. Attempt ALL the questions.

1. By first comparing the coefficients of x^3 in the identity $x^4 - 5x^3 - 19x^2 + 29x + 42 \equiv (x^2 + ax + 3)(x^2 + bx + 14)$
and then comparing the coefficients of x, find the values of a and b.
Solve the equation $x^4 - 5x^3 - 19x^2 + 29x + 42 = 0$.
What are the solutions of the equation $y^4 + 5y^3 - 19y^2 - 29y + 42 = 0$?

2. The nth term of a Geometric Progression is λ times the first term. Prove that the common ratio, r, of the Progression is given by $\log r = \dfrac{\log \lambda}{n-1}$, where the base of the logarithms is optional.
At the end of 1970, the population of Newtown was 46,650 and by the end of 1975 it had risen to 54,200. On the assumption that the population increased annually in a Geometric Progression between 1970 and 1975 and continued likewise afterwards, find

   (i) the common ratio of the Progression, giving the value correct to 3 significant figures,

   (ii) the population at the end of 1985.

3. Determine the range of values of x in each of the following cases:

   (i) $x^2 > 3x$,

   (ii) $\dfrac{2}{x-2} < 1$.

4. Find the value of $\dfrac{dy}{dx}$ at the point with co-ordinates $(1,2)$ when $y^3 = 8x$. Hence, find the equation of the normal at the point $(1,2)$ on $y^3 = 8x$.

SECTION B. Attempt any FOUR questions.

[Seven questions are given. Two are reproduced here.]

8. Write down the expansions of $\ln(1+x)$ and e^{-x} as far as the term in x^4.

Given that $f(x) \equiv 1 + x - \ln(1 + x)$, prove that the expansion of $g(x) \equiv (1 + x)f(x)$ as far as the term in x^4 is $1 + x + \frac{1}{2}x^2 + \frac{1}{6}x^3 - \frac{1}{12}x^4$.

Given that $G(x) \equiv (1 - x)F(x)$ where $F(x) \equiv 1 - x - \ln(1 - x)$, write down the expansion of $G(x)$ as far as the term in x^4.

Prove that the expansion of $h(x) \equiv e^{-x}g(x)$ as far as the term in x^4 is $1 - \frac{1}{8}x^4$.

14. Express $w = \dfrac{16 + 13i}{4 - i}$ in the form $a + bi$, where a and b are real.

(i) If $w = (c + di)^2$, where c and d are real, find the values of c and d. Hence, or otherwise, give the square roots of w.

(ii) If $|z - w| = 5$, sketch the locus of points represented by the complex number z.

Source: Southern Universities' Joint Board for School Examinations. *Examination for the General Certificate of Education, 1987*, Advanced Level and Special Papers. Bristol, England, paper No. 9203/1. (Courtesy University of Cambridge Local Examinations Syndicate, Cambridge, England.)

France: Mathematics

Baccalauréat Examination Paper, Mathematics, 1990
(Series A1, Académie Paris-Creteil-Versailles)

[The test lasts three hours.]

Exercise 1 (5 points)

C represents the set of complex numbers and P the complex plane projected on to an orthogonal framework $(O;\ u,\ v)$.

1. Solve in C the following equation: $z^2 - z\sqrt{2} + 1 = 0$

z_1 denotes the solution of the imaginary positive part, z_2 is the other solution.

Compare z_2 and $\bar{z}_1$.

M_1 and M_2 are the reflections of z_1 and z_2 respectively on P; locate M_1 and M_2 on the plane P.

2. Solve the following equation in C: $z^2 + z\sqrt{2} + 1 = 0$

z_3 denotes the solution of the imaginary negative part, z_4 is the other solution.

Compare z_4 and $\bar{z}_3$, z_3 and z_1, then z_4 and z_2.

M_3 and M_4 are respectively reflections of z_3 and z_4 in P; locate M_3 and M_4 on the plane P.

3. Show that $M_1M_2M_3M_4$ is a square whose center is 0.

4. a. Calculate z_1^2 and z_1^4; derive from these z_2^4, z_3^4, and z_4^4.

b. D'Alembert wrote in *L'encyclopedie methodique*: "In algebra, it is a given that an equation has as many roots as the highest power of the unknown; for example, a second degree equation has two roots, a third degree equation has three . . ."

Using this statement, find from the preceding questions the solutions in C of the equation $z^4 + 1 = 0$.

Exercise 2 (4 points)

A clock factory makes a series of watches. Production consists of two phases. The first reveals defect a in 2% of the cases; the second phase shows defect b in 10% of the cases.

1. One watch is selected at random. The following events are specified:
A: the watch has defect a;
B. the watch has defect b.
Conditions A and B are assumed to be independent of one another.

Calculate the probability of the following:

C: the watch has the two defects;
D. the watch has neither of the two defects;
E: the watch has one and only one of the defects;

2. Five watches in succession are selected at random from the production line. The number of watches is large enough to ensure that the production of defective watches will remain constant throughout the selection. Determine the probability of F: at least 4 watches have no defects. Give the exact value of this probability, and the decimal value to the nearest thousandth.

Problem (11 points)

Let us consider the function f defined on [0,∞] by:

$$f(x) = \frac{1 + \ln x}{x}$$

where ln represents the Naperian logarithm.
The plane P is projected onto an orthogonal frame (0; i, j) (graph unit: 4 cm). C is the curve f in P.

A

1. Examine the variations of f.

2. Calculate $\lim_{x \to 0+} f(x)$.

3. Calculate $\lim_{x \to +\infty} f(x)$.

B

1. Determine the coordinates of the following points of C:

a. M_1, abscissa x_1, intersection of C with the axis of the abscissas.

b. M_2, abscissa x_2, in which the tangent at C passes through the origin.

c. M_3, of the abscissa x_3, in which the tangent at C is parallel to the axis of the abscissas.

d. M_4, of the abscissa x_4, in which the second derivative f'' becomes 0.

2. Draw the curve C and place M_2, M_2, M_3, and M_4 on C.

3. Prove that the four numbers x_1, x_2, x_3, and x_4 are four consecutive terms in a geometric sequence (give your reasoning).

C

1. Calculate $I(\lambda) = \int_1^\lambda \dfrac{1 + \ln x}{x}\, dx,\ \lambda > 0$

2. Calculate the areas A_1, A_2, and A_3 of the three parts of the plane contained by the axis of the abscissas, the curve C and, respectively:

for A_1 the lines $x = x_1$ and $x = x_2$;

for A_2 the lines $x = x_2$ and $x = x_3$;

for A_3 the lines $x = x_3$ and $x = x_4$.

What can be said about the three numbers A_1, A_2, and A_3?

3. More generally, consider a geometric sequence k^n, $n \geq 1$, $k > 0$.

Calculate $J_n = \int_{k^{n-1}}^{k^n} f(x)\, dx$ as a function of n and k.

Prove from this that the terms J_n form an arithmetic sequence.

Select $k = q$ where q is defined as in question B.3.; compare J_1 and A_3.

Source: Marie-Dominique Danion and Marc Gourion. *Sujets 90 Corrigés: Maths: Terminal A/B* (Paris: Editions Nathan, 1990), pp. 59–61. (Courtesy Librairie Fernand Nathan, Paris, France.)

Germany: Mathematics

Abitur Examination Paper, Mathematics—Grundkurs/Basic Course, Province of Nordrhein-Westfalen

[Candidates answer questions selected from two of the three available topics: analysis/calculus, vector/analytic geometry, and probability. The test lasts five hours.]

I. *Analysis/Calculus*

1. The graph of an entirely rational cubic function, f, intersects line g, whose equation is $g(x) = x + 1$, at $x = -1$. At the point W (1,?) the graph has an inflexion tangent t, whose equation is $t(x) = -3x + 5$.

(a) Determine the equation of function f.

(b) Discuss the characteristics of function f, and graph f and g over the interval $I = [-1,5;3]$.

(c) Show that the graphs of f and g enclose two equal areas, and calculate the size of the areas.

3. Given the set of functions, $f_{k:\ x \to -x^4 + kx^2}$, with $k \in R\backslash\{0\}$.

(a) Discuss f_k.

(b) Determine the equation of the set of functions g_k, on whose graph the extrema of f_k lie, given that $k > 0$.

(c) Determine $f \in f_k$ and $g \in g_k$, so that the graphs of f and g enclose an area of 32.4 square units in the first quadrant.

(d) Use the results of (a) in the function f given in (c), and present the graphs of f and g in the interval $I = [-4,5;4,5]$ (1 linear unit on the x-axis = 10 units on the y-axis = 1 cm).

(e) The line joining the maxima of f cuts the y-axis in C. A triangle that is symmetrical about the y-axis has one of its corners in C; the other corners A and B are on the graphs on f, between their maxima. Determine the coordinates of A and B, so that the area of the triangle ABC is as large as possible. Sketch!

II. Vector/Analytic Geometry

Notes: (1) In all the questions in the section a Cartesian system of coordinates in three dimensions is assumed.

(2) The Greek letters λ, μ, and v stand for parameters for real numbers.

6. The point $A(2,1,-1)$ and $C(3,1,1)$, and the vector $\overrightarrow{AB} = \begin{pmatrix} -1 \\ 1 \\ 1 \end{pmatrix}$ are given.

(a) Determine the coordinates of points B, D, and E so that the rectangle ABCD forms a parallelogram with diagonals intersecting in E.

(b) State in normal and parameter form the equation of the plane E_1, in which the parallelogram ABCD lies.

(c) Determine the equation of the intersecting line g between the plane E_1 and E_2:

$$\overrightarrow{r} = \begin{pmatrix} 0 \\ 0 \\ 0 \end{pmatrix} + \lambda \begin{pmatrix} 0 \\ 3 \\ 1 \end{pmatrix} + \mu \begin{pmatrix} -1 \\ 3 \\ -1 \end{pmatrix}.$$

(d) Calculate the size of the angle of intersection of the planes E_1 and E_3: $2x + 3y + 4z - 5 = 0$.

III. Probability

8. Two machines, M_1 and M_2 produce transistors. M_1 turns out 40% of total output with an error rate of 3%. M_2 produces the remaining 60% with an 8% error rate.

(a) Show that 6% of the total output is defective.

(b) One transistor is randomly selected and is defective. What is the probability that it was produced by M_1? by M_2?

(c) What is the probability that there will be in the total output:

    c1) at most 2 defective transistors among 15 transistors?

    c2) at least 10 and at most 18 defective transistors among 250?

(d) A customer orders 4,000 transistors, of which at most 5% may be defective.

    (d1) A sample test by the customer reveals 12 defects among 200 transistors. With what measure of confidence can there be a complaint?

    (d2) How must the producer mix the outputs of M_1 and M_2 in order to secure the 5%-quality level with 99% certainty?

Source: *Grundkurs Mathematik: Schriftliches Abitur: Abitur Prüfungsaufgaben Gymnasium Nordrhein-Westfalen* (Freising: Stark, 1989), pp. 1, 5–6, 9–10. (Courtesy Starkverlagsgesellschaft mbH, Freising, Germany.)

Japan: Mathematics

Joint First Stage Achievement Test, Mathematics, 1988

[There are two parts, Mathematics 1 and Mathematics 2. Mathematics 1 is presented in its entirety below; of the three compulsory questions in Mathematics 2, the second is given here. Candidates provide answers by substituting numbers for the boxed question marks. One question mark indicates a one-digit answer, two question marks together, a two-digit answer. The test lasts one hundred minutes.]

MATHEMATICS 1

1. Given two equations: $2x^2 - 2ax - a + 1 = 0$ 1
$$x^2 - 2(a-1)x - 2a + 1 = 0$$ 2

(1) In equation 1, when $a = \boxed{??} \pm \sqrt{\boxed{?}}$, there is a dual solution,

$$x = \frac{\boxed{?}}{\boxed{?}} a.$$

(2) The roots of equation 2 are:

$\boxed{??}, \boxed{?} a - \boxed{?}$.

(3) When equations 1 and 2 have a common solution, the pairs of solutions for a and x are:

$(\boxed{?}, \boxed{?}), (\boxed{??}, \boxed{??}), (\boxed{?} / \boxed{?}, \boxed{?} / \boxed{?})$

2. The equation of C is: $y = x^2 - 3x$. Point A on C has y=coordinate, a. Point $P(x,y)$ moves along line C. When P is at the point $B(b,c)$, the distance AP is at a minimum.

(1) The y-coordinate of the maximum point of C is $- \boxed{?} / \boxed{?}$.

(2) $AP^2 = (y - a + \boxed{?} / \boxed{?})^2 + a + \boxed{?}$.

(3) When $a > \boxed{??} / \boxed{?}$, $c = a - \boxed{?} / \boxed{?}$.

When $a \leq \boxed{??} / \boxed{?}$, $c = \boxed{??} / \boxed{?}$.

(4) When $a = -3/4$, $b = \boxed{?} / \boxed{?}$, or $\boxed{?} / \boxed{?}$, and $\boxed{??} = \sqrt{} \boxed{?} / \boxed{?}$.

3. In triangle ABC, AB = 5, BC = 8, and $\angle ABC = 60°$.

(1) The area of triangle ABC is $\boxed{??} \sqrt{} \boxed{?}$.

(2) AC = $\boxed{?}$, cos $\angle$ ACB = $\boxed{??} / \boxed{??}$.

(3) Point P is on AB, point Q is on AC. When triangle ABC is folded over on the line PQ, point A lies on point M, which is the center of BC. Therefore:

AM = $\sqrt{} \boxed{??}$, MP = $\boxed{?} / \boxed{?}$, MQ = $\boxed{??} / \boxed{??}$.

MATHEMATICS 2

4. A parabola C: $y = ax^2$ ($a > 0$) intersects a straight line, $y = 1$, at the points P and Q; and $P_x < Q_x$.

(1) The equation of the tangent of C at Q is

$y = \boxed{?} \sqrt{} \boxed{?} x - \boxed{?}$

(2) The tangents of C at P and Q intersect at the point R($\boxed{??}$, $\boxed{??}$)

(3) The area enclosed by the lines PR, RQ, and the parabola C is

$\boxed{?} / (\boxed{?} \sqrt{} \boxed{?})$

(4) The equation for a parabola C', which is symmetrical with parabola C at the line $y = 1$, is

$y = \boxed{??} x^2 + \boxed{?}$

If the figure enclosed by parabola C' and the lines PR, RQ is revolved on the y-axis, the volume of this body is

$(\boxed{?} / \boxed{??}) \pi$

Source: Joint First Stage Achievement Test, Test Booklet, Mathematics, 1988, pp. 4–9, 12.

Soviet Union: Mathematics

Cards for the Oral Graduation Examination, Algebra and Elementary Analysis, 1988–89

[The oral examination in mathematics is compulsory only for candidates in the evening and part-time secondary schools, not in the regular day schools. Candidates choose a card from among a number arrayed facedown on the examiners' table. Each card contains three questions based on the topics listed. See Chapter 5 for a description of the oral examination procedure.]

Card 1

1. Properties and the graph of linear function.
2. Area of a region under a curve.
3. Proving trigonometric identities.

Card 2

1. Exponential functions, their properties and graphs.
2. Solving the trigonometric equation $\cos x = a$.
3. Finding the domain of a given function.

Card 3

1. The derivative of a function, its geometrical and mechanical meaning.
2. Solving the trigonometric equation $\sin x = a$.
3. Evaluating a given integral.

Card 5

1. Properties and graph of the function $y = x^{\frac{1}{2}}$.
2. Differentiation rule for two products (formulated and illustrated via examples).
3. Solving a trigonometric equation.

Card 6

1. The sum and difference of sines, cosines (proof of one of these formulas).
2. Basic logarithmic identities (formulated and illustrated via examples).
3. Identifying the intervals over which the given function is increasing or decreasing.

Card 19

1. The addition formulas for sine and cosine (proof of one of these formulas).
2. Applying the first and second derivative test for quadratic functions (illustrate via examples).
3. Finding the derivative of a given function.

Card 20

1. Definition of the integral. The Newton-Leibnitz formula.
2. Derivative of a function $y = x^n$, n is a whole number (formulated and illustrated via examples).
3. Solving a given trigonometrical inequality.

Source: Ministerstvo narodnogo obrazovaniia RSFSR, Glavnoe upravlenie soderzhaniia obrazovaniia, metodov obucheniia i vospitaniia, *Bilety dlia vypusknykh ekzamenov za kurs srednei shkoly na 1988/89 uchebnyi god* (Cards for graduation examinations for secondary school courses, 1988–89 academic year) (Moscow: Prosveshchenie, 1989), pp. 26–29.

Examination Paper in Mathematics for Entry into the Chemistry Faculty of the Moscow State (Lomonosov) University, 1989

1. Solve the inequality $\dfrac{2x}{x+1} < 1$.

2. The sequence of numbers b_1, b_2, b_3, . . . is a geometrical progression. Given that $b_1 \cdot b_2 \cdot b_3 = 8$, find $b_2 \cdot b_8$.

3. Solve the equation $\log_2 = (3\cos x - \sin x) + \log_2(\sin x) = 0$.

4. In the rectangle LMNK the diagonals LN and MK intersect in point 0. The triangles MON and MO'N are symmetrical relative to the each side of MN. Angle MON is twice as large as angle LO'K. Find the sides of rectangle LMNK, if it is given that the area of the pentagon LMO'NK is $5\sqrt{3}$.

5. Solve the equation $(2x+1)(1+\sqrt{((2x+1)^2+7)})+x(1+(x^2+7))=0$.

Source: *Kvant*, 1990, no. 2, pp. 67–68.

Sweden: Mathematics

Central Test, Mathematics, Third Year, February 3, 1988

Time allowed: 225 minutes. Recommended time allocation: Part A, about 90 minutes; the remainder for Part B.
Part A: 10 questions, each graded 1 or 0 points.
Part B: 5 questions, each graded 3, 2, 1, or 0 points.

PART A. Answer the following questions.

1. Determine the median from the graph.

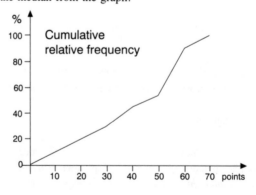

2. Three classes in a school have the following average scores on the central mathematics test:

S3a: 2.83   S3b: 2.69   S3c: 3.38

The number of pupils per class are:

S3a: 21   S3b: 16   S3c: 31

Calculate the weighted average for all pupils, correct to two decimal places.

3. A salary agreement resulted in a 2-year contract in which pay was increased by 12% the first year and by 5% the second. Determine the total salary increase in percent over the two-year period.

4. Give in simplest fraction form the number lying at the midpoint between 1/7 and 1/3.

6. At the beginning of 1987 Adamsson sold his house for 585,000 kroner. It cost him 350,000 kroner at the beginning of 1975. Give the average annual percentage increase in price, correct to one decimal place.

7. A coffee blender mixed x kg. of coffee costing a kroner/kg with y kg of coffee costing b kroner/kg. Give a formula for the price per kg of the blend.

8. A manufacturer makes screws. The lengths of the screws are normally distributed, with an average value of 50.0 mm and a standard deviation of 1.5 mm. What percentage of the output is made up of screws longer than 51.5 mm?

9. Olle Nilsson makes 11,250 kr. a month. After a new contract, his monthly salary increased to 11,650 kr. Using the table, calculate the tax rate on his increase.

Salary (kr)	Tax (kr)
11101–11200	4458
11201–11300	4513
11301–11400	4588
11401–11500	4623
11501–11600	4678
11601–11700	4733
11701–11800	4792
11801–11900	4853
11901–12000	4910

10. In 1976 Lena had a monthly salary of 6,000 kr. By 1984 her salary had risen to 9,000 kr. In current prices, her salary had risen by 50%. How large was the percentage change in fixed prices? In 1976 the Consumer Price Index (CPI) was 382; in 1984 it was 818.

PART B. Answer the following questions. Show your work.

11. Two different alternatives are discussed in a wage negotiation. One alternative provides for a monthly salary raise of 5.0% together with a lump sum addition of 210 kr. The other alternative provides for a monthly salary raise of 7.4%, but with no lump-sum addition. How much must someone earn in order for the two alternatives to have equal value?

12. Points A $= (3, -2)$ and B $= (-4, 10)$ are given. A straight line L, parallel to the line joining A and B, cuts the x-axis at $(-3, 0)$. Determine the coordinates of the point where line L cuts the y-axis.

13. Determine with the help of the derivative the coordinates of the maximum and minimum points of the curve $y = 3x^2 - x^3 + 1$. Sketch the curve.

14. The family Andersson's freezer contains a piece of reindeer meat that has been contaminated with cesium-137. The radioactivity is measured at 8,500 becquerel/ kg, and decreases exponentially with a half-life of 30.2 years. What will be the measured radioactivity after 1.5 years?

15. An enterprise paid into a pension fund at the beginning of every year a sum of 15,000 kr. The fund has a yearly growth rate of 10%. The first payment was made in 1987 and the last will be in 2010. The pension fund will continue to grow until 2015. How much more will the enterprise have in the fund at the beginning of 2015, if it pays in the same amount as above, but the rate of growth is 15%?

Source: Centralt Prov Matematik: Ak 3 SE, 1988-02-03. Skolöverstyrelsen/Prim-Gruppen vid Högskolan för lärarutbildning i Stockholm.

United States: Mathematics

College Board Achievement Tests, Mathematics Level II

[This is a one-hour, fifty-question, multiple-choice test for students who have taken college-preparatory work for at least three years. The following sample questions are reproduced from a College Board publication intended to enable candidates to familiarize themselves with the actual tests.]

Sample Questions—Mathematics Level II

Directions: For each of the following problems, decide which is the best of the choices given.

Notes: (1) Figures that accompany problems in this test are intended to provide information useful in solving the problems. They are drawn as accurately as possible EXCEPT when it is stated in a specific problem that its figure is not drawn to scale. All figures lie in a plane unless otherwise indicated.

(2) Unless otherwise specified, the domain of a function f is assumed to be the set of all real numbers x for which $f(x)$ is a real number.

Algebra

13. For what real numbers x is $y=2^{-x}$ a negative number?

(A) All real numbers x
(B) $x>0$ only
(C) $x\geq 0$ only
(D) $x\leq 0$ only
(E) No real number x

14. If $Z=p+qi$ and $\bar{Z}=p-qi$ are two complex numbers and p and q are real numbers, which of the following statements is true?

(A) $Z=-\bar{Z}$
(B) $(\bar{Z})^2$ is a real number.
(C) $Z\cdot\bar{Z}$ is a real number.
(D) $(\bar{Z})^2=Z^2$
(E) $Z^2=-(\bar{Z})^2$

15. A teacher gives a test to 20 students. Grades on the test range from 0 to 10 inclusive. The average grade for the first 12 papers is 6.5. If x is the average grade for the class, then which of the following is true?

(A) $0.33\leq x\leq 6.50$
(B) $3.25\leq x\leq 6.50$
(C) $3.90\leq x\leq 6.50$
(D) $3.90\leq x\leq 7.90$
(E) $4.00\leq x\leq 7.90$

Solid Geometry

Figure 6

16. In Figure 6, R and T are the midpoints of two adjacent edges of the cube. If the length of each edge of the cube is h, what is the volume of the pyramid $PRST$?

(A) $\dfrac{h^3}{24}$ (B) $\dfrac{h^3}{12}$ (C) $\dfrac{h^3}{8}$ (D) $\dfrac{h^3}{6}$ (E) $\dfrac{h^3}{4}$

Coordinate Geometry

17. Which of the following figures represents the rectangular-coordinate graph of

$\begin{cases} x=2\cos\theta \\ y=4\sin\theta \end{cases}$?

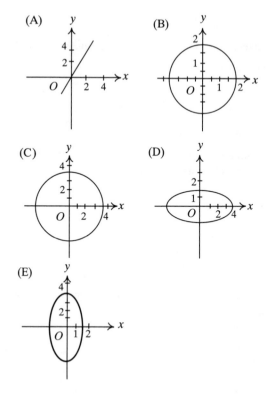

18. In Figure 7, shaded region S has area 10. What is the area of region T, which consists of all points $(x-1, y+4)$ where the point (x,y) is in S?

(A) 40   (B) 30   (C) 20   (D) $10\sqrt{2}$ (E) 10

Trigonometry

19. $\sin\left(\text{Arcsin }\dfrac{1}{10}\right) =$

(A) 0   (B) $\dfrac{1}{10}$ (C) $\dfrac{1}{9}$ (D) $\dfrac{9}{10}$ (E) 1

20. If $0 < y < x < \dfrac{\pi}{2}$, which of the following must be true?

I. $\sin y < \sin x$
II. $\cos y < \cos x$
III. $\tan y < \tan x$

(A) None
(B) I and II only
(C) I and III only
(D) II and III only
(E) I, II, and III

Elementary Functions

21. If $f(x) = 2x$ and $f(g(x)) = -x$, then $g(x) =$

   (A) $-3x$ (B) $-\dfrac{x}{2}$ (C) $\dfrac{x}{2}$ (D) $2 - \dfrac{x}{2}$ (E) x

22. If $f(x) = 10^x$, where x is real, and if the inverse function of f is denoted by f^{-1}, then what is $\dfrac{f^{-1}(a)}{f^{-1}(b)}$ where $a > 1$ and $b > 1$?

   (A) $\log_{10} a - \log_{10} b$

   (B) $\log_{10}(a - b)$

   (C) $\dfrac{\log_{10} a}{\log_{10} b}$

   (D) $\dfrac{10^b}{10^a}$

   (E) None of the above

Miscellaneous

23. For all positive real numbers, $a \text{ J } b$ is defined by the equation $a \text{ J } b = \dfrac{ab}{a+b}$. If $2 \text{ J } x = 3 \text{ J } 4$, then $x =$

   (A) 12   (B) 8   (C) 6   (D) 4   (E) 3

24. The probability that R hits a certain target is $\dfrac{3}{5}$ and the probability that T hits it is $\dfrac{5}{7}$. What is the probability that R hits the target and T misses it?

   (A) $\dfrac{4}{35}$ (B) $\dfrac{6}{35}$ (C) $\dfrac{3}{7}$ (D) $\dfrac{21}{25}$ (E) $\dfrac{31}{35}$

Index